In the
Circles
of Fear
and Desire

William Patrick Day

In the Circles of Fear and Desire

A Study of Gothic Fantasy

The University of Chicago Press
Chicago and London

The University of Chicago Press, Chicago 60637
The University of Chicago Press, Ltd., London

94 93 92 91 90 89 88 87 86 85   54321

Library of Congress Cataloging in Publication Data

Day, William Patrick.
In the circles of fear and desire.

Bibliography: p.
Includes index.
1.   Horror tales, English—History and criticism.
2. Gothic revival (Literature)   3. Fantastic fiction,
English—History and criticism.   I. Title.
PR830.T3D39   1985   823'.0872'09   84-28004
ISBN 0-226-13890-9
ISBN 0-226-13891-7(pbk.)

Okay, first one who sees the vampire,
scream his ass off.

—Lieutenant Morgan in
The Return of Count Yorga

Contents

Acknowledgments

In rereading this book in preparation for its publication, several points have become clear to me. In attempting to define it as a genre, I have necessarily slighted two aspects of the Gothic fantasy. First, I have not been able to deal in any detail with the style of the novels. My focus made it virtually impossible to draw the distinction between the writers who are extraordinary stylists (Radcliffe, James, Stevenson, and Poe) and those who write a serviceable, journeyman prose (Lewis, Shelley, and Stoker). However, the Gothic fantasy places a great deal of emphasis on events and story, rather than on style, so I feel somewhat justified in not dealing with the individual qualities of these writers.

Nor have I been able to do full justice to the complexity and fascination of the works I have discussed. I think this is an inevitable limitation given what I wished to accomplish, but recognizing this, I feel the need to affirm my sense of the value of the novels and stories as individual works. My interest in the Gothic grew from my enjoyment of these works, and I was sustained in the writing of this book by the fact that as my understanding of the significance and importance of the Gothic grew, so did my pleasure in rereading the works that make up the genre. The initial and primary importance of these stories lies in the pleasure they give us. My hope is that I can send readers back to the stories I discuss with new perspectives and new enthusiasm.

I am aware of debts that can be paid only in the inadequate form of acknowledgments. My work as both a scholar and teacher has been shaped by two men: Jerome J. McGann and Lawrence I. Buell.

Their advice and counsel has been of great value to me; their example, as critics and teachers, has been even more important. I also owe a great deal to former colleagues at the University of Pennsylvania. Robert F. Lucid and David J. DeLaura were always ready with encouragement and help. Christopher Dennis, Vickie Mahaffey, and particularly Wendy Steiner were tremendously supportive and responsive and spent a good deal of time listening to me talk about Gothic novels they had never read.

My friend Robin Roberts read the manuscript of this book in all three of its major phases; I may not have fulfilled her charge to "make it more feminist," but her influence on me has been more important than she realizes. Joyce Zonana not only typed an earlier version of the book—and thus made revisions possible—but provided critical insights and ideas, as well as encouragement, that were of the highest value to me. Two other friends, Jenny Egan and Ann Hostetler, read the manuscript and made helpful responses that shaped my revisions.

This material has appeared in a variety of incarnations in various courses I have taught over the past four years. Like Dracula, it has, in one form or another, risen to stalk a graduate course on the Gothic imagination, a freshman seminar on fantasy literature, an advanced undergraduate course on films of suspense and terror, and at both the University of Pennsylvania and Oberlin College, a course entitled "Nineteenth-Century Mischief." While taking a seminar on the teaching of fantasy literature, a group of graduate students humored me to the extent of teaching freshman seminars sharing with mine a common syllabus. To all the students in all these classes, I am indebted for their ideas, insights, and enthusiasm—which over and over confirmed my sense of the vitality and importance of this material—and for their tolerance in letting me try out my occasionally half-baked theories on them.

In the preparation of the manuscript, Robert Lucid was invaluable in helping me to get funds for typing at the University of Pennsylvania; David Love performed a similar service at Oberlin College. At various times, this manuscript has been typed—and retyped—by Janet Schwandt, David Coleman, Barbara Marshall, and Patt Clarkson, as well as Joyce Zonana. Without them, I have no idea what would have become of the project.

I owe a debt of thanks to the Major League Baseball Players Association and the NFL Players Associations: their strikes provided me with an unusual amount of free time, which I funneled into the writing of this book.

As for Beth, who is a medievalist and interested in *real* Gothic literature, I can only say that her support sustains me in ways beyond expressing.

Introduction

Of all the genres of popular literature that have arisen since the eighteenth century, the Gothic fantasy has proved the most enduring. Though the strength of our desire to be frightened varies from time to time, and the genre periodically undergoes transformations in order to adjust to contemporary taste and preferences in the matter of terror, the Gothic has persisted as an unbroken tradition since 1763 when Horace Walpole published *The Castle of Otranto* and gave the genre its name. In this study, I explore the Gothic fantasy from its origins in the late eighteenth century, when, in the novels of Anne Radcliffe and Monk Lewis, it truly becomes popular, through the end of the nineteenth century and the conclusion of its first major phase in such novels as *Dracula, The Turn of the Screw,* and *The Hound of the Baskervilles.* In the last chapter, I explore the persistence of the Gothic fantasy into the twentieth century through film. Though the development of the new medium modified certain aspects of the genre, on the whole I think the continuity between the nineteenth- and twentieth-century Gothic fantasies is greater than their differences. Because of this, I conclude my discussion by tracing the ways in which the tradition affects modernism and by examining its relationship to Freudian theories of psychology. In examining the relationship between the Gothic fantasy and these two twentieth-century cultural developments, we shall be able to see how the former has become a part of our cultural mainstream. The paradigms and dynamics of the Gothic fantasy have been revised and redirected in modernism and Freudianism, and this revision and redirection of the imaginative and cultural energy and tension embod-

1

ied in the genre have only partially come to terms with its underlying concerns and problems.

I have not attempted to deal with the Gothic through a chronicle of its literary history. This study does not survey the fantasies published over the first one-hundred-and-fifty years of the genre's existence, nor do I deal with all of the hundreds of B-grade vampire movies made since Bela Lugosi first said "Good evening" to his unsuspecting victims in Ted Browning's 1933 film *Dracula*. I do not deal at all with the vast body of throw-away Gothics, the nineteenth-century equivalents of the supermarket and airport paperbacks of our own day, whose memory remains, when it remains at all, only because of the list of popular novels in *Northanger Abbey* or because, like *Varney the Vampire*, they have become curiosities, bits of Victorian exotica. Rather, I have defined a canon including those texts that either were perceived as Gothic by their authors and contemporary audiences, or that have, like *Vathek* and *Caleb Williams*, been inextricably linked to the tradition in the years since their publication. In either case, the books I have chosen have been classified as Gothic throughout most of their existence. I have also chosen to deal with novels and stories that have remained to some degree an active part of our literary and imaginative life. All of the books and stories I deal with enjoyed some degree of popularity in their own day, and all have appeared in popular editions within the past twenty-five years, though some, admittedly, have been largely confined to the college classroom. I have eliminated from my study, not only those ephemera that have passed from anybody's consciousness, but also those canonical works that have strong affinities with the Gothic. *Wuthering Heights, Jane Eyre, Moby Dick, Pierre, The House of Seven Gables,* all of which bear a cousinly relationship to the Gothic fantasy, are mentioned peripherally, if at all.[1] Elements in these books certainly indicate the progressive infusion of the Gothic sensibility into the mainstream, but though these texts are doubtless important vehicles for the diffusion of the style throughout our culture, they do not belong to the genre itself. Emily Brontë develops Gothic motifs and paradigms in *Wuthering Heights,* as does Melville in *Moby Dick,* but they look away from the central tradition of the genre; they use the tradition, but they are not of it. Brontë and Melville do not feed back into the genre, becoming part of its development. The very individuality that marks their use of the Gothic places it outside the genre. As a popular literary form, the Gothic operates within relatively strict conventions and formulas, and throughout the nineteenth century, writers defined their place in the tradition and contributed to its communal growth and metamorphosis by their adherence to and use of these formulas. When Henry James wrote *The Turn of the Screw*, he wrote a Gothic fantasy because, despite his status within the canon, in this instance he stepped into the popular tradition and accepted its formulas and conventions.[2]

The books that we have defined as Gothic, novels such as *The Mysteries of Udolpho* and *Uncle Silas,* are neither subliterary nor quite part of our conventional list of works that achieve the status of "art." The texts I deal with form a bridge between the canon that establishes the continuity and dominant form of our literary culture and the popular novels that exist alongside that literary culture, influence it, but usually disappear after a few years. In the Gothic tradition, though, we have a group of popular texts that have achieved an imaginative existence of their own. The power and endurance of the Gothic, its hold on our imaginations, our fascination with its particular pleasures, are revealed in the virtually mythic status of such creations as Frankenstein, Dracula, Dr. Jekyll and Mr. Hyde, and Sherlock Holmes, who is also a fundamentally Gothic character. These four—or five, depending on how one views Jekyll and Hyde—are among the best-known characters in English and American literature. They, and characters based on them, appear in books, films, television shows, and commercials. Their likenesses are instantly recognized by people who might have only the vaguest idea who Hamlet is, and their names have become the labels for whole classes of phenomena: "He's created a Frankenstein," "He's a regular Dr. Jekyll and Mr. Hyde." Our uses of these characters seem endless and our fascination with them inexhaustible. In examining how such compelling creatures came to be, we will also be able to understand more fully why they exercise a hold on us still.

The Gothic fantasy achieves its importance because its very existence expressed an essentailly modern dilemma. How do individuals in a complex urban and technological society undergoing rapid change find amusement for their increasing leisure time? The Gothic came into existence and endured because it gave pleasure and satisfaction to its readers.[3] To understand the genre will help us understand the nature and status of pleasure, particularly imaginative pleasure, in the nineteenth century. The Gothic fantasy is one way that people cut off from the traditional rural culture of their forebearers, on the one hand, and on the other, from the high art of past eras define for themselves the boundaries of imagination and pleasure. The underlying story of the Gothic is, then, the story of the imaginative life of the middle class in the nineteenth century. Yet at the same time, this style of fiction that began as middle-class escapism becomes an important part of the whole imaginative life of the nineteenth century and a shaper of that life in the twentieth.

In the rest of the introduction, I will outline the basic structure of my argument. Much of what I say here will appear at best as interesting, unsupported speculation, but I offer this section as a guide to the book as a whole. In the end, I hope to have shown that what at first seems only assertion is in fact the case.

Approaches to the Gothic

In order to understand the Gothic fantasy, we must deal with it from three perspectives. First, I will define it as a dynamic literary system. In defining the literary form, we also define the Gothic world, which of course has no real existence outside fantasy. We can define the formal and metaphysical shape of the genre by the conventions of character, atmosphere, and structure typical of the fantasies and by the organization and pattern of relationships that underlie and activate those conventions. We will then take up three issues: the relationship of the Gothic fantasy to the figure of the detective, the relationship of the tradition to other conceptions of narrative and reality, and the nature of the imagination embodied and expressed in the novels.

In this process of definition, we shall see that the Gothic fantasy is a creation through conventional narrative of an anticonventional vision of reality. The fantasies, through such techniques as transformation, metamorphosis, and doubling, reverse conventional assumptions about the relation of self to Other, about good and evil, love and hate, pain and pleasure, objective and subjective, masculine and feminine, cause and effect. The protagonists find themselves in a world created by the circle of their own fears and desires, in a state of enthrallment, both thrilling and destructive, to the Gothic world. We shall explore the ways in which the relation of the reader to the text is also a development of the enthrallment of the protagonist. We shall see why the detective is the logical hero of the Gothic fantasy and why the writer must expell him from the Gothic world. We shall discuss the ways in which the Gothic operates as a parody of other narratives and conceptions of the world. Finally, we shall examine the ways in which the Gothic fantasy is based on a conception directly opposed to the romantic vision of the transcendent power and ✓ energy of Imagination.

We shall explore next the themes of the Gothic, the specific material that made it so compelling for contemporary readers. This consideration grows naturally out of the first stage, because we cannot understand the genre without understanding its place and function in the culture that created and sustained it. The thematic focus of the Gothic concerns the nature of masculine and feminine identity and the nature of the family that shapes that identity. Central to the treatment of these themes are the problem of sexuality, the relation of sexuality to pleasure and identity, and the possibilities and problems of androgyny as a response to the conventional concepts of identity and family that dominated nineteenth-century middle-class life. If the central emotion of the Gothic is fear, the source of that fear is anxiety and terror over the experience of the family and the ideals of masculine and feminine identity that hold the family together. The Gothic fantasy is in part an attempt by nineteenth-century culture to both express and relieve its fears about its own concepts of identity. The nature of the family and of masculine and feminine identity are also central themes of the nineteenth-century realistic novel, from Austen through Hardy. Thus the Gothic fantasy is an escape, not only from conventional ideals, but from the realistic novel's ways of dealing with and resolving the conflicts of those ideals. The fear, anxiety, terror, and dread that are both the subject and effect of the Gothic are not, then, free-floating thrills but reflect the essential insecurities of nineteenth-century readers. At the heart of the novels intended to provide escape and entertainment, nineteenth-century readers came face to face with the very thing from which they were trying to escape. The great power of the Gothic stems from its capacity to transform these fears into pleasure.

We must consider the Gothic fantasy, not only as a literary system and as part of its culture, but also as a part of literary and cultural history. We have already suggested that the genre gave birth to the detective and that it stands in a parodic relationship to other types of narrative. However, we must also attempt to explain why it has endured when other popular forms, such as the Newgate novel or the silver-fork novel or cousins like the sensation and the "blood" novel, had their brief lives and disappeared. We could explore the internal dynamics and the relation to contemporary culture of these popular styles just as we discuss the Gothic fantasy. But what sets our novels off from these others is in part the complexity of their interpretation of pleasure and imagination and the relationship of each to the other.

In addition to dealing with this issue, we shall also address the ways in which the Gothic helped define the outer landscape of the wasteland for the modernists and the inner landscape of the psyche for Freudianism. We shall examine the ways in which modernist fiction adapted Gothic paradigms to form the narrator–central character relationship we see in Marlowe and Kurtz in *Heart of Darkness*, which is repeated in so many other modernist novels. In discussing the relationship of the genre to Freud, we shall examine how the fantasies prepared the imagination of the twentieth century to read and understand the nature of dream work. Finally, we shall see how in both the Freudian and modernist vision, the Gothic critique of masculine identity is absorbed and subverted. It will become clear how the Gothic has shaped our ways of looking at and understanding our world—as well as giving us a good scare.

The Gothic and Romance

The Gothic fantasy has its immediate origin in the tradition of the romance that Northrop Frye has described in *The Secular Scripture*.[4] Frye, naturally, sees the Gothic as a form of the romance, for in fact he sees all secular literature as a version of the romance myth. The Gothic is related to the romance; writers in the tradition often referred to their work as "romance"—not necessarily Frye's romance, it is true—but they used many of the its conventions and paradigms, as well as its freedom from strict realism, as a basis of their work. The Gothic fantasy, though, is a peculiar offshoot of the romance, because it subverts its own mythology. For Frye, the romance is a fable of identity, even if the identity achieved by the hero and heroine is ironically qualified. The Gothic fantasy is a fable of identity fragmented and destroyed beyond repair, a fable of the impossibility of identity. In the Gothic, identity is based not on the mythology that Frye calls the "secular scripture," but on the specific concepts and ideals of identity that exist in contemporary culture. The Gothic is a romance that reveals its social and historical, rather than mythological, basis.

The Gothic fantasy employs many of the motifs and archetypes of the romance, particularly, the narrative pattern that Frye calls "the theme of descent," which portrays the movement of hero or heroine from a higher to a lower world, from the Edenic or natural world to the underworld, in search of lost identity. The underworld is a place of "terror and cruelty, "demonized," as Frye calls it.[5] The romance protagonist often descends into the underworld through the medium of a dream or through a process of doubling. There he undergoes a series of transformations and ritual sufferings that lead to the discovery or recovery of the his identity and to either a return to the world left behind or the establishment of a new paradise. In the Gothic fantasy, however, there is no ascent from the underworld, nor is a new Eden established there. The hero never recovers his true identity. Once in the demonic underworld he becomes subject to endless transformation and metamorphosis, his identity permanently and completely fragmented in a world of cruelty and terror. It seems that the only escape from the Gothic world is death, but even this release is an illusion. In the Gothic fantasy, death is neither an escape nor a door through which one can pass to achieve a final humanity. In death, the protagonist becomes, not simply a victim, but fully a part of what tormented him. Death releases the protagonist from the last vestiges of human identity, and he becomes the embodiment of cruelty and terror.

The vampire is the most striking image of a human being fully transformed by the descent.[6] Both more and less than human, it reappears from beyond the grave, the walking, if not precisely living, representation of the Gothic world. This symbol of a truly Gothic identity is an inversion of human identity, a new creature, at one with the landscape of fear and terror in which it lives. The descent into the underworld leads to the rejection of human identity and the embracing of the monstrous. Death, the ultimate descent, results neither in transfiguration, as in a religious vision, in a return to inert matter, the scientific view; nor in a reaffirmation of human identity. Rather, it leads to the creation of a new being, the monstrous parody of the human. The Gothic does not simply create ambiguous or ironic romance, but subverts the mythology of the whole genre. ✓

While the Gothic fantasy uses the themes of the romance to subvert its parent, it also parodies its sibling, realistic fiction. Frye tends to see the realistic novel as parodying romance, even as it maintains the underlying romance structures.[7] But just as the Gothic uses romance devices and techniques to antiromance ends, so too does it deny and invert the principles upon which the realistic novel is based: the stability of personality and identity, the process of cause and effect, and the essentially social nature of human identity. Its power over our imaginations comes in part from its double-edged

parody and transformation of both romance and realism. The motifs
and paradigms of the romance create the expectation of an empowering, affirmative myth in which identity is recovered or created. The
Gothic fantasy defeats this expectation and calls into question assumptions that are fundamental to the realistic vision of self and the
world. It seems to propose a way of imagining the world that is
neither romance nor realism, although not completely unlike either,
but in fact unlike any world in which human beings might exist. The
Gothic world is one of unresolved chaos, of continuous transformation, of cruelty and fear, of the monstrous that is the shadow and
mockery of the human.

The Gothic fantasy occupied a world between romance and realism, a world controlled by no conventional or traditional vision of
reality. In subverting these literary forms it also subverted the cosmological visions that lay behind them. By denying the conventional
expectations and assumptions evoked by the romance, the Gothic
undermined the mythic vision of reality that supported that genre.
At the same time, its use of romance forms also rejected assumptions
that supported realism, which were essentially the assumptions and
cosmology of Newtonian science. Thus the Gothic fantasy occupied
a region not only between romance and realism, but between myth
and science. Nevertheless, the Gothic was not an attempt to generate
a new mythology, as was romanticism. The Gothic writers created a
form that became an indefinite and infinite gesture of revolt against
two cosmological visions that, in conflict with each other, proved
essentially unsatisfactory for the nineteenth-century imagination.

The romance, according to Frye, represents a secular vision of
myth. In a culture that functions in mythic terms, the demarcation
between things visible and invisible, marvelous and ordinary, is not
quite clear. None of our modern oppositions—fact or fiction, true
or false—quite apply, nor does our equation of truth with fact. The
romance reflected the tendency of a prescientific world to move from
the visible, ordinary, and everyday to the invisible, marvelous, and
mythic with relative ease. The romance and such collateral styles as
allegory, pastoral, and utopian vision could make true statements
about reality even if they were not factually true. The dominant
mode of thought in the prescientific West, Christianity, affirmed a
belief in a transcendent, eternal reality beyond the material world.
Thus religion and secular literature would have affirmed that the
ordinary material world was not reality, and that the path to truth
did not lie through literal fact. Since any narrative could be treated

allegorically or archetypally, even the most entertaining romance could also reflect a higher reality, however fantastical and marvelous its events might be.

With the publication of Newton's *Principia* in 1686–87, a new system of thought came into existence that defined the real as material objects and forces, acting under invariable laws, which could be studied, demonstrated, measured, and quantified through repeatable experiments.[8] The physical world became the real world, and fact became truth. The material realm could exist on its own without the support of unseen realities. Indeed, science banished the marvelous and fantastic from reality, and the immeasurable became the unreal. Imagination and fantasy would simply cloud one's perceptions of the material world. Romance, which had been a representation of reality, ceased to be so in the face of this new idea, and in the drawing of a circle defining reality as the material world, fantasy was created. To deal with the world beyond the material, beyond the senses, beyond that which science could define, was to deal in moonshine and nonsense. As romance and allegory lost claim to a transcendent reality, they decayed. Because realism claimed to present the world in a way that corresponded to scientific conceptions of reality, its prestige and power rose.

The techniques and motifs characteristic of the romance were, then, cut loose from "serious" literature and from a serious cultural function. In the eighteenth, and particularly the nineteenth, century, people would find their acceptable fables of identity in realistic fiction. Fantasy could not tell the truth about the world since it referred to a world that did not really exist. Since the fantasy world did not really exist, it could not offer moral truths either. As romance and allegory turned into fantasy, they turned into pure entertainment. Those qualities that made a piece of fiction art in the nineteenth century—the capacity to tell the truth about the world, to express moral truth—were reserved for realistic fiction.[9]

Despite the fact that it was perceived as mere entertainment, the Gothic fantasy retained the symbolic qualities of the romance. Detached from the mythic, it used the techniques and devices of romance without the content, becoming a free-floating form, apparently completely self-referential, for it referred only to its own world, which existed no place else. However, mythic ways of thinking are natural to human beings, and the system acquired a content to go with its form.

The Gothic fantasy began, not as a popular genre, but as the private fantasies of two eccentric aristocrats, Horace Walpole and William Beckford, who in their fiction and in their extravagant mansions, Strawberry Hill and Fonthill Abbey, were busily constructing private, self-referential fantasy worlds. By the 1790s, these private worlds had become public ones, and the Gothic fantasy was transformed from aristocratic hobby to middle-class entertainment. Emancipated from the traditional content of the romance and the dominant scientific conception of reality that controlled realistic fiction, it gathered cultural and imaginative energy that had no other way of expressing itself. In defining the possibilities of leisure and escape, the Gothic defined imaginative possibilities beyond the intractable physical world. The realistic novel had given the new, urban, middle-class readers a definition of reality, of their outer, social lives, and their public fables of identity. The Gothic fantasy provided this same group with internal definitions of the reality they felt and experienced, definitions that might not fit with the public fables. It helped shape its readers' sense of their own subjectivity. In this way, the Gothic is part of that process by which we move from thinking of our inner life in terms of souls to thinking of it in terms of psyches. Nevertheless, the Gothic fantasy could provide no empowering, positive mythology of identity, a vision of self integrated and fulfilled. It addressed those parts of the nineteenth-century reader's inner life that were disordered or fragmented, giving expression, not to their ideal or their best self, but to their fears and anxieties about their own fragility and vulnerability.

Of course, the process was not explicit much of the time. The Gothic fantasy seemed simply a source of entertainment, at best not to be taken seriously, at worst, to be despised. But the imaginative life of a culture is not necessarily fully embodied, or most intensely and significantly expressed, in socially acceptable forms. In the space between the worlds of religion and myth and science, between romance and realism, between soul and psyche, between inner and outer life, nineteenth-century readers saw the source of their anxiety and fear, that is, in the failure of religious, scientific, and philosophical systems to create a sense of wholeness and unity in the self and in the world, which would have allowed individuals to define their own existence. The Gothic fantasy occupied this empty space, filled it through parody of these systematic visions that did not quite account for the world, and turned the anxiety and fear in that cultural gap into pleasure, articulating and defusing the anxiety and fear that called it into existence. As parody, it could articulate, reflect, invert, but it could not create a mythology of its own. But in its fertile suggestiveness, the Gothic fantasy could be used in the creation of empowering mythologies; its diverse progeny are the detective story, modernism, and Freudian psychology.

1

The System of the Gothic Fantasy

Our first step in understanding the dynamics that underlie each Gothic fantasy requires that we reconsider briefly the truism that we cannot separate form from content. At first, as "mere entertainment," it might appear that the Gothic fantasy has no meaningful content. It is simply a sensational spectacle, a product designed to shock its readers with sadomasochistic tales of monsters and demons, incest and violence. On the other hand, readings that affirm the meaningful content of the genre tend to see it allegorically. Freudian critics transform its monsters and demons into the id, while critics emphasizing its religious or philosophical significance use the allegorical lens to see a "Dark Romanticism" or the repetition of the essential anxieties and problems of English Protestantism.[1] Useful truths exist in all of these approaches, the Gothic fantasy is indeed designed to jolt its readers, and we can also find reflections of patterns of thought—romanticism, Freudianism, Protestantism—that swirl around it. However, the relationship of the text to the world outside it is not allegorical, but parodic. The content of the Gothic fantasy lies, finally, in the interaction between the assumptions and expectations of its audience with the fears and anxieties produced by those assumptions and expectations and in the way it treats conventional versions of reality and identity, as well as fear and anxiety.

A central fact about the genre is its announcement of its own discontinuity with the real world; it always makes it own artificiality and fictiveness clear. It represents a world that does not in fact exist. All literary works, of course, are discontinuous with the real world,

13

but the Gothic fantasy makes this discontinuity an essential aspect of its existence. This was especially striking in the nineteenth century, when the mimetic and truth-telling qualities of literature were highly prized and it was generally assumed that good fiction did refer to the real world, with some moral intent. Not only were Gothic fantasies obviously not true to life, but, unlike the allegorical fantasies of writers such as Kingsley or Macdonald, they did not point toward a higher, spiritual truth.[2] The Gothic fantasy, in individual cases, might appear to be used for didactic purposes, and, indeed, to be intended as Christian allegory—Charles Maturin's *Melmoth the Wanderer* is a good example—but the nature of the form seems always to subvert this interpretation. Maturin's Christianity seems ill-considered and tacked on; his dream of horror we take seriously.

Because the text presents a purely imaginary world, we cannot on a strictly analytical level distinguish between its content (its vision of the Gothic world) and its form (the conventions and devices by which that world is described and that appear and reappear throughout the history of the genre). The text defines its world, which exists only within the text.[3] The surface of the Gothic fantasy is its substance. As a product of the human imagination, it does, in the end, refer parodically to the outside world, an issue we will take up later. At the same time, to describe the dynamics of the Gothic world and the Gothic fantasy without recourse to language and concepts derived from outside the tradition is impossible. However, at this stage of our discussion, it is important to be as purely descriptive as possible.

The Gothic fantasy is the intermediary between the world it describes and the conventional world, which is fundamentally different in form and structure. Indeed, the Gothic world, which is in the Gothic fantasy the world beyond death, has no form or shape of its own. It is unknowable in conventional terms. It is made manifest in a kind of translation, in which that which is unnameable and unknowable is given name and form, made knowable through the conventional language of narrative. The Gothic fantasy describes in terms of characters, actions, and plots a world that has none of these things. It defines, not the whole of the underworld, but that part we can comprehend. Beyond the dimly lit corridors of the text, through the metaphor of death, lies the rest of the Gothic world, one suggested by the image of Dracula lying in his coffin, dreaming dreams we cannot imagine. Thus, the Gothic fantasy defines a world but defines a portion of that world as unknowable. Mystery and suspense serve as signals to us that what we can see, illuminated by the conventions of the genre, is only a part of what is there. The sense that something unknown and unknowable lies beyond the terrors of the world we do see is the essential fact of the Gothic fantasy.

The Conventions

The interaction between a set of stable, popular literary conventions and the intuition of an unknowable world is one of the sources of the continuing vitality and flexibility of the Gothic novel. Because the center of the text is the unknowable, individual stories are themselves interpretations of the dark center of the Gothic world. Using the same conventions, individual authors draw their own maps of the unseen to articulate the unutterable. The system of relationships, the dynamics of the interaction, the metaphysical, and finally, the thematic visions of the genre remain recognizably one thing, Gothic. But each author in the tradition brings to this dynamic a different set of values. Writers as diverse as Radcliffe, Lewis, Poe, and Wilde all found that they were imaginatively stimulated and provoked into creation by the Gothic fantasy. Thus, we have reactionary Gothic fantasies, as in the novels of Anne Radcliffe, and radical Gothic fantasies, as in Godwin's *Caleb Williams*. But as we recognize all of these fictions as Gothic, we see that they were shaped by the genre as much as they were able to shape it. Each novel and story in the genre is a response to its fundamental power. We must examine the powerful fantasy that drew writers to the tradition. Our discussion of the Gothic, then, must begin with those conventions that define its boundaries and its internal dynamics.

The conventions fall into three types: conventions of character, conventions of atmosphere, and conventions of plot.[4] Each of these elements interacts with the other; on the deepest level we cannot really separate plot from character, nor character from atmosphere. However, despite the interpenetration of these conventions, we can for the sake of analysis discuss them independently. Because of the identity of form and content, to discuss conventions of character in the Gothic means we are also discussing the nature of the self. In discussing atmosphere, we will also be discussing the nature of a world that is "not-self," or "Other"; while in discussing the conventions of plot, we will be exploring the nature of action—the relationship of self to Other.

Heroes and Heroines, Victims and Victimizers

The most important aspect of the conventions governing the Gothic protagonist is the disappearance of the romance hero. The fantasies have a heroine, derived from the female protagonists of the sentimental romance, and a male antihero who shares some characteristics with the quest hero of the romance but who is also marked by a demonic quality as well as Faustian egotism.[5] We have real difficulty distinguishing between Gothic "heroes"—Victor Frankenstein and Manfred of Otranto, toward whom we are to feel some sympathy— and out-and-out villians, such as Schedoni in *The Italian* and Dracula. Three Gothic versions of the romance hero exist, Theodore in *Otranto*, Valancourt in *Udolpho*, and Vivaldi in *The Italian*, but these characters are all unable to fulfill the requirements of the quest hero. Each is reduced to the position of passive observer rather than active participant in the events of the story. In *Melmoth the Wanderer*, Moncada, who calls himself a "hero of submission," demonstrates how male heroes in the Gothic fantasy take on feminine qualities of passivity and endurance, rather than the conventional hero's capacity for action. The romance hero virtually disappears from the tradition after *The Italian*, for the Gothic world cannot allow for a character who is both capable of significant action and truly heroic. The fantasies cast of characters, then, reflect on one hand the collapse of the quest hero and his replacement by an ambiguous, egocentric, self-destructive antihero and, on the other, a revision of the sentimental heroine. The heroine does not step forward and take the center stage in the Gothic fantasy as a successful version of her romance original. Though the conventional heroine is not disposed of as is the quest hero, she too proves a self-contradictory, self-destructive style of identity.

The heroine of popular novels that today can be found in bookstores under the section marked "Gothic Romances"—or sometimes just "Gothics"—is the direct descendant of the Gothic heroine of the 1790s. Derived from sentimental fiction, this young woman is well-bred, passive, and respectable; her original is Emily St. Aubert in *The Mysteries of Udolpho*, though the female characters in *The Castle of Otranto* sketch out her lineaments.[6] She reappears in Clara Wieland, Maud Ruthyn of *Uncle Silas*, and the nameless governess of *The Turn of the Screw*. These characters are, on the whole, thrust into the underworld through no apparent fault of their own. The worst that can be said of them is that their virtuousness makes them prey to villains;

for example, Emily St. Aubert's respectable refusal to run away with Valancourt in book one of *Udolpho* in a sense leads to her subsequent imprisonment. Elena, in Radcliff's last novel, *The Italian,* is so respectable that she hesitates, only momentarily it is true, to escape from being immured in a convent because she is not quite sure of the propriety of running off alone with Vivaldi, her rescuer. These characters are obviously and inescapably victims. Their conceptions of themselves and of proper behavior render them passive in the face of terror. Paradoxically, this passivity and acceptance of victimization is their greatest strength, allowing them to escape from the Gothic underworld. They desire nothing more than to return to the conventional world and establish themselves as wives and mothers. Nevertheless, the relentlessly virtuous Emily and Elena, who are presented as unequivocally good, become in their late incarnations much more ambiguous figures as LeFanu and James, particularly, explore more rigorously the implications of this style of feminine identity, an exploration that illuminates the degree to which this heroine is a part of the Gothic world not by accident, but by her very nature.

The Gothic hero, or more properly, antihero, is a version of the Faust character, an overreacher seeking power, pleasure, even godhood. These characters are essentially active men, attempting to realize their desires through the efforts of their own will; above all, they are men engaged in the process of creating, or recreating, their own identities. Though such characters are often intelligent and daring, they need not be so. Robert Wringham in *The Private Memoirs and Confessions of a Justified Sinner* is cowardly and obtuse, while Charles Brockden Brown's Edgar Huntly is rather stupid, though he is daring enough. Dracula possesses courage of a brutal type and is certainly assertive, but both Henry Jekyll and Dorian Grey are in many ways cowardly men and partake of the tendency to passivity common to Gothic heroines. All the male protagonists, though, share the qualities of egotism and monomania; they seek to dominate their world, rather than accommodate themselves to it as the female characters do. The male protagonist always enters the Gothic world of his own free will, even though he surely does not understand what he is getting into. His attempt to assert his power leads him to this world, and his actions there lead to his destruction. The archetype of this figure is Manfred in Walpole's *Castle of Otranto;* the line descends from him through every male protagonist to Dracula.

The male protagonist shares two qualities with his female counter-

part. Like her, he is a victim, but he is overtly the victim of his own
desires and actions, rather than the passive victim of another. In the
Gothic fantasy, victimization is the natural state of all individuals.
The male and female characters also share with the sentimental heroine a heightened imagination and curiosity. Even such a virtuous
young woman as Emily St. Aubert, thrust into the Udolpho
through no fault of her own, soon finds that she cannot contain her
curiosity. She wanders the halls of the castle, looking into strange
rooms and behind mysterious hangings, and she cannot control the
tendency of her imagination to construct horrors out of her own
ignorance and uncertainty. The male characters usually have a more
active imagination and curiosity: Melmoth wishes to know what exists beyond death and to test his power against God's, while Frankenstein wishes to know the secret of life and make himself a god.
Henry Jekyll wants to know more of the pleasures he has forbidden
himself for the sake of respectability, and Dorian Grey is fascinated
by the process of watching his soul transform itself through the medium of the portrait.

The male and female protagonists of the Gothic fantasy share a
third characteristic: neither is capable of effective action. The heroine
is by definition passive. Her escape, if it comes, comes by accident, as
when Emily St. Aubert discovers that she can simply walk out of
Udolpho and no one will notice her absence. This occurs because
Radcliffe, having defined her as essentially passive, must allow circumstances to free Emily, who cannot free herself. The hero is usually engaged in furious action, but this gets him no farther than
passivity does his Gothic sister. However hard Ambrosio the Monk
seeks pleasure and power, he acts only in ways that lead to his damnation. This is true of all Gothic heroes; even those who appear to
have achieved what they desire are only marking time, moving in a
circle that leads to their destruction. This is true of Frankenstein, of
Jekyll, of Dorian Grey; it is even true of Dracula, whose "life" consists of the endless repetition of the act of vampirism, to no end but
the ceaseless and meaningless replication of himself. Dracula's triumph is the celebration of his own monstrous life-in-death state.

The hero and heroine almost never hold the center stage together.
The Gothic fantasy characteristically has only one protagonist, either
a man or a woman. If the fantasy has a woman as its central char-
acter, then the male will appear as a villain: Montoni in *Udolpho*,
Schedoni in *The Italian*, Silas Ruthyn in *Uncle Silas*, Quint in *The
Turn of the Screw*. If the central character is a man, the heroine may

appear in subsidiary roles: Matilda and Isabella in *Otranto,* Elizabeth in *Frankenstein.* But because the male protagonist can be his own victimizer, he does not need the heroine, while the heroine, to be persecuted in appropriately Gothic style, must have a villain to assail her. Most important, though, is the fact that the protagonist is always alone. The fantasy defines its world as a place where there exists one self; everything else in that world is Other, an enemy to the desires and integrity of the self, whether that self wishes to become a god or simply to escape and get married. Everything and everyone else conspire against the protagonist, and victimization and isolation are the central features of both the masculine and feminine self in the Gothic fantasy.

The relationship between self and Other is defined by the struggle between the impulse to domination and the impulse to submission. The hero seeks to dominate his world through action, thus creating his own identity; the heroine seeks to protect her identity through passivity.[7] In these attempts though, the Gothic world comes to dominate and control the protagonists, whatever their course of action, reducing them to the state of nonbeing, absorbing them into the Other. The pattern of all relationships in the Gothic fantasy, then, operates on the dynamic of sadomasochism. One asserts one's power either by inflicting or enduring pain, or both. However, the isolated protagonists can never inflict or endure enough pain to maintain their independent identities. This pattern defines, not only the dynamics of the self-Other relationship, but also that of the protagonist's own identity. The heroine accepts domination, accepts the position of masochist, because the assertion of her identity, tied up as it is with the qualities of passivity and respectability, demands she accept this role. The hero, who seeks to dominate his world and acts out the role of sadist, is also inflicting pain and suffering on himself, as all of his actions lead to his own destruction. This internalization of the sadomasochistic pattern is the logical precondition for the Gothic fantasy's repeated use of the double. The self is both sadist and masochist, both dominated and dominator, at once submissive and assertive.

From the very beginning of the genre, we can see this clearly in the male protagonist. In *The Castle of Otranto,* everything Manfred does, from the time the giant helmet falls from the sky and kills his son Conrad, is designed to take control of his world and to assure his continued identity as duke of Otranto. But each of his actions in fact moves him closer and closer to the collapse of his line and his own loss of identity. Victor Frankenstein creates a being who will worship him as a god, acting out the role of dominator, but he finds himself terrorized by the creature. Each duplicates the sadistic acts of the other, in the destruction of the creature's mate by Victor and the murder of Elizabeth by the monster. In *Caleb Williams,* Caleb comes to view Falkland as a monster who dominates and controls his life, destroying him; but when he confronts his tormentor at the end of the novel, Caleb realizes that Falkland holds exactly the same view of him. They have become mirror images of each other, each the sadist to the other's masochist.

Caleb Williams allows us to see the essential instability of the domination and submission patterns in the Gothic fantasy, and how that instability results in the creation of doubled identities, in which characters either, as in Godwin's novel, become versions of each other or, as in *Jekyll and Hyde,* literally become two people. The figure of the double, transforms the self-Other relationship into a self-self relationship. Rather than finding the Gothic protagonist isolated in a hostile world, we see that the Other resolves itself into a version of the self, a fragmentation and externalization of identity that destroys the self as fully and as surely as the overt attacks of its nemesis.[8]

This transformation of the relationship of self to Other into the relationship of self to self occurs for both male and female protagonists, particularly later in the nineteenth century, when Laura finds her double in Carmilla, and the governess her double in Miss Jessel. Early in the history of the genre, female characters rarely find the self-Other relationship transformed into a self-self dynamic. The passivity of such characters as Emily St. Aubert and Clara Weiland makes this transformation impossible, for by refusing to act, they never manifest the dominating, sadistic side of their own identities that would redefine them as doubled selves. We must be aware, though, that the passivity and acceptance we see in the heroines is not a surrender to their situation, but a style of resistance and self-assertion. Though submissive in form, it is in content equivocal, embodying both the impulse to submit and to dominate, the sadistic and the masochistic dynamic. Clearly the male and female protagonists of the Gothic fantasy act out, not only romance archetypes of masculine and feminine identity, but the dominant archetypes of Western culture. What is important here is that both these archetypes are shown to be self-destructive and inadequate, leading, not to the fulfillment and fruition of identity, but to its fragmentation and destruction.

The only identity possible within the Gothic world is the identity achieved by Dracula, the parody of life embodied in the vampire. Dracula's relationship to the world, to the Other, is sadistic and dominating, but he defines his own identity through submission. He has accepted his own death as the basis of his "life" and he reenacts this ultimate masochistic experience every morning when he returns to his coffin. He has completely internalized his submissive and masochistic impulses and achieved a stable, but monstrous relationship to the world of the Other. He has, as we can see in *Dracula,* achieved his identity only by becoming the embodiment of the Gothic world, by submitting complictly to the Other that he appears to dominate.

Because the self embodies within it both sides of the dynamic of all relationships in the Gothic world, and because the self manifests this duality through the creation of doubles, we can see that the encounter of the self with the Gothic world leads to the transformation and metamorphosis of the self into its opposite, either into the Other or its own hidden double. In many instances, we see the male protagonists attempt to assert their power and identity by taking control of these processes. In *Otranto,* Manfred marrys his dead son's fiancée, thus metaphorically transforming himself into his own son through an act of technical incest. Since Manfred no longer has a son to carry on the family name and preserve Manfred's identity, Manfred must simply become a new being and do the job himself. In *Frankenstein,* Victor transforms death into life and seeks to make himself into a god through his control of these powers. We also see, though, that he unwittingly unleashes his own double in the creature he has made. In *The Monk,* Ambrosio transforms himself into a monster in search of pleasure and sensual satisfaction; the same is true of both Henry Jekyll and Dorian Grey. All three men delude themselves into thinking that they are in control of the process of transformation and metamorphosis, when in fact their creation of alternative identities in an attempt to extend and complete their original, limited selves is an exercise in self-destruction.

We can thus add to our list of aspects of the character of the protagonist in the Gothic fantasy. It is victimized, isolated, in a sadomasochistic relationship both to the Other and to itself. It is in a constant process of transformation and metamorphosis, which is the manifestation of its doubled, fragmented nature. Doubling, then, is not simply a convention, but is the essential reality of the self in the Gothic world. Once the protagonist enters that world, the identity begins to break up. The line between the self and the Other begins to waver, and the wholeness and integrity of the self begins to collapse. As we have seen in *Otranto,* everything Manfred does to preserve himself leads to his destruction. At the end of the novel, he murders his daughter, Matilda, ending his family and his line. In *The Monk,* Ambrosio's search for pleasure leads him to create a new identity, the inversion of the celibate, austere, disciplined monk. But this new identity, without limits or discipline, operating only on the spark of desire, leads Ambrosio, too, to slaughter and rape his way through his own family, albeit unknowingly, destroying the source of his human identity.

In *The Mysteries of Udolpho,* the terrors of the castle and its mysterious passages evoke in Emily's imagination terrors even greater than those that are actually there. The castle functions as the externalization of Emily's own imagination, the Other, as physical environment, made into a double. The same situation appears in *Uncle Silas* and *The Turn of the Screw.* In LeFanu's novel, Maud's experiences at Bartram Haugh are the reverse of the relationship with her uncle she has fantasized, while the house itself becomes a metaphor of her uncertainty and confusion. In *Turn of the Screw,* even if one believes in the existence of the ghosts, the governess's sensitivity to their presence indicates that they express some aspect of her own identity. In the Gothic fantasy, metamorphosis and transformation are the rule: everything contains and becomes its opposite, the self is found in the Other, and the Other is in fact a face of the self. The isolation of the Gothic protagonist is complete, because as the line between self and Other disappears and the integrity of the self vanishes, the protagonist is left alone with the fragments and shards of identity, unable to distinguish between what is me and what is not-me, what is real and what is imagined, or whether such distinctions really make any difference.

The Gothic world, then, as we shall deal with in more detail in our discussion of atmosphere, is a world of utter subjectivity. This to some extent is the nature of any fantasy: it exists, but only as a projection of an individual mind. The Gothic, though, exploits this to create terror and fear. The collapse of the self is frightening exactly because it subverts the conventional assumption of the integrity of the self: held together by the soul or by sense impression or by a train of associations, the self was for most people one thing. Jane Austen could conceive easily of people having desires and impulses they did not acknowledge, that they might know themselves imperfectly, but she would never have comprehended the unstable and fragmentary self presented in the Gothic novel. The realistic novel,

on the whole, dealt with identity in terms of character and personality, the way the self manifested itself in society. The romantics dealt
with the self as, essentially, a connection between the human and the
numinous. For the Gothic fantasy, the self might simply divide and
fragment until it disappeared or the two sides of the self would lock
in combat until they destroyed each other.

Enthrallment

We have described the masculine and feminine versions of the
Gothic protagonist and seen how each character's quest for identity,
whether active or passive, leads to the fragmentation and metamorphosis of the self into its own double and the disintegration of
the integrity of the self, the loss of the distinction between self and
Other. How, exactly, can we explain the nature of the protagonist's
relationship to the Gothic world? How can we characterize the
nature of this state of fragmentation?

The protagonists, whether male or female, find themselves in a
state of enthrallment, first to the possibilities of the Gothic world,
then to its horrors. Each approaches the Gothic world, whether vol-
untarily or not, with a heightened apprehension and a restless curi-
ousity about what may lie beyond conventional reality in its underworld. The vision of the Gothic world evokes in the protagonist
both fear and desire. The stimulation of desire comes from the apparent possibilities of self-creation and gratification inherent in the
underworld. By their descent to that world, Manfred can become his
own son and preserve his identity, Victor Frankenstein can create
new beings and become a god, Ambrosio can satisfy his desire for
sensual variety and self-indulgence. Henry Jekyll can experience the
thrills and pleasures respectability forbids him, and Dorian Grey remains forever young, forever untouched by any indulgence, however
evil or destructive. Yet for each of these men, the possibilities of the
Gothic world, the prospect of infinite desire infinitely satisfied,
proves an illusion. What had been an object of desire becomes an
object of disgust, as Ambrosio finds when he has raped and stabbed
his sister Antonia in the caverns beneath the convent. "She, who had
so lately been the object of his adoration, now raised no sentiment in
his heart other than aversion and rage." Dorian Grey, who had
looked upon his portrait with excitement when he first realizes what
is happening to it, comes to regard it with fear and loathing:

> He wondered and hoped that some day he would see the change
> taking place before his very eyes, shuddering as he hoped. . . . For
> there would be real pleasure in watching it. He would be able to

follow his mind into its secret places. The portrait would be to him the most magical of mirrors.[9]

In any number of instances—Dorian Grey, Henry Jekyll, Caleb Williams, Edgar Huntley, Carwin in *Wieland*—the impulse to voyeurism is an essential aspect of the initial stages of enthrallment. Not only does the Gothic world promise satisfaction of all the protagonist's desires, but it offers the opportunity for him to regard his own fulfillment as a spectacle that is in itself a heightened satisfaction and fulfillment of desire. Yet, just as Victor Frankenstein recoils from his plans and dreams made real in his creature, the protagonist finds himself repelled and afraid of that which he had sought: Frankenstein reacts this way to his creature, Jekyll to Hyde, Dorian Grey to the portrait. The alternation from one state to the other is made clear in Caleb Williams's two responses to his discovery of Falkland's guilty secret. First, he experiences the state of enthrallment, the possibilities of heightened pleasure, as the language of the passage suggests, simultaneously sexual and religious:

> I exclaimed in a fit of uncontrollable enthusiasm, "This is the murderer! The Hawkinses were innocent! I am sure of it! I will pledge my life on it! It is out! It is discovered! Guilty upon my soul!" . . . I felt as in my animal system had undergone a total revolution. My blood boiled within me. I was conscious of a kind of rapture for which I could not account. I was solemn, yet full of emotion, burning with indignation and energy. In the very tempest and hurricane of passions, I seemed to enjoy the most soul ravishing calm. I cannot better express the then state of my mind than by saying I was never so perfectly alive as at that moment.[10]

Caleb goes on to say that this state lasted "several hours." When, though, Caleb finds himself the object of another's voyeurism, when he is discovered by Falkland searching his trunk for evidence, he experiences the other side of enthrallment, the fear of his own implication in what he has just enjoyed:

> All chaos and uncertainty was within me. My thoughts were too full of horror to be susceptible of activity. I felt deserted of intellectual powers, palsied in mind, and compelled to sit in speechless expectation of the misery to which I was destined. To my own conception I was like a man who, though blasted by lightning and deprived forever of the power of motion, should yet retain forever the consciousness of his situation. Death-dealing despair was the only idea of which I was sensible.

The possibilities of the underworld, particularly of voyeurism, a topic to which we shall return shortly, turn quickly into horrors, and the protagonist is paralyzed, caught between desire and fear, seemingly opposed emotions that have fused. The fusion of fear and desire is the resolution of the dialectic of sadomasochism that dominates the relationship with the Other and with the self; the fragmentation of the self and the creation of the double is the natural result of the protagonist's inability to resolve his state of enthrallment. As fear and desire become one, the self divides, and the protagonist finds himself locked in combat with himself, as Frankenstein battles with his creature, identity itself becoming the ultimate object of fear and desire.

For the male protagonist, whose impulse is to continue his attempt to dominate and control the Gothic world, to conquer fear by achieving the object of his desire, the enthrallment can only deepen with each action, for all objects of desire become objects of fear, and all objects of fear become objects of desire. His goal becomes what he flees from, what he flees from becomes his goal. In obtaining what he desires, Ambrosio destroys himself; Frankenstein creates his creature, seeks to destroy him, and finally embarks on an endless chase across the frozen wastes, unable to distinguish pursuer from pursued. For the female protagonist, the state of enthrallment is not usually so overt or so violent; able to sit and wait, enduring rather than attempting to dominate, she achieves a degree of release. Emily St. Aubert, through the aid of Radcliffe, escapes Udolpho, and Clara Wieland never has to fully acknowledge the peculiar attractions to both Carwin and her brother Theodore that underlie her own experiences of terror. The governess in *The Turn of the Screw* does not connect her own desires and fantasies about the distant uncle-employer with what goes on at Bly. The ability to supress desire, to convert it into passive acceptance of the Gothic world, rather than active pursuit of it, allows these characters to extricate themselves from their situations, though the underlying dynamics remain the same in each text. Modern readers inevitably recognize desires to which James's governess—and perhaps James himself—did not admit. In LeFanu's *Uncle Silas* and *Carmilla,* the heroines are much more overtly implicated in the dialectic of fear and desire. In *Uncle Silas,* Maud Ruthyn fantasizes romantically about a youthful portrait of her uncle, as well as about a more open and loving relationship with a father figure than she has achieved with her own father, Austin Ruthyn. But by the conclusion of the novel, Silas Ruthyn, a

shadowy, perfume-drenched, white-robed dope addict and murderer, has become an object of fear to Maud, her jailer and would-be
murderer. She escapes the consequences of her enthrallment only
through the magic of authorial intervention. Laura's encounter with
her ancestor-lover in *Carmilla* ends with an image of continued enthrallment, though here desire seems to dominate fear:

> It was long before the terror of recent events subsided and to this
> hour the image of Carmilla returns to memory with ambiguous
> alternations—sometimes the playful, languid girl; sometimes the
> writhing fiend I saw in the churchyard; and often from a reverie I
> have started, fancying I have heard the light footsteps of Carmilla
> at the drawing room door.[11]

The combination of horror and longing, the union of the playful and
the fiendish, the girlish and monstrous, contained in the dreamlike
existence in which Laura passively awaits the return of the lover who
is also a vampire sums up the state of enthrallment, particularly for
the female protagonist. In any given novel, the mixture of fear and
desire will vary, and the exact mood and quality of the enthrallment
changes from text to text as authors interpret this essential Gothic
state according to their own inclinations. But the dynamic, however
formed and proportioned, reappears in all Gothic fantasies.

As we have seen, the state of enthrallment encompasses and explains the sadomasochistic actions of the Gothic protagonist and explains the underlying causes for the fragmentation and doubling of
the self. Enthrallment to the possibilities and terrors of the Gothic
world becomes a type of self-hypnosis; as the protagonist watches
pleasure and terror metamorphose into a single experience, he responds by a similar, but inverted, transformation. The self, which
had been one, becomes two. Unable to resolve the paradox of the
unity of fear and desire, the self seeks to escape its paralysis through
division, attempting to obtain the capacity to act by reestablishing
the division between fear and desire, self and Other, terror and pleasure. But this division only deepens the paralytic self-hypnosis, and
the fragmentation of the self destroys the identity it was meant to
preserve. Whether, like Laura, the protagonist responds to enthrallment by passive dreams of the double or, like Frankenstein, through
rejection and flight from the double or, like Ambrosio, by attempting to embrace his new identity and actively participate in his own
transformation, the result is the same: the enthrallment is unbreak-
able, trapping the protagonist forever in the Gothic world.

A truly successful hero or heroine in a Gothic fantasy would be a character capable of entering the underworld, entering the state of enthrallment, and yet able at the same time to escape the self-hypnosis, paralysis, and disintegration of identity this state engenders. The character who can achieve critical, analytical distance from the state of enthrallment, its revelation of the fragility of the self, can escape both the enchantment of its possibilities and enslavement to its horror. Out of the Gothic fantasy comes such a character, the detective. He is neither a hero of action nor of submission, but a hero of understanding. In exploring the possibilities of this new type of character, conceived in the tensions and contradictions of the Gothic fantasy's subversion of the romance, writers create a new genre, the detective story. It is less subversive of the romance tradition than the Gothic, for it revolves around a new version of the romance hero. Although throughout the Gothic fantasy we find characters who try to fulfill the functions of the detective and thus break out of their enthrallment, in the central tradition of the genre, all such characters fail, because for them enthrallment is inevitable and inescapable.

The Gothic Atmosphere

Subjectivity as Nightmare

As we have seen, the descent into the Gothic underworld becomes a descent into the self in which the protagonists confront their own fears and desires and are transformed, metamorphosed, doubled, fragmented, and destroyed by this encounter. However, the conventions of the genre always externalize this process, presenting the psychic experience of the protagonists in terms of their encounters with exotic places, creatures, and events. Readers have come to recognize this world as characterized by what we call Gothic atmosphere: the sense of mystery, suspense, and fearful anticipation, the sense of being in the presence of the strange or different that marks all Gothic fantasies. This atmosphere is the natural counterpart of the disintegration of the self, a reflection of the breakdown of divisions between self and Other. Gothic atmosphere is in part, then, a function of subjectivity and is thus an extension of what Richardson was doing in such sentimental novels as *Pamela* and *Clarissa* and, in a very different key, of what Sterne was doing in *Tristram Shandy*. We may in fact say that it represents an important phase in the discovery—or perhaps invention might be a better word—and definition of the subjective that begins in the eighteenth century, not only in

sentimental fiction, but in the rise of autobiography as a recognizable literary form.

However, the atmosphere of the Gothic fantasy differs from the
subjective experience of reality embodied in Richardson's novels or
even in such realistic novels as *Emma*. In those works, the relationship of self to Other, of subjective perception to objective reality,
may be confused or limited for the protagonist, but this is not, on
the whole, true for the reader. That is, in *Clarissa* or *Emma* or, later
in the century, in *Middlemarch* or *Great Expectations,* we have no
serious question about the existence or nature of an objective reality,
however mistily Emma, at the beginning of Austen's novel, may perceive it. A novel like *Tom Jones* has really no atmosphere at all, no
distortion of objective reality, no troubling sense of subjectivity intervening between us and the world, though of course certain
facts—such as Tom's parentage—are not known. Fielding's point of
view is resolutely objective. Even his caricature of Blifil and Thwac-
kum is not a subjective distortion but an objective revelation of their
actual natures or perhaps more exactly, of actual personality types. In
those realistic novels that do place a subjective consciousness between us and reality, the intrusion is a function of point of view, of
our seeing essentially through the limited perceptions of one or several characters. But in the Gothic novel, the sense of a veil of subjectivity hiding the real is an aspect of the Gothic world itself. There
time and space are not absolutes through which characters can perceive a common reality and act in more or less secure relationship to
the world. Rather, they become, like identity, relative functions of
perception. The protagonists find that conventional measures of
time and space break down into aspects of their own experiences.
The frequency with which characters faint, lose consciousness, fall
into swoons, or undergo blackouts is one way in which the collapse
of time and space are portrayed in these novels. The Gothic atmosphere mirrors the collapse of the self, for just as the self is fragmented into a doubled identity, it loses its ability to place itself in
relation to an objective world. The only relationship possible in the
"subjectified" Gothic world is the relationship to the fragments of
the self. The metamorphosis of the self is extended into the transformations of time and space. By dissolving the objective, the Gothic
fantasy also dissolves the concept of the subjective; as one becomes
the other, they become indistinguishable. The peculiar qualities of
Gothic atmosphere anticipate a number of aspects of modernism,
with its emphasis of the subjectivity of reality and the collapse of
objectivity and the self.

The earliest writers in the genre, Walpole and Beckford, do little to exploit the collapse of objective and subjective relationships. *The Castle of Otranto* and *Vathek* seem almost as devoid of atmosphere, at least in this sense, as *Tom Jones*. In the works of such writers of the 1790s as Radcliffe and Charles Brockden Brown, though, we see the full development of this aspect of Gothic atmosphere. Suspense, anticipation, uncertainty, pervasive twilight and the darkening scene are the conventional devices by which this atmosphere is achieved. A very good example of this comes from *Wieland*. Large sections of the novel dramatize the passing of a few moments in Clara Wieland's house as she listens to the voices that Carwin, the ventriloquist, produces to frighten her for his own, obscure, purposes:

> Suddenly, the remembrance of what had lately passed in this closet occurred. Whether midnight was approaching or had passed, I knew not. I was, as then, alone and defenceless [*sic*]. The wind was in that direction in which, unaided by the deathlike repose of nature, it brought to me the murmur of the water-fall. This was mingled with the solemn and enchanting sound, which a breeze produces among the leaves of pines. The words of that mysterious dialogue, their fearful import, and the wild excess to which I was transported by my terrors, filled my imagination anew. My steps faultered [*sic*] and I stood a moment to recover myself.
>
> I prevailed on myself at length to move towards the closet. I touched the lock, but my fingers were powerless; I was visited afresh by unconquerable apprehensions. A sort of belief darted into my mind, that some being was concealed within whose purposes were evil. I began to contend with those fears, when it occurred to me that I might without impropriety, go for a lamp previously to opening my closet. I receded a few steps; but before I reached my chamber door my thoughts took a new direction. Motion seemed to produce a mechanical influence on me. I was ashamed of my weakness. Besides, what aid could be afforded by a lamp?
>
> My fears had pictured to themselves no precise object. It would be difficult to depict, in words, the ingredients and hues of that phantom which haunted me. A hand invisible and of preternatural strength, lifted by human passions, and selecting my life for its aim, were parts of this terrific image. All places were alike accessible to this foe, or if his empire were restricted by local bounds, these bounds were utterly inscrutable to me.[12]

This passage illustrates quite clearly the typical conventions for intensifying Gothic atmosphere through the interpenetration of subjective and objective reality. Clara begins with a clear sense of her separation from the external world and finds that world a source of "enchanting sound." However, her fears transform the sounds of nature into the memory of "that mysterious dialogue," and her imagination fills the world with terror. Time stops, space disappears, and the world around her becomes a reflection of her fears. Finally, in the third paragraph, Clara's fear detaches itself from her imagination and becomes objective reality, an "image," but an image with no dimensions or form, a reality with no location in time or space, with no describable characteristics and knowing no bounds, "utterly inscrutable" to the human being from whose imagination it appears to have sprung.

At moments like this, Clara and other Gothic protagonists encounter the Gothic world in its purest form: all atmosphere and no substance, all suggestion, possibility, inference, and suspense, totally without certainty. Similar passages can be found in *The Mysteries of Udolpho* and *The Turn of the Screw,* and the effect occurs in virtually all Gothic fantasies. In *Melmoth the Wanderer,* poor Moncada, whom Maturin subjects to every imaginable torture at the hands of the evil Catholics, finds himself confined to what we can now see as a primitive sensory deprivation chamber, a room beneath the monastery sealed off from contact with the outside world. In this room, dark and virtually soundless, time and space vanish, and Moncada finds that he has become "my own clock."[13] Objective reality, symbolized by the image of the clock, fuses with subjective, experiential measures of time into a single image of a nothingness that is also everything. Moncada and his world become the same thing. The terror that underlies the Gothic is not that some monster shall emerge; such moments are, for the reader and often for the protagonists, moments of relief. The true terror lies in the possibility that the Gothic atmosphere will take over completely and that the conventional, stable division between self and Other will disappear forever. The direct representation of such a state is, of course, beyond the resources of the novelist, particularly the Gothic writer whose audience demanded a plot, characters, and action. As I have suggested, the fog, moonlight, twilight, and darkness, the protracted suspense and mystery of the texts are the devices by which the Gothic fantasy represents the metaphysical state of fusion of subjective and objective into identityless horror.

Thus the common intuition that the Gothic world is a dreamscape, a land of nightmare, stems from this characteristic blurring of reality so central to its atmosphere. The world of the Gothic fantasy is an imitation of the world of the dream, the hallucination, in which that which is real and that which is imaginary fade into one, creating a reality that subverts our perceptions. We will return to the similarity between the Gothic fantasy and the dream and nightmare when we discuss the conventions of plot and action. For now, we simply need to see that by using it as a model in popular literature—*Otranto*, *Frankenstein*, and *Dr. Jekyll and Mr. Hyde* all, according to the authors, had their origins in dreams[14]—the genre validated and formalized the dreamscape. The Gothic fantasy is not literally dreamlike, except occasionally, at particularly intense points in the narrative or when characters actually dream. However, by articulating fantasy in terms similar to the world of dreams, the Gothic writers made dreams and nightmares a part of the real world, not as visitations from beyond or the result of physiological causes, but as an aspect, uncontrolled and dim, of human desires.

The Exotic and History

In the early years of the tradition, writers often achieved atmospheric effect through the use of exotic settings and remote time periods. The locales of the early fantasies are Spanish, Italian, German, and Middle Eastern, and they are made more remote and exotic by setting the stories in the past. Of course, the Italy and Spain of the Gothic fantasy bear little resemblance to the real Italy and Spain, nor do the writers manage to capture any real sense of history in their portrayal of the past. Even Brown, who uses contemporary settings and and places his novels *Wieland* and *Edgar Huntley* on the edge of the American wilderness, does little to evoke either real time or place. The exotic possibilities of the American frontier are what attract him, and thus, despite his proclamation that he is trying to achieve peculiarly American effects in his fiction, his attitude toward the American scene is very much the same as Radcliffe's attitude toward Italy: it is a strange place.[15] Among the major Gothic writers up to the mid 1820s, only William Godwin places his story in a recognizable time and locale:—the present, in England. This is a function, not of the Gothic aspects of *Caleb Williams*, though, but of Godwin's political purposes.

Clearly, the writers' indifference to the representation of real places and historical circumstances in their fiction stems from their use of time and setting to further separate the Gothic world from reality. The locales of these novels were, for an English audience, already exotic and strange; in transforming Italy into a fantasy world, this effect was doubled. The transformation of history and geography into aspects of fantasy emphasizes the discontinuity between the Gothic and the conventional world and further emphasizes the suspension of conventional ideas, such as the laws of cause and effect and the nature of identity. The Gothic writer exploits the past as the location of the other reality of fantasy, a world released from the rules of the here and now. Leslie Fiedler has said that the Gothic fantasy embodies the fear of the past and is thus either implicitly or explicitly revolutionary, marking an attempt to break with the old, feudal order.[16] This is certainly to some extent true, but the past that creates fear in the Gothic fantasy is not so much the past of the ancien régime as it is the immediate past of parents and family. Even in such novels as *The Italian* and *Melmoth the Wanderer* in which the Catholic Church is an obvious symbol of the old order, the corruption and horror of the family lurks behind the corruption and horror of the Church. In both of these books, Maturin and Radcliffe, English Protestants, appear to argue that the Church has corrupted the family. Moncada's weak and venal parents turn their son over to the horrors of the ex-Jesuits because of the sinister influence the priest known only as the Director exercises over them. But in *The Italian,* the evil of the Church and the Inquisition are really only extensions of the familial evil of Schedoni and the marquessa, who plots to kill her own son, apparently because he might make an embarrassing marriage. The fantasy plays upon fears generated by the historical past, the terrors of a feudal, Catholic, authoritarian society, and fears generated by the relations between generations and the power of parents over children. But as the two versions of the past, the historical and the familial, come together in a novel like *The Italian,* we can see that it reflects, not simply fear and rebellion against an actual past, but against the very concept of pastness embodied in a modern conception of history. The creation of the Gothic fantasy world is an assertion of the existence of a timeless reality outside history, one in which historical reality can be used as a source of imaginative pleasure and in this way controlled. This attitude toward history can be seen more clearly if we briefly compare the Gothic fantasy to the historical novel, another popular genre of the nineteenth century.

This historical novel is essentially an attempt to imaginatively reconcile the individual to the fact of history and to the idea that the past, though it is the cause of the present, is in fundamental ways irrevocably lost. In *Waverly,* Scott recreates the vanished Scottish past, which serves as a standard against which change can be measured and in this way revives and restores the past to the present. *Waverly* also shows the reader a way of life that has been lost and cannot come again, because it is simply irrelevant to the world of the nineteenth century. Even in its nostalgia about vanished traditions and values, the historical novel effects a momentary union between past and present. The Gothic fantasy, in contrast, embodies, and even glorifies, the alienation of the individual from history. In the world of cardboard battlements and mock-monasteries that dot the landscape of the early Gothic novels, the past vanishes into an aspect of the mind, a projection of fantasy. As Emily St. Aubert finds the world of Udolpho turning into the mirror of her own fears, so the world of Italy becomes that of the author's and reader's imagination. By making the past vanish into fantasy, making it into a function of exotic atmosphere, part of the literary dreamscape, the author and reader both accept the disappearance and irrelevance of history and replace the past with a world outside of time. Historical processes are disrupted and replaced by dreams; indeed, the obvious artificiality and nonhistorical qualities of the Gothic fantasy are, essentially, a rejection of the very idea of history as something to be taken seriously. When Scott defended *The Castle of Otranto* in his preface to the 1811 edition of the novel, he defended it as a historical novel. His defense is clearly more relevant to his own work, for in fact, *Otranto* stands as a type of prescient parody of the historical novel. The Gothic world's transcendence is perhaps best embodied in Dracula, a man of the Middle Ages who breaks the bonds of time, bridging the feudal and modern worlds in his attempt to conquer England as in the past he had conquered Transylvania. For the Gothic fantasy, as for Dracula, historical time is an illusion.

After the 1820s, exotic settings tend to disappear from the genre, along with the extravagant romance style and diction. To a lesser degree, it loses its strictly aristocratic cast of characters, though the writers can never completely resist the allure of a lord or an occasional count. Poe does use noncontemporary settings, and LeFanu and Stoker both send their readers to that "whirlpool of imagination," Transylvania, but on the whole, Gothic fantasies are set in the present or the recent past in England and America. *Frankenstein* moves into the present, and *Melmoth the Wanderer* and *The Private Memoirs and Confessions of a Justified Sinner* move their stories closer to England (presumably Ireland and Scotland were both near and strange).

In the last two thirds of the nineteenth century, the Gothic fantasy appears to indulge in elaborate shows of ordinariness, in many ways mimicking the language, setting, and characters typical of realistic fiction. We can hardly be surprised that writers respond to the dominant literary conventions of their eras or adjust their work to their audience's experience and taste, but their abandonment of Inquisitions, ex-Jesuits, Italian love, and Italian vengeance is more than simply the following of fashion. While nineteenth-century authors could not truly produce eighteenth-century novels, exotic settings and extravagant writing are not unknown in nineteenth-century fiction. The fantasies of writers such as Morris and MacDonald show this quite clearly. The Gothic writers abandon much of their exotic machinery because the internal logic of the genre made this the most reasonable course to follow. The atmosphere of the novels is heightened by a more subtle interpenetration of the exotic and ordinary after 1820. The wild intrigues of the Inquisition are less exotic and less of a signal of the strange, discontinuous landscape of the Gothic than the appearance of Dracula at high noon in Picadilly. The early fantasies disrupt the continuity of history by making the past into part of an imaginary world; later works disrupt the present, juxtaposing the conventional and unexceptional with the strange and inexplicable. The immediacy of the exotic in the later fantasies heightens Gothic atmosphere and compensates for the loss of the extravagant settings of the 1790s. This substitution of a single bizarre event—a vampire walks the streets of London, a man's soul enters his portrait, a scientist learns how to split himself into two distinct persons—for a whole exotic world also reflects the submergance of the romance form into the realistic novel. The vitality of the genre depended on its recognizable link to the form it subverted; as romance mythology and archetypes appear in realistic forms, the Gothic fantasy follows this transformation like a shadow.

The Supernatural and the Monstrous

Another convention of Gothic atmosphere is the presence of the supernatural or the monstrous; we know we have entered the Gothic world when we begin to encounter vampires and demons. Like the exotic locale, the appearance of the monstrous or supernatural corrodes the vision of reality that confines such things to the world of nothingness. As we have seen, the supernatural being, the monster, is part of the distortion of reality common to the tradition. It abolishes time, space, and all other expectations: Melmoth the Wanderer lives both inside and outside time, and though he can act within the conventional world, he does so by suspending its rules; he is always its enemy, always challenging it. Frankenstein's creature and Edward Hyde are also beings, natural rather than supernatural monsters, who intrude upon otherwise ordinary worlds and whose appearance signals the crumbling of reality, which dissolves into insubstantiality at their touch. The creature destroys Frankenstein's world as he destroys his family, and Hyde not only destroys Jekyll and his dream of respectability and self-indulgence, but he destroys Lanyon, Jekyll's friend, whose nerves and heart cannot endure the shock of discovering his double identity.

Yet at the same time, the supernatural and even, strictly speaking, the naturally monstrous are not actually a necessary part of the Gothic fantasy. *The Mysteries of Udolpho, The Italian, Wieland, Edgar Huntly, Caleb Williams,* and *Uncle Silas* contain no such beings or events, and the same is true of a number of Poe's tales. The narrators of stories like "The Black Cat" and "The Tell-Tale Heart" claim to have had supernatural experiences, but what they describe could also be the result of psychosis or extreme guilt, leading to hallucinations. Frankenstein's and Dr. Jekyll's monsters are the products of scientific investigation and thus within the world of the text explicable in terms of natural laws. Shelley and Stevenson are not really at all "scientific," but we cannot simply ignore the fact that they take the trouble to invoke science in their stories, however vaguely. Radcliffe hints at supernatural events but at the end of her novels always reveals perfectly rational and natural explanations of everything that has happened. In *Edgar Huntly,* Edgar claims that it has been given to him "to o'er leap the bounds of time and space," and, indeed, he does perform prodigious feats. However, on closer examination, we see that none of his deeds is supernatural; he has remained within the bounds of time and space despite the illusion that he has overcome them. The supernatural and monstrous are a matter of effect rather than substance. Again, it is the impression of strangeness, the sensation that one is in the presence of that which suspends and calls into doubt the laws of the universe that is essential to the Gothic, even if this effect is later explained away.

Devendra Varma and Judith Wilt both maintain that the Gothic fantasy embodies contact with the numinous, or spiritual, reality.[17] On the contrary, I would argue that it portrays the disintegration of the spiritual. Just as Gothic atmosphere subverts the physical, world of science, the laws of time and space, it also subverts the world of the numinous, which is transformed into the monstrous or freakish, the strange and exotic. It does not represent an order or a plan of reality higher than that of physical reality. The supernatural, or the sense of the supernatural, when it occurs in the Gothic fantasy, is the manifestation, not of transcendent order, but of chaos and disruption.

The rejection of the spiritual appears first in the works of Anne Radcliffe. Though she herself was a conventionally religious person and doubtless believed in a divine providence that watched over human beings, her novels always insist on the impossibility of supernatural events or manifestations. For Radcliffe, everything is explicable and so while presenting a Gothic world, she also claims that reality fits the classic eighteenth-century mechanistic model. The supernatural, for Radcliffe, is the product of a "distempered imagination," not an aspect of the real world. Radcliffe was apparently comfortable with a clockwork world, for her conception of the clockmaker is God. But in *Melmoth the Wanderer,* this image is a source of horror. The monastery of the ex-Jesuits is repeatedly described as a mechanism, and the monks as automatons; Moncada's terror stems from his fear of becoming absorbed into this soulless, rational system. Maturin, like Radcliffe, believes in a benevolent God behind the mechanism, but since his mechanism creates even more horror than Radcliffe's and the existence of God is affirmed mainly through his absence, we are left with the frightening picture of a world that seems to function without providence,

Frankenstein and *Jekyll and Hyde* are further developments of the Gothic fusion of the scientific, rational world with a monstrousness that is an inversion of the numinous. Both Victor Frankenstein and Dr. Jekyll are scientists, and their creations should fall within the laws of the physical universe. Instead they transform the natural world into a source of the monstrous. Jekyll and Frankenstein are caught in the paradox that by purusing the logic of scientific investigation and the powers inherent in the understanding of the laws of the universe, they have created beings that are antinatural, that seem to call into question the order and comprehensibility of the material world. Nor do these creations lead us to the apprehension of a spiritual reality that could give meaning to the apparently fractured world of materialistic science. The effect of the creature and of Hyde both on Frankenstein and Jekyll and on the reader is, as Varma and Wilt suggest, similar to an awareness of the numinous, but this awareness leads to no understanding of a higher reality. The creature and Hyde remain what they began as: monsters, products of the physical world called forth through thoroughly natural means.

They are, to some extent, special cases in the Gothic canon, for they imply the numinous without actually being so. Yet they are also archetypal, as we see in even those novels that present the monstrous as supernatural beings. Dracula, for example, gives the impression of belonging to a spiritual or nonscientific reality, when in fact he calls into question, and in effect cancels, the very concepts of either scientific or spiritual meaning in the universe. The Gothic, by use of the monstrous and supernatural, divests the physical and spiritual worlds of their power to impress a sense of order on the human mind. Such monsters as Falkland and Caleb Williams become to each other— here not even science intervenes to create the monstrous, which is simply a product of human imagination and ego—emphasize the fact that the Gothic world is a *naturally* monstrous universe, a logical paradox in which all principles of order cease to operate. The Gothic world is at once physical and supernatural but unbounded by the laws of the material world and without divine or spiritual order. Just as the Gothic atmosphere blurs, and, at its utmost extreme eliminates, the distinction between the objective and subjective, so it dissolves the concepts of physical and spiritual reality.

However, certain Gothic texts do employ supernatural events and charaters, rather than relying on the creations of science, rationalistic explanation, hallucination, or psychological imbalances to give the impression of the presence of the otherworldly and the strange. True monsters and demons appear in *Otranto, Vathek, The Monk, The Private Memoirs and Confessions of a Justified Sinner, Melmoth the Wanderer,* and *Dracula*. In the last two works, both Maturin and Stoker appear to believe in God and to use the Gothic world to justify this belief. The question still remains, Are such texts, as I have claimed, essentially the same as those in which the monstrous is not an aspect of the supernatural or do they constitute a different class of Gothic fantasy and create a different type of Gothic world?

The texts that rely on supernatural events and characters fall into two categories. In the first four, the supernatural functions purely to set the stage of the genre; they signal the conventionality of the supernatural as a peculiar aspect of the imaginary reality of the Gothic world. They do not reflect anything like belief in a spiritual or supernatural reality outside the text. In these works, the Gothic remains resolutely nonmimetic of spiritual as well as physical reality.

The supernatural as it appears in *Otranto, Vathek, The Monk,* and

Private Memoirs is rendered to some extent ludicrous. The first event in *Otranto* is the death of young Conrad when a giant helmet falls from the sky and he is "dashed to pieces and almost buried beneath it."[18] The giant helmet is certainly out of the ordinary, certainly monstrous, and, as we discover later, the first signal of the supernatural vengeance about to overtake Manfred. Nor do I underestimate the unpleasantness of being dashed to pieces, however improbably. However, we recognize that this is, at best, a silly manifestation of the supernatural. When we learn that Manfred's grandfather escaped divine justice by making a deal with a local saint to have his punishment put off, we can be confident that we are dealing with a purely formal representation of the supernatural, a representation so formalized that it is drained of content, except as an aspect of the Gothic world. The same situation is true in *Vathek*. In this novel, the characters live comfortably with the marvelous and supernatural as everyday occurrences. When the Giaour rolls himself into a ball and literally bowls over the caliph's servants, and the queen's mutes and negresses disport themselves with ghouls, we are in the presence of completely conventionalized uses of the supernatural, uses that devalue and subvert the idea as fully as does Radcliffe's explaining the mysterious events of her novel away. The supernatural events in these novels function in much the same way as the marvelous events in *Alice in Wonderland:* they let us know we are in wonderland and should adjust our imaginations accordingly. Walpole may have taken his giant helmet seriously, though Beckford appears to have intended the comic effects of the supernatural in *Vathek*. Whatever the intent of either author, though, the effect remains: the supernatural is deprived of its force as an aspect of the real world, as a serious principle of order.

In *The Monk*, the appearance of such characters as the Bleeding Nun and the Wandering Jew are again self-enclosed supernatural conventions, existing for the effect of the fantasy, not to reflect a serious encounter between the physical and spiritual worlds. At the conclusion of the novel, when Ambrosio makes his pact with the devil and Matilda is revealed as a demon sent to tempt him, Lewis may seem to be seriously invoking the Faust tradition. However, the actual presentation of the demonic in this text undercuts itself. Lewis's devil is a hideous winged creature out of a medieval illustration: he is a stylized figure of artistic and literary tradition, not a genuine devil, a manifestation of the numinous. Ambrosio's punishment for his final pact with the devil is pictured in purely physical terms, in a long paragraph of hideous torment, as he is beset by insects and eagles. When "the corse of the despairing monk" is borne away by the waters of the flood, this is the last we see of him.[19] Lewis does not imagine supernatural torments for Ambrosio, for his supernatural world is a part of the Gothic world, which is beyond conventional ideas of heaven and hell.

A more sophisticated devil appears in *The Private Memoirs and Confessions of a Justified Sinner*. Gil-Martin is not the winged monster of *The Monk*, but a suave and urbane gentleman who happens to be the Prince of Darkness. He tempts Wringham, uses supernatural powers on his behalf—as Matilda does for Ambrosio—and finally takes his victim off to hell and eternal damnation. Hogg's circumspect and polite devil, though, creates no more sense of an actual devil than does Lewis's. Since from very early on in Wringham's narrative, we know Gil-Martin is the devil and are also aware that Wringham is so egocentric and obtuse that he does not, Gil-Martin becomes in many ways an ironic device, not "real". We are aware of him, not as a demon, but as an illuminator of Wringham's nature This devilish sophisticate proclaims his literary qualities every bit as fully as the winged monster in *The Monk*.

Further, in both *The Monk* and *Private Memoirs*, the real focus is not on the encounter of the physical and supernatural worlds. Ambrosio wills himself to become a monster, and Wringham follows out the implications of his own personality and values to their logical extreme. The devils have no real power over their victims, except insofar as their victims give them power. The forces that shape Ambrosio's and Wringham's destinies are, not the power of the supernatural nor that of the material world, but rather the force of their own natures. The devils in these books function, not only as images of the monstrous, meaningless supernatural of the Gothic world, but also as doubles, as projections of the monstrousness of the human characters. That which seems supernatural in these novels does not truly come from without, but from within. Had the spiritual world real power or meaning in either text, then we would, by definition, be out of the Gothic world and into genuine religious allegory.

In *Melmoth* and *Dracula*, the supernatural does seem to have real force. Not only do both novels present powerful demonic figures, but each seems to represent a conventional vision of the nature of the spiritual and its relation to earthly life. The human world is the battleground between the forces of good and the forces of evil, independent spiritual realities whose existence gives the universe meaning.

Nevertheless, both authors were employing traditional notions of good and evil as pure conventions defining the world within the fantasy. The question remains, then, to what extent can Maturin and Stoker reverse the subversive tendencies of the genre?

When we examine *Melmoth* closely, however, we can see that Maturin's intent, as explained in his preface, is apparently outmaneuvered by his imagination: the power of the Gothic fantasy overtakes his announced intentions. Melmoth, who represents the demonic in the novel, is in fact a symbol of humanity. He wanders the earth, one of the living dead, seeking someone who will join him in his rejection of God and his power. As we see in the Indian's Tale, in which Melmoth falls in love with Immalee, to pursue damnation and human love are essentially the same thing. Melmoth's quest to damn souls is also a quest for a fully human world, independent of God, sustaining existence purely through human love and power. Only God makes the terrible suffering of the various characters Melmoth tempts meaningful; Melmoth asks them to substitute pleasure and satisfaction in the human world, the physical world, for the prospect of salvation after death. Melmoth is a very Enlightenment demon and comes to represent, not the devil or the principle of evil as it exists in the world of the numinous, but rather the search for a fully human alternative to a spiritual reality whose essential manifestation for human beings is pain. Melmoth is truly a Gothic being, rather than a supernatural one, existing in limbo between the purely physical and the truly spiritual. This is the meaning of his peculiar state beyond death in the human world, with power over time and space but still existing in terms of time and space. The reality represented by Melmoth is what really fires Maturin's imagination. The irony of Maturin's attempt to make the case for God is that while he can portray the Job-like suffering and excruciating horrors undergone by the various victims in the novel, he is unable to make God's restoration and the prospect of salvation in any way convincing. Both the physical world—the world of Spain, the ex-Jesuits, and the Inquisition—and the spiritual world are, in *Melmoth,* simply the sources of pain and suffering.

Like Melmoth, Dracula is also a supernatural being whose qualities actually identify him as part of the peculiar Gothic world in which material and spiritual intermingle. If Melmoth was a Gothic version of Englightenment man seen through Maturin's particular brand of Calvinism, Dracula is the image of modern man. Jonathan Harker comments, early in his visit to Castle Dracula, that the count "would make a marvelous solicitor,"[20] and this, despite his feudal origins and supernatural powers, is really the count's keynote.[20] Like Melmoth, Dracula possesses power over time, space, and nature, but he has achieved this only by rejecting the spiritual world. To become supernatural, Dracula in fact has become more a part of the natural world, not less. Dracula's kingdom is of this world, founded by denying death, by refusing to leave the material world. His immortality is completely physical, a reversal of biological processes, for he is death feeding on life, rather than life feeding on death. Dracula's powers over time, space, and nature are nevertheless limited by natural forces. He is no more powerful than an ordinary man between noon and sunset, he must sleep in his native soil, and he can be barred entrance and held at bay by garlic, the branch of the wild rose, and running water. Of course, he also fears the cross and the host, the symbols of the spiritual world he has rejected, but he can be destroyed only as one would destroy a living human, by cutting off his head or driving a stake through his heart. Insofar as Dracula is death incarnate, the individualized representation of death, its kingdom and power, he represents, a physical or material reality, not a spiritual or truly supernatural, reality. He is modern man in that he lives only for himself; in a purely physical and material reality, in which only his own desires and wants shape his relationship to the world, unrestrained by any system of order or any meaning beyond himself. Such supernatural or spiritual reality as exists for him, he creates himself. If Melmoth seems at times a forlorn and melancholy searcher after a human utopia, Dracula is engaged in a quest for dystopia. In both instances, though, each character represents a world neither physical nor spiritual, in which neither the scientific nor the religious or mythic vision of reality and its meaning is powerful.

Thus, the Gothic cosomology is completely humanized. It is created and defined by the collective fears and desires of nineteenth-century culture, the culture that called the Gothic into being and that sustained it. It refers only to the human emotions and impulses that shaped it, not to a vision of reality and order that exists independent of the human act of fantasizing. As an imaginative projection of the nineteenth-century, the Gothic refers back and appeals exclusively to the human world from which it came. At the same time, it reflects perfectly the alienation of that world from both the intractable physical order of science and the eternal order of myth. The Gothic fantasy is a realm created by the human imagination, into which the

human imagination retreats. Nevertheless, it also represents the alienation of the human imagination from its own products. To escape
anxiety and terror, the imagination creates fantasies of anxiety and
terror; the experiences that cause our alienation reappear in our escapes from it. The human world dramatized in the Gothic fantasy is
a historyless, orderless abyss. Thus, not only is the human world
alienated from the visions of science and myth, but it is also pro-
foundly self-alienated. In the Gothic fantasy, the human imagination
can only externalize the fears it finds in itself.

The Gothic Fantasy and Narrative Form

Narrative is fundamentally action is a meaningful sequence. Through
the use of different kinds of action in various types of sequence,
narrative form defines the world in a fictional text; we can see how
this happens in the contrast between Tom Jones and *Tristram Shandy*. In *Tom Jones,* the narrative and the world portrayed in the narrative are a series of intricate, interlocking physical events. Fielding
imagines a world in which "reality" is a sequence of causes and effects; understanding the structure of the narrative leads to an understanding of the meaning of the fictional world and, for Tom, the
discovery of his own identity. The form of the narrative in *Tom Jones*
reflects the patterns of cause and effect that are the essence of the
world imagined in the novel. In *Tristram Shandy,* narrative form portrays reality as a series of interlocking perceptions, associations, and
memories; the world of physical action, the *"Tom Jones"* world is
subsumed into mental or subjective action. The form of Sterne's
narrative also derives from the nature of the reality he imagines. In a
romance or allegory, the narrative form reflects the underlying mythos or system of ideas, as in *The Fairie Queen;* both the sequence
and the nature of the action are shaped by the logic of their under-
pinnings. Obviously none of these texts offer the reader anything but
a stylized version of actions in reality, whether physical, mental, mythic or allegorical. But in all these genres, narrative form implies a
pattern of order and meaning that has significance in the world of
the text and in the world outside it. Narrative form mediates between the world of the text and that of the reader. By these apparent
correspondences, we are able to mesh our imaginations with the
imaginary world of the story. Thus, conventionally, the narrative
both creates the world of the text and reflects the relationship of that
world to reality.

The writers of Gothics though, make no claims upon the real

world in their works. The Gothic fantasy certainly makes no attempt to portray life as it really is, nor does it seem to be attached to any systematic vision of reality. Certainly its world is not one of literary realism as we find it in Fielding, Austen, or Scott, nor is it the inner world of Sterne; it rejects the mythos of romance and is attached to no allegorical system. The Gothic fantasy portrays a world spun purely out of the human imagination. It appears, at times, to contain aspects of the realistic novel's vision, of the romance mythos, allegorical systems, or of Sternian interior consciousness. It is made up of the fragments of other versions of the world, versions that the Gothic reveals as incomplete and inadequate to describe its imagined world.

The novelist, then, must devise a form that will both express the strangeness and unreality of the Gothic world and yet allow the reader access to that world. The Gothic narrative takes as its model the dream, nightmare, or hallucination. Such modes have as part of their essential quality a pervading strangeness and fragmentation, a sense of the familiar rendered bizarre. By using the dream as a model, Gothic narrative form creates this familiar strangeness, and it is never dispelled in the course of the narrative. The fantasy remains both accessible and strange, in the same way that dreams or hallucinations are.

Yet the dream, nightmare, and hallucination are not narrative forms at all; they lack action in meaningful sequence. Sterne's portrayal of inner consciousness has a structure, however chaotic it may appear, but the dream form needs no structure or order. The novelist is caught in a dilemna: the form that can both portray the imagined reality of the Gothic world and allows access to that world for the reader is not, strictly speaking, narrative and offers no guiding principle of order except apparent orderlessness. One cannot write books that are really like dreams; the writer's task is the manipulation of conventional narrative structures in such a way that dreamlike strangeness is maintained. Thus, throughout the Gothic fantasy, we see over and over the elusvie fragments of other types of narratives, the images of our own stylized versions of reality. These fragments, though, serve only to frustrate us, for we can never succeed in converting the Gothic fantasy back into a realistic novel or a romance. We search in its narrative form for the rules by which the Gothic dream world brings these fragments together, only to discover that the real rule is the parody and subversion of the forms enlisted in the creation of a sense of formlessness. By creating a "formless" narrative, the genre calls into question the capacity of narrative to portray reality. It subverts conventional modes of storytelling, which make either explicit or implicit appeals for validation to ideas about the "real" world and asserting the correspondence of narrative form to objective reality. Writers like Sterne and Fielding, of course, recognized that the form of narrative was never more than an analogue to reality, but their work seems to rest on the assumption that such analogues are possible. The writers in the Gothic tradition create narratives that advertize their discontinuity with the real world, subverting and parodying the analogues to the real world that appear in the fantasies as the fragments of a dream or hallucination.

The Gothic fantasy does more than call into question the capacity of narrative form to comment on and represent reality. It undermines fundamental modern conceptions about the nature of reality. The Gothic subverts the notion that reality consists of meaningful chains of cause and effect, that meaning resides in patterns of action, that action may result in progress or even bring about change. Its rejection of action in favor of dreamlike or hallucinatory narrative structures creates another problem for the Gothic writer, since sequences of action are the substance of narrative. Again, the novelist does not do away with sequences of action, but rather portrays action in such a way that it is revealed as meaningless. In the Gothic world, no action can really occur.

By "action" we do not mean simply energetic motion, for the Gothic is full of this sort of activity. Manfred in *Otranto* is nothing if not busy, and a great deal happens to Henry Jekyll. But in the Gothic, no action can ever achieve its intended result. Meaningful action, action that moves from point a to point b, either physically or psychically, is impossible. Manfred cannot become his own son and Henry Jekyll cannot successfully split himself into two people. Each of these attempts collapses back in upon itself. The Gothic world, like a black hole in space, allows no energy to escape, but traps it in a closed system. Action can never be progressive, only circular; whatever the protagonist tries to do, his actions must result in his own disintegration. The more energetic his motion, the sooner this will occur. Gothic fantasies portray actions that move from point a back to point a, except that in this movement, the identity of the actor erodes. The Gothic protagonist achieves only the illusion of meaningful action, for every movement is in fact the same movement: a downward spiral to destruction. Whenever the protagonist in a Gothic fantasy attempts to accomplish anything, we recognize almost immediately that he is doomed to failure. In Hogg's *Private Memoirs,* we see that Gil-Martin is the devil right away, and we know that all Wringham's efforts to prove himself one of the elect move him toward damnation. As when in a dream we find ourselves powerless to act, so in the Gothic we intuitively recognize that action is hopeless; we see this in Manfred, Ambrosio, Jekyll, and all the other Gothic protagonists. Those who act, whatever their intent, destroy themselves; only those who are passive, who refuse to be drawn into the illusion of action, can be saved. In the Gothic, to act is to plunge into meaninglessness and oblivion; in denying the meaningfulness of action, the genre denies the meaningfulness of the objective, physical world, the world that meant reality in the nineteenth century.

The Gothic draws heterogenously and parodically on other forms in the creation of narrative; this tendency explains why early Gothic fantasies appear to be mock versions of the romance (*Otranto*), the oriental tale (*Vathek*); or the sentimental novel (*The Mysteries of Udolpho* and *The Monk* and, to a lesser degree, Brown's *Wieland* and *Edgar Huntly*). Each of these texts bears a resemblance to a more familiar form but always subverts the conventional expectations the reader brings to such genres. In *Otranto,* Theodore, the nominal hero, proves an ineffective cipher; in *Vathek* the oriental tale, conventionally a "moral story" or apologue, is transformed into an experiment in excess, and the moral seems almost an afterthought. The Gothic versions of the sentimental novel extend and twist the conventions until they subvert the very values they appear to affirm. Radcliffe's affirmations of sentimental virtues in the marriages of Emily and Valancourt and of Vivaldi and Elena are forced happy endings that contradict the novels' essential mood of gloom and horror.

As the Gothic fantasy becomes a tradition of its own, the need to draw overtly on other genres lessens. LeFanu and James can look back to Radcliffe and invoke her uses of the sentimental tradition. The development of the Gothic fantasy as a genre with its own narrative rules includes the development of highly unreliable narrators and of competing narrators within the same text. The earliest fantasies use third-person narrators but tend to subvert this seemingly reliable point of view. Radcliffe's and Lewis's narrators violate their apparent omniscience. Radcliffe arbitrarily withholds information from the reader in both *The Mysteries of Udolpho* and *The Italian;* she refuses to tell the reader what Emily sees behind the curtain in

Udolpho, for instance. Lewis, in *The Monk,* declines to reveal
Matilda's true identity and Ambrosio's parentage. We may decide
that the information withheld is hardly something a reasonably intelligent reader might not deduce, but the very transparency of what
the narrator withholds calls attention to itself. In both instances, we
are made conscious of the artifices of narrative strategy, breaking the
illusion that the version of reality presented in the text meshes with
reality outside the text. We also see that the Gothic fantasy violates
its own apparent narrative rules.

In *Wieland* and *Edgar Huntly,* we are confined to the viewpoint of
a first-person narrator; both Clara and Huntley not only fail to understand events as they occur, but they never come to an adequate
understanding of events after the fact. The use of the retrospective
first person is characteristic of the genre. We see this strategy in such
stories as Poe's "The Tell-Tale Heart" and "The Fall of the House of
Usher," in LeFanu's *Uncle Silas* and *Carmilla,* and James's *The Turn
of the Screw.* Each of the stories interposes, not only the perspective
of the narrator between the reader and reality, but also the veil of
memory, since each of them is recollected. The Gothic fantasy is a
tale retold, memory turned into narrative, rather than action embodied in narrative. This structure emphasizes the origin of the Gothic
world in the individual imagination and also the fact that the narrative is a story, an artifice that self-consciously recounts a sequence
of action, not a portrayal of an actual sequence of action. By enfold-
ing *The Turn of the Screw* within the brief introduction, James places
the governess's story in the context of other stories, rather than in
relation to reality. The introduction is full of red herrings—Is the
governess's story a true story or just a story she has made up? What
was her exact relationship to Douglas?—which lead us to examine
the narrative as a construct, instead of as a representation of reality or
an expression of the romance myth.

Gothic fantasies, even those using a single point of view, resolve,
implicitly or explicitly, into narratives that embody multiple points
of view. As we recognize in reading *Wieland* that Clara's understanding and retelling of the story is not adequate, we come to realize that
even though we hear no voices other than hers, other voices must
exist. The failure of Clara's point of view to fully explain what has
happened demands that other points of view exist, even if we can
only fantasize about them. The most fully "Gothic" narrative structures exploit the multiplicity of voices and viewpoints implied by all
narratives of the genre. In *Frankenstein,* Walton's story frames Vic-

tor's story, which frames the creature's story, which frames the story of the family of "the excellent Felix," the DeLacys. The real narrative structure is, not a sequence of actions, but a sequence of stories. The action in the novel is shattered and fragmented. Each story within the story appears to form a sequence of events in the style of a realistic or "objective" narrative, but in fact this linear chain of cause and effect is subordinated to the real units of narrative, the stories that embody the characters' interpretations of the events that have happened. The meaning, the coherence, of the narrative lies, not in the actions, but in the juxtaposition of the various viewpoints within the text. Each narrative is a mirror, a double, of the others, and the actions of the stories are subordinate to larger patterns that derive from the act of telling stories. The overall form of *Frankenstein* is a circle: we return to where we began, with Walton still facing the same questions, shall he continue his quest, strike out on his own, or return to the world where he might find companionship and friendship? The novel's form makes progress or self-discovery or awakening impossible. Tom Jones may find his mother, Emma marry Knightly, Pip come to understand fully the meaning of his expectations, but in the world of the Gothic, transformation and metamorphosis lead only back to the place from which one started, and thus further into the underworld.

The structure of *Melmoth the Wanderer* also moves the reader further and further away from the world of action, as we pass through narrator after narrator, through a labyrinth of voices, until we arrive at the story of Guzman's family, a tale within a tale, within a tale, within a tale, within a tale. This process of refraction and reflection diverts us, keeps us from seeing the novel as an analogue to reality, from the idea that a sequence of actions has meaning apart from the tales in which they occur, refocusing our awareness on the act of fantasizing itself. The Gothic fantasy dissolves conventional expectations about reality and truth. Objective and subjective become a double spectacle: a display of violence and horror but also a display of storytelling. The disintegration and chaos of the fantasy coexist with the order created by the act of storytelling.

The use of the enfolded tale is, of course, an old device, going back to *The Golden Ass* of Apuleius. Indeed, Fielding uses it in the story of the Old Man of the Hill in *Tom Jones*. In *Tom Jones*, though, it does not become a principle of organization calling into question the nature of the real. Further, the Gothic fantasy does not simply use the enfolded tale derived from earlier tradition but develops a type of narrative that extends the strategy. *The Private Memoirs and Confessions of a Justified Sinner* is composed of three sections: a third-person narrative about the death of George Colwin; a first-person account by Colwin's brother, Robert Wringham, revealing that Wringham has been involved with the devil; and finally, a second third-person narrative, whose connection to the initial one is unclear—they may or may not be by the same person. This third narrative seems to cast doubt on the previous two, suggesting, for instance, that Wringham's tale is an allegory, not an account of actual dealings with the devil. The novel is not really a series of enfolded narratives, since each section exists independently of the others: the various tellers never meet, and the three sections have no natural unity within a single narrative frame. This form subverts the possibility, not simply of an objective, reality, but of any common perception at all.

Each tale represents a different conception of reality. The first narrative is a collation of various accounts of the murder of George Colwin and the Colwin family history, but it cannot make the sequence of actions it recounts meaningful. Objective on its face, constructed on the model of cause-and-effect sequence, it reveals what Poe in "The Black Cat" calls a "chain of facts," but not a chain of meaning. The second narrative, confined to Wringham's obtuse, even psychotic, explanations, presents a viewpoint we must take as impossibly skewed, but that is nonetheless a real sequence of mental acts, as well as one interpretation of reality. The final section neither confirms nor denies what has been said before. Indeed, rather than settling questions we may have about the relationship between the earlier stories, it simply raises more questions, for it presents "facts" that do not exactly conform to the version of events presented in either of them. Hogg himself even appears as a character in this third narrative, but is shown to be either a liar or at least an inept observer. By appearing in his own book as a character who is not the narrator, Hogg playfully calls into question his own relation to the accounts: not only can we not trust the narrators of the three parts of the novel, we may not even be able to trust the author, who suggests that he be regarded as simply another storyteller within the tale. By playing with the relationship of author to text, Hogg makes it difficult, at best, for us to appeal to even an implied source of narrative authority.

Without this authoritative voice, the relationship of the narratives to each other reduces to simple proximity within a larger text and some overlap in subject matter. We get from *Private Memoirs,* not a text that represents action, but one in which the primary focus is on the problem of point of view and the relationship of one story to another. Rather than a unified, coherent whole with a beginning, a middle, and an end, it is a series of fragments, each of which seems to be complete in itself, but whose position in the text reveals its fragmented quality in relation to the other narratives. The juxtaposition of the three sections emphasizes their incompleteness and the impossibility of a narrative that could represent reality or even be a complete story. *The Private Memoirs and Confessions of a Justified Sinner* leaves us with a sense of indefiniteness. The novel contains three narratives, but it could easily contain four or five or six; we see nothing inevitable or complete about it, except for the arbitrary limits set by the ending of the last of the three accounts. The realization that the story is over, but without any sense of closure, confirms the dreamlike atmosphere of the Gothic fantasy, whose experiences end similarly, at the arbitrary moment when we awaken or are shaken out of our hallucination by some event in the real world. Because the Gothic fantasy is made up of a set of narratives, rather than a representation of action, it becomes a hall of mirrors, a series of stories doubling and reflecting each other. A story leads only to another story, which is a repetition of the dynamics of the genre. The novel becomes a series of stories, all of which are in fact the same story. This echoes the collapse of meaningful action in our texts. The more the text becomes a series of enfolded and enveloped narratives, the more conventional narrative structure disintegrates.

The characteristic narrative form of the Gothic fantasy is designed to create a sense of formlessness and refuses to obey our assumptions about narrative as a meaningful sequence of action or to serve as an analogue to the world outside the text. The closure and logic essential to the realistic or romance form are avoided to create a narrative whose order appears arbitrary and chaotic. The denial of our expectations creates in the reader a sense of unease and uncertainty. We find the flickering shadows of a dream, rather than the substantial coherence of a reasonably ordered story. The Gothic fantasy becomes a series of allusions to other narrative forms, and a series of illusions, in which conventional expectations are raised, only to be frustrated. The characters in the fantasy act, but do so in a way that denies the possibility of action; narrators tell stories that are somehow incomplete, that lose their coherence in a jumble of other narrators telling other stories or in the muffled voices of speakers trying to tell stories we cannot hear.

This apparently infinite ambiguity is exploited by James in *The Turn of the Screw,* in which he creates a story that suggests many possible stories, many plausible interpretations, but that continually frustrates our efforts to say exactly what the story is about, or even exactly what happens, as long as we bring to it expectations based on narratives outside the Gothic tradition. The implication is that we can trust neither the teller nor the tale. Out of the need to halt this tendency toward absolute instability evolves the figure of the detective and the genre that responds to the instabilities of the Gothic fantasy, the detective story.

The Gothic and the Creation of the Detective

From the Gothic fantasy comes the detective story; so goes the critical commonplace. We can even locate quite precisely the link between the two in the work of Edgar Allan Poe: the author of such classic Gothic stories as "The Fall of the House of Usher" also creates the first detective, M. Dupin, and writes the first detective stories, "The Purloined Letter" and "The Murders in the Rue Morgue." Noting the link, though, is easier than explaining why and how the detective story emerges from this tradition. Poe's dual status is not merely fortuitous. His invention of the detective follows from his insight and understanding of the dynamics of the earlier form; the detective story develops because the inner logic of the Gothic demands such a development. The detective story is a natural response to the Gothic vision. As Dupin is to Minister D.—a twin brother and mirror image—so the detective story is to the fantasy.[21]

All Gothic fantasies are mysteries: Who is the real heir to Otranto? What lies behind the hanging in Udolpho? Who, or what, causes the strange apparitions in *The Italian?* Is Silas Ruthyn trying to murder his neice? Who is Edward Hyde? Why is the beautiful Miss Lucy Westenra sick and dying? But though each tale is a mystery, none is concerned with the solution of that mystery. Most often, the solution we get comes from the unraveling of the logic of horror, not from the intervention of a character before the unknown destroys the protagonists. At best, in works such as *Udolpho, The Italian,* or *Uncle Silas,* the solution that saves the protagonists comes from outside the text, from the author's manipulation of the plot, which allows Emily to escape from Udolpho or Maud Ruthyn be rescued in a nick of time. The Gothic fantasy lacks an effective hero, a character who through his own efforts can resolve the mystery and put an end

to horror. The figure of the detective develops from the tension created by the lack of a true hero. He is, in effect, the hero the Gothic
world needs but cannot sustain. The presence of such a character
revises the balance and dynamics of the genre, focusing on the restoration of order and meaning rather than on the steady disintegration
of identity and the absolute instability of the world in which the
characters live. Out of the Gothic fantasy's critique of the romance
grows a revised version of the romance, and the romance quest hero
returns in the guise of the detective.

We can see this process clearly in three of Poe's stories, "The Black
Cat," "The Tell-Tale Heart," and the "Imp of the Perverse." Each of
these stories comes from the heart of the Gothic abyss; the protagonist has committed his crime, has been discovered, and now,
quite mad, tells the story of how he has come to the moment of his
own destruction, how his own actions have uncovered his crimes. In
each of these stories, Poe offers "a chain of facts" but never an explanation of those facts. Why does the narrator of "The Tell-Tale
Heart" have to kill the old man? Why does the narrator of "The
Black Cat" torture and kill animals? Is his murder of his wife really
just a grotesque accident, as he tries to slaughter the supernatural cat
that has come to haunt him? Why do these characters, and the narrator of "The Imp of the Perverse," confess to their crimes? Poe
never offers an explanation, and his characters are unable to do so.
Each is completely in the grip of the Gothic world. The stories do
reveal a sequence of events, but nothing about the meaning of this
sequence, about the chain of cause and effect that leads to the
murder, the confession, and the moment of execution. Each story is,
then, an image of meaningless violence, insanity, and horror.

However, we cannot accept this vision of meaninglessness, of actions and results that seem unmotivated and inexplicable. In "The
Imp of the Perverse," Poe's narrator names "perversity" the root
cause of all the evil but the very notion is a perverse explanation, for
it simply elevates to a principle of order the unmotivated action the
story recounts. Indeed, "The Imp of the Perverse" is itself a superb
example of contrariness, for it seems to begin as an essay, only to
turn into a Gothic fantasy in the last few paragraphs. Simply label-
ing chaos does not explain it, and so we must interpret the stories,
discover somehow the principles that make the protagonists' acts
intelligible, if not acceptable. One may read "The Black Cat" as a tale
of supernatural vengeance or one may construct an allegory around
the events of the story. One may read "The Tell-Tale Heart" as a

dramatization of the psychology of guilt. But whatever our interpretation, we have no warrant for assuming that it is more true than any other interpretation. In attempting to make sense of these stories, to become, in effect, the detective who, though the crime has been "solved," explains its motive, we can only impress upon the story our own ideas about how the world works. Our interpretation is the revelation of our own fantasies of order and meaning. It is the barrier we erect against Poe's Gothic vision. Whatever we say, though, the world of the story remains stubbornly chaotic and unexplained on its own terms.

Poe invents the detective to provide within the world of the story a character who can explain and organize the events into a meaningful pattern. The detective's essential task, as Sherlock Holmes says in *The Hound of the Baskervilles* is "the creation of narrative" through "the scientific use of imagination."[22] Dupin insists on the same thing when he emphasizes that he and his opponent, Minister D., are both mathematicians and poets, scientists of the imagination. The detective rearranges the seemingly chaotic and arbitrary events of the mystery story, and in doing so, discovers who is a criminal and who is not, why the crime has been committed, and thus frees the innocent from the terrors of guilt and uncertainty. In a Gothic fantasy, the Gothic world overwhelms the human world, for no character can understand, or stand against, its evils. The detective challenges the encroachment of its terrors, the disorder brought on by crime and the monster in the shape of the criminal, returning the world to order and stability.

Holmes's charge to the detective—the creation of order through the scientific use of imagination—is dramatized in Wilkie Collins's two great detective novels, *The Woman in White* and *The Moonstone.* Here Collins transforms the Gothic narrative structure into a form that dramatizes the detective's restoration of order. In these novels, the detective organizes the various eye-witness accounts into a coherent text that mirrors his process of tracing the line of cause and effect, that is, his solution to the crime. Walter Hartwright and Franklyn Blake are more than detectives who solve the mystery of the woman in white and the theft of the moonstone; they are also the primary forces behind the creation of order in the form of narrative structure. Rather than the feeling of unease and incompletion we experience in *Dr. Jekyll* or *Private Memoirs,* these narratives achieve genuine closure. Nevertheless, in the resolution of both *The Woman in White* and *The Moonstone,* Collins recalls the origins of the detective story in the instability of the Gothic fantasy. In *The Woman in White,* we recognize how accidental Walter's success is and see, not only the happiness of Walter and Laura, but the existence of a world of secret societies that reach out to destroy the powerful and brilliant Count Fosco. In *The Moonstone,* the mystery is solved, but the gem returns to India, the world of chaos from which it came. Thus Collins reminds us that the detective's triumph is only temporary.

We can see how the detective grows out of the dynamics of the Gothic fantasy, and how he resolves the instability of both the Gothic world and the Gothic narrative. But what qualities must this character have to perform such functions? How is he different from the figure of the romance hero he revives and revises? First, the detective is much less a man of action than the quest hero. He reacts to the actions of others through mental rather than physical activity, making observations and asking questions. Second, the detective, unlike the quest hero, is not in search of his identity. Indeed, he can react effectively to the encroachment of the Gothic world exactly because he knows who he is; for the other characters, the crime creates uncertainty about their own identities, about their own guilt or innocence. The detective has no such questions, and this means that he is often closer to the criminal, who knows his own monstrousness, than he is to the good, ordinary people whom he protects.

The reactive nature of the detective means that his identity depends, not on the ordered world, but on the Gothic world. The detective must wait for a crime to occur before he can respond to it; he cannot be who he is or do what he does without the actions of criminals. He can never rid the world of crime, never restore the victim to life, never erase the other characters' glimpse into the Gothic abyss. This limitation stems both from his reactive relationship to, and his dependence on crime and criminals for self-definition. To eliminate crime completely, to banish totally such monsters as Fosco or Minister D., would in effect destroy him.

The doubled relationship of the detective to the criminal is another commonplace. In his analysis of "The Purloined Letter," Richard Wilbur argues convincingly that Minister D. and Dupin are brothers. Thus Dupin can think just like Minister D., and his theft of the letter D. has stolen becomes, not a defense of order and value, but part of a deadly game between two versions of the same identity. In "The Murders in the Rue Morgue," Dupin's ability to solve the case again depends on his relationship to the "criminal," though in this story, the doubling is not with the sophisticated and shrewd Minister D., but with an orangutan. In both instances, though, Dupin does what Victor Frankenstein, Dorian Grey, Henry Jekyll, and Caleb Williams cannot do: he confronts his double and survives, indeed, for the moment at least, triumphs. The detective, unlike the Gothic protagonist, can confront his double without anxiety. He can live comfortably with the fact that he has within him the potential to become something monstrous, that he belongs, in part, to the world he opposes. This acceptance of his own doubled identity frees the detective's powers of understanding and analysis. Thus, he cannot be enthralled by the images of fear and desire he encounters because he accepts that he does both fear and desire what he sees when he looks over the edge of the abyss.

In *The Hound of the Baskervilles,* in which Doyle constantly flirts with the possibilities and motifs of the Gothic fantasy, we can see exactly how the detective relates to his doubles and the Gothic world. In this novel, Holmes has three doubles. One, Watson, is his foil, as well as his voice to the conventional world. He uses Watson as his eyes and ears within Baskerville Hall. Holmes also has two criminal doubles: Stapleton, clever, intelligent, who actually uses the name "Sherlock Holmes" while in London; and Selden, the brutal, animalistic murderer who hides on the moors at the same time as Holmes. Both criminals are egocentric and sadistic, and these qualities, though muted, are found in Holmes. Like Selden, he is a man of great physical strength and fortitude, who can endure life on the harsh world of the moors. Holmes, like Stapleton, whom he calls "a foeman worthy of our steel," uses his intellect to dominate the world around him; like Holmes, Stapleton is a man of disguises and multiple identities. Holmes reveals his egotism when, thinking that Sir Henry has been killed by the hound, refers to his client's death as "a blow to my career." Even the sadism of Selden and Stapleton finds its echo in Holmes's genial bullying of Watson. His treatment of his friend perhaps reflects his attitude toward the respectable world in general.

Holmes's ability to adapt to the moors, a primeval wilderness, dotted with the remains of prehistoric man, also reveals his kinship with the Gothic world. The wild, trackless moors are a place out of a nightmare. Even Stapleton, who knows the moors well, can become lost and fall into the mire. Of Holmes, Selden, and Stapleton, only the detective survives his encounter with the moor. Holmes can live in the Gothic world, but he can also find his way out of it, and he is equally at home in London or in Baskerville Hall. Stapleton is finally betrayed by his egotism, by his brutal nature. Only Holmes can keep these aspects of himself under control and thus survive his journey into the nightmare world. When Watson sees a figure on the tor one moonlit night, not realizing it is Holmes, he thinks

> There, outlined as black as an ebony statue on a shiny background, I saw the figure of a man upon the tor. . . . He stood as if he were brooding over that enormous wilderness of peat and granite which lay before him. He might have been the very spirit of that terrible place.[23]

Watson is correct, though he does not understand who he sees or the implications of what he says: Holmes is indeed the spirit of that terrible place.

The question still remains, how can the detective accept his doubled nature and survive? Why does he not go down into the abyss, like his double or like the Gothic protagonist? The answer lies in his ability to reconcile the qualities of the male protagonist with those of the Gothic heroine. Like her, the detective is essentially a reactive character. Neither figure initiates action; instead they respond to the actions of others. Unlike the Gothic heroine, though, the detective's is not submissive or passive but analytic; where she accepts and endures, he frees himself through understanding.

The heroine often occupies the place in the Gothic narrative that the detective takes in the detective story. Emily St. Aubert confronts several mysteries in *The Mysteries of Udolpho*—What is behind the curtain? Who is the singer on the steps of the castle? Where is her aunt?—though she never actually solves any of them. The same is true of Maud Ruthyn in *Uncle Silas,* who needs to discover whether or not her uncle is a murderer. Clara Wieland is also confronted by a mystery she is unable to solve in *Wieland.* These heroines cannot solve the mysteries that confront them for two reasons: first, their sense of identity as women is based on passive respectability and endurance, not the active pursuit of knowledge and understanding; and second, they are simply too afraid of what they will discover. Moreover, what they fear is also what they desire, and they cannot accept the unity of these two things. We see this most clearly in characters such as Maud and Clara; Maud wants to love her uncle and has unacknowledged incestuous fantasies about him, and Clara is attracted to both her own brother and Carwin. Should Maud discover her uncle wants to kill her, or Clara discover that the voice in the closet threatening her with rape and murder is that of a man to whom she is attracted or, worse, her own brother, the tensions would become intolerable. In contrast, the detective neither fears the loss of his identity nor the discovery that he desires what is terrible, frightening, and forbidden.

The detective and the heroine can both return to the conventional world, but she remains spellbound nevertheless. When Maud Ruthyn constructs her narrative of her experiences beyond the edges of order, we can see that she is still enthralled to her vision of that world. Clara Wieland's version of her encounter with the Gothic reveals a willful obtuseness, a refusal to accept that what happened could not have been prevented by prudence and foresight. The act of analysis by which the detective turns chaos into narrative, though, means that he breaks the bonds of fear, desire, and ignorance by accepting the fact that he is part of the Gothic world.

I would argue, then, that the detective deals successfully with these tensions because he is essentially an androgynous character. He combines elements of the male and female protagonists, and in doing so creates a whole identity that can accept the fact of his participation in the Gothic world. From the hero, he takes intellect and egotism; from the heroine, the ability to restrain himself, to be reactive rather than active. However, the detective's androgyny is not a complete solution to the problem of identity. He remains an essentially isolated character; Watson's vision of Holmes, brooding upon the wasteland before him, defines the aloneness of the detective. Neither Dupin nor Holmes show much capacity for human warmth or intimacy. Dupin has no real relationship with anyone except his brother, Minister D., and Holmes's relationship with Watson is based to a great extent on the latter's ability to accept his continual bullying and making fun of him. Modern detectives—Miss Marple, Hercule Poirot, Philip Marlowe, Lew Archer—are also loners. Complete unto themselves, their relationship to the conventional world, as well as to the Gothic world, is more an analytical than an affective one. At home in both worlds, the detective is truly at home in neither. A romance hero who already knows who he—or she—is, the detective is really a hero without a quest, whose only goal is the temporary repair of the barrier between the Gothic world and ordinary reality. The only time the detective is ever at home, ever truly complete, is when the two realms momentarily interpenetrate; his nature, though, demands that he restore the barrier and make himself homeless once again.

However, once the Gothic fantasy has formed the basis for the creation of a new genre and its hero, it is not done with him. Its writers play with the figure of the detective, further revising and experimenting with him in ways that dissolve him back into the chaos from which he initially sprung. The most successful Gothic detective figure appears in *Dracula*, which uses the fragmented narrative form that Collins adapted to the detective novel and Stevenson used for *Dr. Jekyll and Mr. Hyde*. At first, *Dracula* appears as a series of fragmented texts, commenting on and reflecting on each other, but never coming together as a work whose external unity— its unity in the experience of the reader—is matched by an internal coherence within the vision of the characters. Up to Lucy's death, the narrative structure evokes the same sense of unease and anxiety we experience in *Jekyll and Hyde*. Shortly after her death, though, we learn that what we are reading is not an unconnected set of fragments, but rather a collation put together by Mina Harker. Thus, the stories achieve an internal unity—a relationship to each other within the text—and become the basis upon which the characters unite to defeat Dracula. The creation of the complete and coherent text is the analogue to the emergence of understanding that puts an end to Dracula. The count recognizes this and tries to destroy Mina's narrative. He is defeated because she has the foresight to make another copy.

Mina is a version of the detective, for it is she who really enables the humans to destroy Dracula; she accomplishes this because she has the two important qualities of the detective. When forced to drink Dracula's blood, she becomes his double, inextricably linked to him, but she is able to accept this linkage and use it against him. Under hypnosis, Mina can tell the men where he is and thus allows them to head him off before he reaches his castle. Also, Mina is an adrogynous character; Van Helsing says she has "a man's head and woman's heart." This combination of intellect and feeling makes her the true leader of the crusade against the vampire. One might think that Van Helsing seems more the leader—and thus the detective— of the novel, but in fact he fails in this role. He cannot save Lucy, his insistance that Mina be kept out of the fight against Dracula actually puts her in danger, and it is Mina who plans the final campaign against the count. Van Helsing's knowledge of the vampire is invaluable, but he himself is not a very effective vampire hunter. Mina, with her ability to create narrative and her courage is Dracula's real enemy, and the count knows it: he attacks her, not Van Helsing.

Within the Gothic tradition, a number of much less successful versions of the detective appear. Utterson in *Dr. Jekyll and Mr. Hyde* sets out to find out who Edward Hyde is and what his hold over Jekyll might be, but he is completely baffled; he "solves" the case only in the sense that he discovers Jekyll's account of what has happened. The narrative he creates as a result has the same fragmentary, incoherent, inconclusive quality as Hogg's in *The Private Memoirs*. I would also argue that the narrator in "The Fall of the House of Usher" is Poe's version of the detective trapped in the Gothic world. He is called to the house to help his old friend, and from his narrative, the reader can easily deduce exactly what the problems of the Ushers are. We are quite aware that Madelaine is not dead when he helps Roderick screw down the coffin lid. His story reveals the crimes of the Usher's—incest and murder—and he witnesses their destruction in a tableau of love and violence, but he never establishes an analytic relationship to the narrative he tells. Indeed, he resolutely refuses to understand anything he sees, a fact Roderick recognizes when, as Madelaine stands before the door, he leaps up and cries "MADMAN!" Structurally, the narrator of "Usher" stands in the place of the detective, but passive and repressed, he cannot even recognize, let alone break, his enthrallment to the Gothic world.

The most interesting revision of the detective occurs in *The Turn of the Screw*. The governess discovers what she takes to be a truly Gothic crime, demonic ghosts plotting to corrupt and destroy the souls of Miles and Flora, her little charges. And, indeed, the governess creates out of her experience a narrative, a chain of cause and effect, that tells how she "solved" the mystery at a terrible cost. But though clearly the governess believes that Miles and Flora have been "dispossesed" and that she has succeeded in saving Miles's soul, if not his life, we are not so sure. She has created a narrative and used her imagination in doing so, but has she been "scientific"? Is her tale the "true" version of what has happened? Many readers have been convinced by her account, but many others have found her self-deluded and deeply neurotic, creating the evil she claims to be fighting. The dynamics of the Gothic fantasy demand that the detective fail, or, as is the case here, be rendered a completely ambiguous figure. The governess of James's novella is, finally, as opaque to us as are the criminal narrators of Poe's short stories. She may have solved the crime, she may be correct about the ghosts—or she may not. We cannot know, and thus, the detective is drawn back into chaos. Miss Jessel and Quint may be the doubles the governess defeats or they may be the projections of her own hopelessly divided nature, fragments of herself that she cannot accept. Miles's death thus may be a result of her desperate attempts to deny her own position within the circle where fear and desire become one. Once again, the narrative has no closure, and its mystery no solution. Here, though, the mystery focuses on the figure of the detective, who cannot illuminate but only deepens the terrors of the Gothic twilight. Finally, even the detective cannot fully escape his Gothic origins.

The Gothic Parody

The twilight world of the Gothic fantasy is made out of fragments, bits and pieces of the romance, the realistic novel, religious and scientific versions of reality. The heroes and heroines of these myths of identity break into fragments, and the lines between fear and desire dissolve. The genre even draws the detective back into the world of horror and uncertainty. No element of that world is benign: everywhere we look we see monsters in the shadows and fragments of the familiar. The relationship of the Gothic to the conventional world, and to the literary forms from which it derives, can best be described as parodic.

When we use the term "parody," we must recognize that although it is usually used to comic or satiric ends, it is not intrinsically satiric or comic.[24] Parody is a literary technique based on the creation of doubles. The parodist begins with the original and produces a copy that renders it ludicrous or monstrous. Swift's "A Modest Proposal" reveals the essential inhumanity beneath the reasonableness of English attitudes toward Ireland. His parody implicitly invokes Christian values and ethical principles against the monstrousness of English attitudes. Wilde's *The Importance of Being Earnest* parodies conventional English social values by exaggerating and distorting them, ridiculing them rather than condemming them. Wilde does not appeal to a set of values in opposition to, for instance, Lady Bracknall's, nor does he suggest that her values are in fact very harmful. The solution to her ludicrous demands is itself appropriately ludicrous, when Jack discovers he "really" is "Earnest." Parody becomes satiric when it reveals its original as monstrous, ugly, or harmful and invokes, implicitly or explicitly, alternative values or norms; parody is comic when the target is shown to be absurd and ridiculous, but essentially harmless. However, the technique can be employed in a third way, metaphysically. The Gothic parody functions in this way. The Gothic reveals its originals as both monstrous and ridiculous, but it implies no alternative. It becomes a metaphysical statement because the object of parody is, not one aspect of society or a literary text or type, but all the world, both human and literary. The world of fantasy created in the Gothic is the double of everything else. Thus, the Gothic parody creates a state of metaphysical uncertainty and anxiety: through its distorted lens, we see the whole world. Insofar as we recognize our world in the Gothic, we are left without solid ground upon which to base our sense of ourselves. The parody renders the world grotesque through its fragmenting and doubling of both conventional ideas about reality and other literary genres.

This impulse appears clearly in the works of Poe, as Daniel Hoffman has noted.[25] His earliest stories, "Metzengerstein," "The Assignation," "Berenice," were all intended for a collection to be called *The Tales of the Folio Club*. Each story was to be accompanied by a sketch of the teller, and the volume was meant to parody the *Blackwood's Magazine* style of Gothic tale.[26] Poe apparently extended his conception of the parodic impulse within the genre to a parody of the tradition itself. Strikingly, many of his works—for example, "The Philosophy of Composition" and *The Narrative of Arthur Gordon Pym*—appear to be parodies at some points and serious and straightforward at others. Poe's affinity for the hoax and the parody stems from his typically Gothic awareness of the doubleness of reality, the tendency of people and objects to transform themselves into their opposites. The parody is above all the metamorphosis of one thing into another. It is, then, a literary device that perfectly embodies the mystery basic to the Gothic fantasy. Out of one thing comes two; the second subverts the first but is dependent upon it. While the parody subverts the original, it also affirms it, since it is a likeness of the original. The exact meaning of a parody, particularly in the Gothic, is always somewhat ambiguous. What, exactly, remains of the original? If it retains any of its integrity and validity, what aspects of these survice, and how do we know? And if the parody has totally demolished the original, what is the nature of this afterimage, the negative of the original? The pervasive parody of the Gothic, as opposed to the limited and directed parody of comedy or satire, is a world of complete uncertainty.

We can see the effect of the Gothic as parody clearly in Poe's story "Berenice." The story is the first-person account of the narrator's obsession with his cousin, Berenice. She is his inverted double: active while he is passive, outgoing while he is reclusive. His obsession finally focuses on her teeth, which are remarkably attractive, at least to him. After Berenice's apparent death—she is one of Poe's vast collection of cataleptics (catalepsy is a parody of death)—the narrator goes completely mad and yanks out all her teeth. When she returns from the grave—the tale ends as his collection of dental instruments and teeth clatter to the floor as he shrieks in horror. It is difficult to point out exactly where one begins to suspect this story is a parody, but by the end, with Berenice coming to look for her cousin and a good set of dentures, we have no doubt that it is and that it is, in a grotesque sense, funny. Yet Poe recognized that within his parody was the source of his "serious" Gothic tales, "Ligeia" and "The Fall of the House of Usher." "Berenice" does not render the Gothic ludicrous, it simply makes its parodic nature evident and manages to combine the fearful and the comic. It is not a reduction of the Gothic tale, but rather an expansion: it can parody, not only the conventional world, but itself as well. Thus the Gothic can parody itself and survive.

Nevertheless, this quality is a limitation on the form. The Gothic parodies everything from ideas about the self to ideas about the nature of the universe; thus it generates no vision of its own, for nothing in it is more than a reversal or inversion. One can, of course, claim that this is the substance of its vision, the ambiguity that comes from questioning our definitions of reality, but this is in fact a statement of the essential unknowableness of the real. For the Gothic to produce anything like a stable vision of reality, it must create a hero, the detective, and then expel him. The genre cannot make positive statements or create an empowering mythology.

Because the Gothic is a reactive form, it is always dependent on its originals for its effect. Without the traditions of the romance and realism, it would disappear. Wtihout conventional ideas about the integrity of the self, the divisions between subjective and objective, past and present, natural and supernatural, its ambiguous and transformative world could not be portrayed. Like any popular genre, it is dependent on the culture in which it exists; it can reflect and comment on that culture—through parody rather than through affirmation—but it cannot transcend it. It can only give back to it its own negative image. This accounts for the fact that so many Gothic fantasies lend themselves to readings that appear to support conventional moral ideals. The Gothic fantasy often appears as a cautionary tale, warning of the dangers of egotism and self-indulgence, the nineteenth-century version of the horror film voice-over of the 1950s, "There are some things man was not meant to know." All popular forms must, at least formally, affirm the ideals of the dominant culture; this is simply a precondition of their being truly popular. But in the Gothic, this is undermined by readers' fascination with its imagined world, their participation in the act of fantasy. The genre presents its face to the world with a large warning sign: Do Not Look at This. But readers, like the Gothic protagonist, must look, and the world they see is so subversive as to outweigh any moral, or any happy ending, that might be attached to it.

If the genre in fact served as any sort of warning to its culture, it was not the warning of conventional wisdom, but a sign that the commonplaces of belief and behavior were torn by contradiction, that they had within the seeds of the Gothic world. The nineteenth-century's fascination with the Gothic tells us a great deal about the inner life of nineteenth-century people; the worlds they were imagining were quite different from the one they thought they lived in. Those texts—*Moby Dick, Wuthering Heights,* "Maud"—that are not in the genre, but reveal a strain of its imagination reflect an impulse to convert the Gothic from a dependent and parodic mode into a genuine alternative vision. The development of such twentieth-century visions as modernism and Freudian psychology build on the Gothic fantasy by making its parody into a description of reality. This impulse is a response to the uneasiness and fear that the genre defines. It is one thing to see the world as ambiguous or as a wasteland; it is another to see it as one monstrous distortion.

Voyeurism, Enthrallment, Analysis: The Reader and the Text

Our understanding of the dynamics of any genre depends, not simply on describing its structure, but on explaining how that structure relates to the reader of the individual text. The nature of the reader's involvement with the text is the final step in defining the Gothic fantasy as a genre.

We can begin to define the relationship of reader and text by seeing that the archetype for this relationship is that of the Gothic protagonist to the world within the fantasy. The reader is drawn into the fantasy just as the protagonist is drawn into the underworld. The reader experiences the Gothic world vicariously; since each fantasy has, not only a single protagonist, but in reality only a single character, the redefinition of self in the novel parallels the reader's identification with that self. This is what makes the Gothic fantasy so compelling.

All readers recognize that the Gothic deals with fear, both as its central topic and as its central effect.[27] Subject and effect are mirror images of each other, just as the experience of the Gothic protagonist mirrors that of the reader. However, as we have seen, the experience of the Gothic world is a process of enthrallment to desire as well as to fear. Indeed, the protagonist's identity is redefined by the unbounded possibilities of fear and desire, and the reader is able to explore their limits. This explains the peculiar pleasure readers take in the painful and frightening events that occur in the Gothic novel. We do not experience the fear we would upon encountering a genuine vampire; rather, we experience a mixture of fear and pleasure—or, in the terms we have been using so far, desire—which renders the overall experience enjoyable. Some readers or filmgoers are in fact unable to share these delightful frissons. They do not read Gothic novels and, if dragged to a horror movie by their friends, spend the evening with their hands over their eyes, refusing to look at the images that provoke such pleasure in their companions.

Essential, then, to its effect is a novel's capacity to reveal the unity of fear and desire, which destroys the self in the Gothic world, as pleasure for the reader. This is, for the reader, an awakening to possibilities and resources of the self that the protagonist never knows. The Gothic reveals to the reader the capacity of fantasy to convert the fearful, anxious, or dangerous into genuine pleasure; fantasy becomes the affirmation of the power of the imagination to control and channel the threatening emotions and impulses. The Gothic has a therapeutic value for it converts tension, anxiety, and fear—tensions about desire—into pleasure. The end effect is the taming of fear and the reassertion of the power of desire. Yet despite this positive function, the exact nature of the Gothic fantasy's relationship to the reader remains ambiguous and potentially disturbing. The Gothic makes its appeal to the reader, not through action, character, ideas, or language, but through spectacle. It is strange and exotic, but its sadomasochistic pattern appeals to the reader's fascination with the forbidden, as well as the unusual.

Voyeurism is a pervasive phenomenon within the genre. Caleb Williams spies on Falkland, who spies on Williams; Carwin watches Clara Wieland from his secret hiding place; Edgar Huntly watches Clithero Edny on his sleepwalking travels; Frankenstein's creature looks at the De Lacys through a crack in the wall; the narrator becomes an enthralled spectator to the bizarre goings-on in the house of Usher; and both Henry Jekyll and Dorian Grey are fascinated observers of their own desires and experiences. The act of observing another person, often, though not always, secretly, is a paradigmatic Gothic motif; it is the act of watching one's self. The characters' experience of watching their own doubles or projections is duplicated in the readers' relationship to the text. The act of reading is itself essentially voyeuristic, for the spectacle of Gothic sadomasochism and horror is an externalized, public, and thus mediated, expression of the reader's fears and desires. The Gothic fantasy articulates and thus confers some degree of acceptability upon otherwise dangerous personal fantasies. From a safe distance, the reader sees his own, perhaps unacknowledged, desires given shape and, further, public expression in a more or less respectable aspect of his culture. We see the best exploration of the voyeuristic qualities of the Gothic experience in an incident in *Melmoth the Wanderer*.

Moncada the Spaniard, imprisoned by the ex-Jesuits, receives a letter from his brother, Juan, explaining that he has arranged for his escape, with the assistance of a monk who has taken vows to avoid punishment for parricide. Moncada and the parricide—known only by the code name "Juan"—attempt an escape through a temporary breach in the wall, which they must reach through the underground tunnels of the monastery. They come up short of their goal, and, since it is daybreak and people are about, they must wait in the tunnels until nightfall. Moncada, who is terrified, can barely stand the idea of remaining in the tunnels with a man he views as a brutal animal. When the parricide falls asleep, though, he reveals himself to be something rather different.

Talking in his sleep, he recounts the murder of his father in lurid detail. Moncada is so frightened by this that he awakens the parricide, who then begins to tell him another story. He recounts the tale of two lovers, a young man and a woman who followed him into the monastery disguised as a monk. When they were discovered, their punishment was to be immured in an underground cell, in the very tunnel in which Moncada and "Juan" are sitting. The parricide volunteered to stand guard over them in order to observe their agonies, for, as he says, "Emotions are my events." The lovers grow to hate each other, and the man even attempts to devour his beloved to assuage his increasing hunger. After a few days, they starve to death. The parricide enjoys this spectacle of horror, even when he discovers that the woman was his sister.

I laugh at all mankind and the imposition they dare to practice when they talk of hearts. I laugh at human passions and human cares, vice and virtue, religion and impiety; they are all the result of petty localities and artificial situations.[28]

Suffering, he goes on to say, "silences all feeble sophistries of conventional life." He is the voice of the Gothic world, with its denial of all life and value and its sadomasochistic fascination with suffering, its impulse to self-destruction embodied in his pleasure at the murder of his father and sister. Yet at the same time, this is also the voice of Moncada and the reader. For just as the parricide has looked hungrily on suffering, so too has Moncada by listening to his story. In the same way, we are drawn into a web of voyeuristic experiences as Moncada narrates his story to John Melmoth. We see the suffering in the parricide's story, which is enclosed in Moncada's, which is enclosed in Melmoth's story. Emotions have become the reader's events as well, and as we watch horror pass through the consciousness of the various characters until it reaches us, we become voyeurs upon voyeurs, the watchers of the watchers. We find ourselves in a state similar to that of the Gothic protagonists, for to continue reading the novel is to acknowledge that it has a hold over us. In that compulsion comes, again, the encounter with the self. The spectacle of the Gothic presents the reader with a self-image. Just as when we daydream and construct idle fantasies for ourselves, the encounter with the Gothic is a moment in which the self defines its internal existence through the act of observing its fantasies. The therapeutic possibilities of this are genuine, but the act of participation embodies the same type of enthrallment that the Gothic protagonist experiences. Readers may retreat from, or reject, the implications of the mirror of the self found in the fantasy, they may use the experience as a basis for analysis, or they may choose to indulge in the spectacle, affirming with the parricide that emotions are their events.

Voyeurism, particularly when the spectacle upon which the voyeur looks is also a self-projection, is at once passive and powerful. The voyeur is outside the world of action and thus should be immune to the horrors and transformations that go on there. Ideally, the voyeur finds those characters and situations looked upon to be what Dorian Grey calls his portrait, "the most magical of mirrors." The object of the voyeur's attention is a mirror of the self, magical because presumably the watcher is protected from the consequences

of the things observed. The voyeur's ability to look on without involvement echoes the qualities of the female protagonists of the
Gothic and of the detective. The heroine remains passive because
respectability demands she do so, while the detective, though much
less passive, has analytical distance from the spectacle. However, this
combination of passivity and the "magical" power that voyeurism
confers is complicated by the fact that the voyeur is dependent upon
what is observed. Insofar as the act of voyeurism is one of self-projection and self-definition, voyeurs come to need the characters they
watch.

This dependent relationship becomes clear in *Caleb Williams,*
Frankenstein, and *Dr. Jekyll and Mr. Hyde;* in all three stories, the
character who begins as the dominate partner in the doubled relationship, the voyeur, is inevitably drawn into an active role in the
pairing. Enthrallment to the spectacle of one's own fears and desires,
to identity made external and visible, means that the voyeur must
always join the spectacle first observed from a safe distance. The voyeur's power and pleasure are potentially infinite, as long as distance
from the innermost desires of the self can be maintained. Once that
distance is lost, though, the protagonist becomes a participant in the
spectacle, which leads to fragmentation and destruction of the self.

An example of this situation can be found in *Vathek.* When Vathek finally reaches the underground domains of Eblis, where all
power and pleasure reside, he discovers that his heart will become a
burning flame, tormenting him and his lover, Nouronihar, throughout eternity.

> Almost at the same instant, the same voice announced to the Cal
> iph, Nouronihar, the four princes, and the princess, the awful and
> irrevocable decree. Their hearts immediately took fire, and they, at
> once, lost the most precious gift of heaven:—HOPE. These unhap
> py beings recoiled, with looks of the utmost distraction. Vathek
> beheld in the eyes of Nouronihar nothing but rage and vengeance
> nor could she discern aught in his but aversion and de
> spair. . . . All severally plunged themselves into the accused multi
> tude, there to wander in an eternity of unabating anguish.[29]

The narrator goes on to explain that this is the inevitable punishment
of humans who seek to transcend the limits of humankind. Though
the novel ends with the conventional Gothic invocation of traditional values, in fact Vathek has become one with his desires. He has
achieved what he has sought and thus ends by destroying himself. In

the realm of Eblis, he can have anything he can imagine. His fantasies and his reality have fused, and this has destroyed him. The quest to achieve the ultimate fantasy—absolute power and absolute gratification—destroys the distance between desire and satisfaction that made each meaningful.

The voyeur in the Gothic fantasy is always forced to join the spectacle observed, becoming entranced by the images of the self discovered in the image of the Other. The reader of the Gothic fantasy, though also a voyeur, has more options than the protagonist. First, the reader may reject the invitation of the Gothic, refusing to see the self in the mirror of the text. At the other end of the scale, the reader may pass through the voyeuristic experience to a state of analytical distance analogous to that achieved by the detective. In this instance, a fuller understanding of the workings of fantasy in general and the forces behind the Gothic in particular might be gained. Ideally, one might achieve enough distance that the alienation and anxiety expressed would be translated from their literary form into a complete understanding of the dynamics and significance of the genre in our culture. This ideal state is unreachable, though, because even this could not transform the conditions that produced and sustained the Gothic fantasy within our culture. As we saw with the detective, understanding does not free one from the Gothic world, even if it makes one's relationship to it more flexible.

The mediating literariness of the Gothic fantasy allows an analytical response, illuminating, defining, and exploring the twilight world of the inner self externalized and projected in the text. At the same time, this makes the fantasy a therapeutic experience, enabling anxiety and alienation to find a temporary release through their safe expression. However, this response may contain relatively little analytical illumination, and though the twilight world may be banished for a moment, it will, presumably, return to haunt and, paradoxically, please the reader once again. A fourth response is the true analogue of the state of enthrallment experienced by the protagonist. This reader uses the Gothic fantasy as a mode of gratification, a source of thrills and a spectacle from which no analytical distance is ever achieved. Moreover, rather than therapeutic release, a reader might simply come away desiring more, immediately, of what has just been experienced. That this literary form has ever truly induced psychosis is unlikely, though Jane Austen's Catherine Moreland seems to have drunk so deeply from the spring that she has become, at least temporarily, intoxicated with the thought that the Gothic world might be the real world. One might argue, too, that De Sade is an example of self-created enthrallment to a body of texts—and actions—not dissimilar to the Gothic fantasy.

Whether the response to the Gothic is rejection, analysis, therapy, or indulgence, one thing seems clear. It proposes no real solutions or alternatives to the situations it dramatizes. It may subvert certain values or attitudes, but it offers nothing in their place, because its "solution," voyeurism, is shown to be no solution at all. The protagonists are destroyed because they cannot maintain their safe position as observers, while the reader is caught in the fact that no possible response really tackles the problems that, implicitly, the genre poses. Any reader's response is probably a mixture in various proportions of the four I have outlined, but none can fully resolve the relationship of the individual to the Gothic fantasy.

The experience is, of course, only a literary one, and thus it does not itself make clear the social and cultural conditions that have called it forth and sustained it. But if the Gothic neither offers answers to its own dilemmas nor solves the problem of fantasy itself, it does function in several important ways that take the reader back to its origin and significance. First, it signals to the reader the problematic status of pleasure in modern culture. The need for escapist pleasure suggests its absence in the real world, a world that inadequately satisfies the desire for pleasure. By its content, terror and horror, the Gothic tells us that this lack, or failure, in the real world generates the pleasures of terror in the worlds we imagine. The fact that we have come to enjoy fear is a sign of the dominance of fear in our everyday lives.

The genre also calls into question the lines between reality and fantasy, fear and desire, self and Other that exist in our society. It suggests the illusoriness of our assumptions about the stability of things as we see them and the unreality of the things we imagine. Yet at the same time it asserts the reality and importance of the inner life, it reveals that life to be a dark and mysterious thing, perhaps essentially unknowable, or knowable only at our peril. The affirmation of fantasy implicit in the Gothic work is undercut because the substance of that fantasy is horror, fear, and anxiety, the disintegration of the very self that performs the act of fantasizing. Only in the state of voyeurism can one be safe, but again, that safety is only an illusion. The protagonist of the Gothic fantasy falls into enthrallment to the world observed, while the reader is expelled from that world back into the reality from which escape was sought. The Gothic fantasy

begins as a flight from the tensions, fears, contradictions, and anxieties of everyday life and ends by presenting the reader with an
imaginary world in which they are reproduced in monstrous forms.
The world of escape is the distorted, parodic mirror of the real
world, and finally we are forced out of this dark mirror back into the
reality from which we came. What the Gothic fantasy finally offers
the reader is knowledge that we must escape and the images of what
we are fleeing from, but it offers no more than a temporary resolution of our problem. It tells us that escape is no escape at all.

Imagination in the Gothic Fantasy

Understanding the dynamics of the Gothic fantasy, particularly the
dynamics of the reader's response to the text, leads naturally to the
issue of the nature and purpose of imagination and imaginative acts
in the genre. Its primary function is escapist; one of its central pleasures is that it allows us to leave and transform the real world. The
content of the Gothic escape intensifies the act of rejection, because
readers can indulge in voyeuristic fantasies of their forbidden desires.
Readers can enjoy what they know ought to be feared and rejected
without the danger and stigma that would come from actually acting
out such desires.[30] Of course, most readers of Gothic fantasy don't
want to do any of these things anyway; they want simply to fantasize
about them. The text externalizes and validates their fantasies, for
their private, inner desires now appear in a more-or-less sanctioned
form. The escapist or reactive operation of imagination functions by
transforming images of the painful and terrifying into sources of
pleasure. In this sense, the imaginative act becomes a mirror that
reveals and at the same time transforms our fantasies; because of this
we are able to indulge our most fearful fantasies. These capacities of
the imagination are central to the Gothic vision of imagination. Yet
the romantic tradition, which arises roughly at the same time as the
Gothic, emphasizes, not the escapist and transformative powers of
imagination, but the transcendent and creative ones. The nature of
the creative capacities of the imagination, and its capacity for transcendence, are in fact called into question by the Gothic, which in
effect becomes a critique of the romantic idea of imagination that
dominated the nineteenth century.[31] The Gothic fantasy does, however, acknowledge a type of creative power in imagination.

The imagination can create narrative, pleasure, and versions of the
inner life that define the self. But these capacities are confined within

the human world of history and society. The creative powers of imagination in the Gothic fantasy are, like the powers of the detective, reactive, a capacity of combining and revising that which is already in existence. The fantasist creates new things, new worlds, new beings, which are at heart versions of real things, worlds, and beings. We return again to the fact that the Gothic fantasy provides an escape that leads readers back to a confrontation with those realities from which they wished to flee. The imagination is bound within history and society, and fantasy, whether private or literary, is an aspect of history and society.

This conception of imagination differs radically from that of the romantic tradition. Indeed, the contrast I have been suggesting is drawn by Coleridge in the *Biographia Literaria:*

> The Imagination I consider either as primary or secondary. The primary Imagination I hold to be the living power and prime agent of all human perception, and as a repetition in the finite mind of the eternal act of creation in the infinite I Am. The secondary imagination I consider as an echo of the former, co-existing with the conscious will, yet still as identical with the primary in the *kind* of its agency, and differing only in *degree* and the mode of its operation. It dissolves, diffuses, dissipates, in order to recreate: or where this process is rendered impossible, yet still at all events it struggles to idealize and unify. It is essentially *vital,* even as all objects (*as* objects) are essentially fixed and dead.
>
> Fancy, on the contrary, has no other counters to play with, but fixities and definites. The fancy is indeed no other than a mode of memory emancipated from the order of time and space; while it is blended with, and modified by that empirical phenomenon of the will, which we express by the word Choice. But equally with the ordinary memory the fancy must receive all its materials ready from the law of association.[32]

We can, I think, have no quarrel with Coleridge's definition of fancy, or fantasy, as we have been calling it. This definition, which serves as a statement of a general, though very complicated, faith in the Godlike power of the imagination, makes it clear that from the romantic point of view, the Gothic fantasy is not an expression of that power at all. However, we also see that the Gothic questions the romantic conception of imagination, and thus the individual's ability to transcend history and the reality of time and space and move into a higher, or as Coleridge suggests, spiritual reality. The basic assumption of the Gothic is that no real distinction between the material world, the fixed and dead world of objects, and a spiritual world can be made. To pursue transcendent goals is to be, like Victor Franken-stein, ensnared in exactly what one wished to transcend.

The Gothic fantasy, then, is a critique of the romantic belief in the power of the imagination and of the particular version of humanism we see in the passage from Coleridge. As Stephan Prickett has point-ed out, this conception of imagination had tremendous prestige throughout the nineteenth century and was, for the Victorians, allied to an ideal of moral insight: to transcend the actual world imagina-tively was to apprehend the transcendent moral values of spiritual reality. Of course, for the romantics, particularly, contact with the transcendent reality was the highest possible experience of pleasure; not only Coleridge, but Wordsworth, Blake, Keats, and Shelley are all clear on this point. This was true even though Blake and Keats, for instance, were acutely aware of the connection between sensual and spiritual pleasure, specifically, the pleasures of sexuality. The fact remains that pleasure gains its fullest significance when touched by the transcendent power of imagination, when, like Porphyrio and Madelaine in "The Eve of St. Agnes," one melts into dreams and, upon awakening, finds the dream true and that truth a path out of the actual world.

For the Victorians, the place of pleasure in relation to the power of imagination was much more problematic. Dreams of pleasure turn into the agonies that precede the definition of identity. Such moments of mortification appear in Austen, as when Emma suffers from Knightley's criticism of her behavior and, later, from the fear that he will marry someone else. Dark nights of the soul and identi-ty-affirming pain come to Dorothea Brooke in *Middlemarch,* Eugene Wrayburn in *Our Mutual Friend,* Jane and Rochester in *Jane Eyre,* and to Bathsheba Everdine in *Far From the Madding Crowd.* These moments of descent lead to moments of vision and self-understand-ing analogous to the moments of imaginative revelation found in romantic poetry, for example, Wordsworth's discovery that "Nature ne'er did betray the heart that loved her" in "Tintern Abbey" or the recollection of "spots of time" in *The Prelude.* In the romantic vision, the power of imagination leads to liberation through transcendent pleasure or joy, while in nineteenth-century realism, the visionary power of imagination lies in suffering, leading to the discovery of moral duty and responsibility, often enforcing the alignment of indi-vidual identity with the necessities of respectability.

The Gothic protagonist, though, can have no such moment of

insight, since neither pleasure, suffering, nor imagination have that power in the Gothic fantasy. There liberation is replaced by therapy, and the sacred powers of imagination are replaced by those of escape and parody. The genre parodies both romanticism and realism's visions of transcendence. The romantic vision becomes the false sense of the numinous that is signaled by the appearance of its perversions and parodies, neither truly natural nor supernatural. Wordsworth's mystical vision of Nature or Blake's wisdom won on the road of excess both fail in the Gothic, leading only to death and the abyss of the Gothic world.

The Gothic parodies the moral vision of the realistic tradition by integrating conventional moral wisdom into the fantasy. Most of the novels can easily be read as cautionary tales; in *Frankenstein* and *Jekyll and Hyde,* for instance, Victor and Henry even provide the reader with an explicit statement of the moral significance of their stories. Both novels seem to warn the reader against pride and egotism, against the excessive pursuit of either power or pleasure. In this explicit moralism, the Gothic fantasy uses the values of the realistic tradition to close the fantasy and return the reader to the conventional world where such values are supposed to function, but it does so in such a way that the moral vision implied in the warnings is parodied and drained of content.

The reader of the Gothic fantasy goes to it as a means of escape from conventional reality; the very choice of the story proclaims some degree of alienation. The content of the fantasy further enforces this alienation, for the Gothic spectacle provides escape through the forbidden and dangerous. The very fact that the reader can find pleasure in it emphasizes that the genre offers a more subversive and daring type of escape than that provided by more benign fantasies, such as Morris's romances or MacDonald's fantasy-allegories. The rejection of conventional values is central to the tradition, and that rejection is direct and overt. However, after fulfilling the reader's need, the fantasy returns him to the real world where those values operate. In part, it does this simply by ending; when the text stops, fantasy stops. The end, though, is also signaled by the affirmation of conventional moral ideals, which then become part of the Gothic fantasy itself. The moral vision becomes part of the parody, part of the obviously fictive world of the fantasy. When used in this purely formal way the moral vision loses its power to refer to the actual world. At the end of *Wieland,* Clara says that had she been possessed of sufficient strength of mind, or had Theodore formed more just notions of the nature of God, they would have been spared their descent into terror; she invokes conventional values, but we are struck by the fact that her analysis of what has happened does not correspond to our sense of the essential irrational horror of the story. Even as Henry Jekyll offers the conventional moral interpretation of his position, calling for the repression of the evil part of man's nature, we are conscious that these categories do not seem to fit very well with his description of either himself or Hyde. Thus, both in its obvious formalism and its inappropriateness to the text, the cautionary moral tale is parodied.

The imaginative experience of the Gothic fantasy can provide neither transcendent visions of a higher reality nor the revelation of moral truths; the Gothic fantasy cannot fulfill the exalted functions claimed for the imagination by either the romantics or the Victorians. As a parody, it cannot claim a cosmological or mythic vision of its own that might allow such a revelation; as a fantasy, it can only work with what is, with what Coleridge calls "fixities." But what then is the function performed by the imagination in the Gothic?

The first function is therapeutic; fantasy releases tensions and anxieties by assigning them objects, by giving them objective expression in the text. The second is to produce, not an imaginative vision, but analytical distance. Like the detective, the reader can break enthrallment to the Gothic spectacle only by achieving a critical relationship to that spectacle and his own voyeuristic participation in it. Since the genre does not offer readers an empowering vision or myth and has parodied conventional values, they are left in an undefined state between fantasy and reality that can only be resolved analytically. A reader may, of course, simply rest in the afterglow of therapeutic release but in doing so remains spellbound. Then, again, to see the limitations of the escape is to see the imitations of imagination, which in Gothic terms cannot create transcendence, but merely restructures our experience of the real world. By firmly linking the imaginative to the social and cultural reality from which it springs and to the conventional values and ideals that it parodies, the Gothic fantasy can localize imagination. It cannot be a complete escape, only the prelude to an understanding of the links between the imagined and real worlds. The problems that the stories temporarily relieve can be solved only in the real world, and thus the they must return us to that world, though with a new understanding and perception of it.

The limitations of the Gothic fantasy's conception of imagination is, then, really its greatest strength. Because it refuses to offer a transcendent vision and empowering mythology, a new cosmology and an ethical imperative, the Gothic escape leads readers directly back to the world in which they must live. They are lead back, though, with a critique of that world that can make alienation the basis for understanding, rather than a cause for flight. By denying readers an alternative world, the Gothic intensifies its critique of the world from which it springs. In the Gothic fantasy, the imagination cannot project its anxieties and desires as their own solution.

2

The Gothic Themes

So far we have focused on the formal structure of the Gothic fantasy and discussed its effect on the reader as a spectacle of fear and desire. While this exploration has told us a good deal about the genre, it can also be approached through its content, its recurring themes and motifs. Through understanding the dynamics of its themes, we will see, not only the genre more clearly, but also its links to its culture, and we will understand more fully its enduring appeal.

The Gothic fantasy is a fable about the collapse of identity, parodying the fable of identity in its romance origin; its vision also inverts its sibling, the realistic novel. In the romance, and to a somewhat lesser degree in the realistic novel, two types of identity exist: masculine and feminine. These personality types are invariably linked to the sex of the individual characters. In the romance, the male hero asserts his archetypal masculine identity, while the female heroine embraces her feminine identity. This correlation of masculine and feminine archetypes with male and female characters is central to the romance's fable of identity; from one point of view, we might say that discovering identity for any man or woman is fundamentally coming to terms with the appropriate archetype. The same is true in realistic novels: Emma Woodhouse becomes a true woman and thus can marry Knightly and fulfill herself, similarly, Dorothea Brooke comes to understand her true self and marries Will Ladislaw. Marriage is the symbol, in both romance and realism, of the fixing of masculine identity in the male and feminine identity in the female and of their reconciliation in marriage.

This pattern does not hold in the Gothic. As we have seen, the double is a central motif in the genre; the individual is not one self, but two. The archetypal masculine and feminine coexist in a single individual. The nature of these archetypes within each male or female character is derived from the patterns of the romance, but it appears in the Gothic fantasy primarily in the dynamics of sadomasochism, bondage, and domination. The masculine archetype embodies selfish, egocentric impulses, often manifested as a desire to become godlike, or even to become God. Rooted in this identity is the impulse to impose one's will upon the world and other people and to do so by breaking moral and social laws; the masculine archetype can be satisfied only with power that is illegitimate. In this way, the Gothic male fuses the romance quest hero, who seeks his true identity and legitimate place—as does Theodore in *Otranto*—with the Faustian figure.

In contrast, the feminine archetype embodies strong affective qualities. She manifests herself in the desire to submit and serve. The archetypal feminine self tends to adhere closely to the moral laws and social conventions of the non-Gothic world; she embodies the will to virtue as opposed to the will to power. The feminine can only submit to legitimate—that is, virtuous—authority. Thus Matilda submits to Manfred's fatherly authority, while Isabella may justly resist his designs upon her, until her own father approves of them. The conflict between the two archetypes turns on the masculine need to transcend legitimate authority by violating it and the feminine need to unite with that authority by submitting to it.

This pattern is repeated in the dynamics of the family in the Gothic fantasy.[1] Each Gothic family—and virtually every major work in the genre is the story of a family—is really two families. One is patriarchal, dominated by the all-powerful father figure. He uses the members of the family as extensions and expressions of his power and authority, instruments supporting his masculine identity. The other family is affective or sentimental; it's central figure is the loving and caring mother. It defines itself as a circle of love and affection; each member finds identity through submergence into the family as a whole. The patriarchal and maternal families thus reflect on a social level the characteristics of the archetypes of individual identity. These two-families-within-one act out the typical Gothic pattern of submission and domination. As with the individual protagonists, the "two families" need each other because they define themselves in terms of difference. At the same time, they need each other for the family to operate. Without the maternal family, the patriarch would have no symbols and instruments of his power; without the patriarch, the family would be powerless, unable to act in its own behalf. Both families strangle their members; the patriarch robs the family members of their identities by forcing them to conform to his will, while the affective family submerges individual identity into the group. Both within the self and within the family, the two archetypes coexist in a necessary but finally destructive relationship, unable to fuse into a truly united whole.

The characters in the Gothic fantasy cannot accept their own double natures; they cannot acknowledge the existence of both a masculine and feminine component in a single person, nor can they even see that their desire for a stable, certain identity can only be fulfilled by the unification and reconciliation of these two halves. They are controlled by the idea that identity is either one thing or the other, never a fusion of both, for masculine and feminine are not simply different, but they are defined by their opposition and conflict with each other. Sharp, antagonistic differences are essential to the very concepts of masculine and feminine in the Gothic, and any easing of that sense of difference threatens the stability of the male in his masculine, and the female in her feminine, identity. The protagonists, though, acknowledge their doubled identities negatively and unconsciously through the violation or repression of one half of themselves. In order to fight the unadmitted and dangerous urge to unification, the protagonist may direct violence or hostility outward, particularly toward a double upon whom the unwanted, "other" half of the self is projected. Violence or repression inevitably turn back upon the protagonist, though, because they are really directed at the doubled nature within.

The collapse of identity stems, then, from two sources. On the simple level, the conflict between the radically different halves of the self does not allow any resolution; by definition, the Gothic protagonist can never become a single self. Yet on a more complex level, the protagonist both desires and fears the possibilities of the androgynous self that results from a fusion with the other identity. On the one hand, it would erase the contradictions and antagonism within, but on the other, an androgynous self would be unstable, neither masculine nor feminine, and thus the meaning of sexuality and our most obvious signs of identity would be called into question. Though the protagonists of the Gothic fantasy never bring this

complex drama to the surface of their own consciousness, this frightening and fascinating vision of a desirable and unattainable selfhood
is central to its thematic appeal.

The enactment of this theme dramatizes the contradictory and
self-destructive attempts of the characters to resolve the tensions
within the self. On the one hand, the protagonists fear their doubled
identities. They try to reject them through repression, self-deception,
or a variety of self-mutilations. In their attempts to escape, they become grotesques, maimed and twisted versions of human beings.
Manfred becomes a hysterical monster in pursuit of masculine
power, and Emily St. Aubert is reduced to terrorized passivity because of her highly developed femininity. Sometimes, a protagonist
will attempt to escape the doubled nature through a relationship
with a double, as Henry Jekyll lets loose his masculine side through
Edward Hyde. Yet the externalizing of the other self maims protagonists as fully as does repression or self-denial, for they are literally rejecting part of their own identities. Naturally enough, all
attempts to reject the unwanted and feared half of the self turn into
acknowledgments of the Other's existence and expressions of the desire to confront the Other. Repression or violence against the double
are expressions of the twin need to deny the doubled nature of the
self and the deep yearning to accept and unite the doubles into an
androgynous whole. In the Gothic fantasy, the quest for identity
becomes a self-contradictory fear of identity, a fear of the mutilated
masculine or feminine half selves and a desire to affirm one or the
other of these unitary archetypes.

We might talk for some time about the conflict between archetypes at a very high level of abstraction; indeed, because the characters are never conscious of this conflict, their stories are rarely
couched in such terms. The Gothic fantasy grounds the airy dance of
abstractions in human situations and characters through the use of
six primary motifs. These articulate the theme of the collapsing self
and allow us to see it in a social, as well as psychological, context and
refine the theme of identity into the problem of sexuality and pleasure as sources of identity.

Repression and Imprisonment, Violence and Incest, Respectability and Inheritance

Two relatively benign expressions of conflict between the archetypes
are repression and imprisonment. Throughout the Gothic fantasy,

characters repress aspects of their dual natures in order to conform more fully to a single archetype, thus stabilizing their identities. Manfred of Otranto denies his natural humaneness and Maud Ruthyn supresses her own desires to conform to the wishes of her dead father, Austin; in doing so, she puts herself in the hands of his evil double, Silas. Henry Jekyll holds down that side of his nature he releases in Hyde, and Laura, the heroine-narrator of *Carmilla*, finds in her vampire lover the expression of sexual desires she refuses to acknowledge. Sexuality is the common target of repression for both male and female characters. Schedoni and Manfred push aside their sexuality to pursue power; Emily St. Aubert, Elena of *The Italian*, and Antonia of *The Mark* are so thoroughly repressed we have difficulty thinking of them as grown women. The classic case of this type is probably the governess in *The Turn of the Screw*, though Robert Wringham in *The Private Memoirs and Confessions of a Justified Sinner* comes close. He has sex only during a six-month period of blackout, after which he cannot remember anything he has done. For male characters in the Gothic, repression is likely to mean a loss of interest in sex. Removal of the repression, as in the case of Ambrosio in *The Monk*, may result in a flood of sexual activity, accompanied by violence. The characters identify sex and sensuality as feminine qualities. In the female characters, repression either means complete denial of sexuality and the adoption of childish or girlish qualities or a deep attraction to a male power figure, which is expressed as daughterly love and obedience. To the female characters, sex and sensuality are also feminine qualities, but ones that must be sublimated if they are to be "truly" feminine.

Imprisonment is an externalized repression, and usually male characters imprison female characters. Imprisonment may be literal: Montoni locks Emily St. Aubert up in Udolpho, and Ambrosio kidnaps Antonia and hides her in the catacombs of the Abbey of St. Clare (Ambrosio's action is also a symbolic murder, leading to a real one). Or it may be symbolic, for example, Maud Ruthyn's "adoption" by Silas, the governess's self-isolation at Bly in *Turn of the Screw*, or Dracula's turning his victims into vampires, mirror images of himself. Dracula also immures himself in his coffin, and Dorian Grey hides his portrait, his soul, in the attic. Moncada in *Melmoth the Wanderer* is imprisoned by the Church, as is Agnes in *The Monk*. The act of imprisonment, whether literal or metaphoric, is usually something the masculine self does to the feminine self, probably because only male characters have the power to literally imprison another person, though powerful institutions, such as the Church and the Inquisition, can do this too. The case of Jekyll and Hyde shows that the pattern can be reversed, though. As an external repression, imprisonment is also a metaphor for the control of sexuality.

Violence is, of course, the natural expression of the masculine in its purest form, the application of force to the world to assert its power and identity. Incest is the desperate attempt to affirm the feminine identity through the power of love. Incest parodies the values of the affective family, transforming emotional and spiritual bonds into sexual ones. Female characters, though, are not always the ones who initiate incest. Often male characters commit or attempt incest in order to reconcile themselves to their own feminine nature by sexually possessing their feminine double, typically, a sister. Incest and violence are thus doubled impulses, the extreme expressions of the masculine and feminine archetypes at their most monstrous. Thus, in the Gothic, sexuality—almost always covertly incestuous— provokes violence, just as violence is always sexualized, expressing a hidden incestuous impulse. As the instruments of assertion of the two archetypes, each inevitably calls the other into being, for they are inescapable halves of a single drive for identity.

The motifs of inheritance and respectability are the sanctioned expressions of the authority and power of the masculine and feminine archetypes and link them to the established power of social institutions. By inheritance, the masculine identity affirms its legitimacy through the patriarchal line. The masculine personality is authoritative and powerful because its source is respectable and legitimate, but in the Gothic fantasy, inheritance is poisoned at the source, and no genuine authority and power—and thus no true identity—can flow from it. The failure of inheritance reverses the romance convention in which the discovery of the hero's identity and proper inheritance are linked, if not identical, events. The Gothic, which rejects the very concept of history, rejects the possibility that continuity with the past can be a foundation of identity. The very first Gothic fantasy, *The Castle of Otranto,* lays out the dynamics of inheritance in the genre.

Respectability, on the other hand, symbolizes the sanctioned and acceptable power of feminine identity. By respectability, we mean here the conventional ideal of female virtue, particularly, chastity. Respectable women are fit to be wives and mothers and therefore are allied to the power of inheritance, which they can marry into and then perpetuate. Respectability is weakened by the collapse of inheritance because that failure means the failure of legitimate male authority. A chaste, respectable female may submit only to legitimate authority—a father or a husband—because only then can she partake in the power of his authority. A woman who is imprisoned, taken by violence, or the victim of incest is not only powerless, but because she becomes disreputable, loses any chance to obtain legitimizing power through marriage and inheritance. Respectability should be a bulwark against victimization, but in fact, as chastity—or in an extreme form, repression—it defines and creates the conditions for victimization. The very need to be respectable and therefore passive—both sexually and otherwise—defines the female as the male's potential victim as well as a possible wife or a daughter.

Clearly all these motifs center on the problem of sexuality. Repression denies sexuality; imprisonment confines it or hides it, as when Ambrosio attempts to confine and hide Antonia in the catacombs of the abbey. Violence and incest, at the other extreme, are the active manifestations of sexuality in its most uncontrolled and disruptive forms. Inheritance, the passing on of identity from one generation to the next, is an attempt to harness the power of sexuality in the service of stability and continuity. Thus, in the romance, marriage, with the implied establishment of a line of succession, is the affirmation of masculine and feminine, male and female reconciled in a stable unity. Respectability controls sexuality simply by confining it to marriage, assuring the purity and security of inheritance. Sexuality is, of course, naturally linked to identity, but we see here also how sexuality and identity are social issues. The values of inheritance and respectability reveal again how clearly the dynamics of individual identity are tied to those of the family.

The Gothic fantasy proved compelling for a nineteenth-century audience and, later, for a twentieth-century one, not because it was an interesting variation in a literary tradition, but because its transformation of the romance mythology reflected the transformations and tensions of the society in which its readers lived. Middle-class readers were attempting to adjust to life in a radically new environment, an urban, industrialized, technological, capitalist culture, in which science was replacing religion as the dominant orthodoxy and the pace of change seemed to increase expotentially. This new world—and it is easy from our late twentieth-century perspective to forget how radically new it really was—clearly required different concepts of what it meant to be an individual, what it meant to be a man or a woman, what a family was. These things could not retain their precapitalist, preindustrial, prescientific form. The knight and the warrior were gone; that form of heroism had disappeared. Moreover, in an increasingly democratic society, in which intelligence and mental qualities were to become more important than physical strength and power, the status of women could not remain as it had been.

Yet in the naturalization of the romance mythology in the realistic novel, modern culture attempted to adapt the fables of the past to the present. No complete break, of course, was possible or desirable, and that people living with an accelerated sense of change should look to traditional conceptions about identity was quite reasonable and understandable. The fables of the past could, as indeed they should, provide a sense of continuity that might stabilize human life. But insofar as these myths could not truly serve a modern world, their adaptations show the strain under which the middle class lived. The fact was, romance conceptions of masculine and feminine identity did not provide very useful versions of what today we would call imaginative role models. Men who had to be businessmen or office workers or bureaucrats could not really imagine themselves questing knights. The aristocratic warrior became the professional soldier, who in a way was simply another sort of businessman or bureaucrat. For women, the romance mythology supported the insistant and crippling nineteenth-century view of women)as sexless, ethereal beings, the "Angel in the House," whose only function was to be pure and motherly.

Thus the literary and social problems melt into one another. The changes in literature reflect changes in society, and the changes in the culture's mythologies become part of the process of social change. That we can now look back upon the nineteenth century and see clearly where and how they failed in their attempts to adapt to their new social situation should not lead us to one more useless condemnation of the bogey of Victorianism. Anglo-American society in the nineteenth century was caught up in a tremendously radical transformation of human culture; that they were able to adapt at all is perhaps more impressive than their very real mistakes.

The transformations most important to the Gothic fantasy were those in the roles open to men and women and hence, those in the nature of the family. In the nineteenth century, the family moved from being a unit of production to a unit of consumption; it ceased to be primarily a structure that passed on and maintained the past through inheritance and became a refuge for its members, existing for emotional and psychic solace and escape from the strains of everyday life. These changes of course were gradual and uneven, but they were part of the transformation of the way Western culture operated. Men increasingly worked outside the home, earning money in economic structures that had no necessary relationship to the family, where the man lived his private life. Middle-class women were more and more tied to the home, where they functioned, not as producers of wealth, but consumers of it, spending the money their husbands earned to maintain the home as a refuge. Thus the family foundation—the men and women who lived as husband and wife, the mother and father—was based on a fragmentation of roles and functions. In a sense, the family created nothing, but it consumed everything. The man's social function as husband and father took place largely outside the home, in the world of business, while the woman had no significant functions outside the home. Within the home and family, middle-class women throughout the past two-hundred years have been confronted with the problem of increasing leisure time. While many worked hard in maintaining their homes, particularly before the advent of labor-saving technology, the fact was that the family and home were increasingly defined as a place of leisure. Woman become divorced from the world of work because in the home, women neither earned a wage nor produced a product, and in a capitalist society, only these activites could be "work." However tentatively, middle-class women were confronting one of the central cultural problems modern capitalist, industrial society created: What do we do with increasing leisure time?

These new situations in male and female roles, these new functions for the family, locate and frame the specific anxieties and fears to which the Gothic fantasy was a response. It was here that the contradictions and tensions between the old myths and new realities took their heaviest toll. The very way in which these people lived posed the questions, What does it mean to be a man or a woman? What does it mean to be part of a family? without providing any clear answer. We can see that both these problems share a common focus and a common axis upon which their answers must turn: sexuality. An essential part of being a man or a woman is defining one's relation to the other sex; a central part of being human is defining one's own sexuality. Whatever the family is, whatever it's economic or psychological functions, it is always a structure for reproduction, in which the male and female identities of the children are defined and shaped. Perhaps the great age of Victorian repression and willful blindness about the reality of sexuality is based on the anxiety caused by modern culture's inability to generate an effective, humane way of expressing sexuality in the mechanistic, technological, capitalist world. That world, of course, was in theory inhabited by "economic man," the creature who made all decisions by calculating the marginal utility of every action and who chose his pleasures as a rational analysis of the possibilities before him. This, combined with the traditionally ambiguous Christian attitude toward sexuality, may well have meant that nineteenth-century people had trouble defining sexuality and, thus, their own identities and the nature of their families. The central emotion that underlies the Gothic fantasy and finds its expression in it is the immediate and pressing fear that wells up from the deformation of identity and family resulting from the unresolved problem of sexuality in modern society.

The problem of identity is, then, the problem of sexuality. Traditionally, the power of sexuality is the power of reproduction; the prominence given to the issue of inheritance and the nature of the family in the Gothic acknowledges that. But the root cause of horror in the genre is the protagonist's inability to control sexuality, to thus define masculine and feminine and create legitimate identity. The identities of the protagonists disintegrate because they cannot control and channel sexuality in a productive way; thus we see the constant sexualization of violence and the transformation of the power of continuity and affirmation into that of destruction and terror. Yet the power of reproduction is not lost to the protagonists of the Gothic; they obsessively exercise this power, which is, metaphorically, the power to regenerate the self. Manfred, Victor Frankenstein, Roderick and Madelaine Usher, and even Dracula are caught up in the process of reproduction. The creation of doubles is also a part of the process: thus Jekyll gives "birth" to Hyde, Wieland becomes a new man at the sound of his Voices, and Ambrosio recreates himself in the awakening of his sensuality. Whether they succeed, as Victor and Dracula do, or fail, as do Manfred and the Ushers, the power of reproduction is within the reach of all Gothic protagonists. Yet their attempts always result in grotesques and monsters—the creature, Hyde, Dorian's portrait. Any success is short-lived. Perhaps the fear of success in recreating their crippled and mutilated selves is what prevents Madelaine and Roderick Usher from continuing their family tradition of incest. The question is, then, if the power to reproduce is not beyond the capacity of the Gothic protagonists, why do their attempts end in failure?

The answer lies, I think, in the other power of sexuality, the power of pleasure. The protagonists can accept sexuality simply as a means of reproduction, but they repress or reject it insofar as they cannot accept that it is also pleasurable. In the Gothic world, the self is defined through conflict, as a giver or receiver of pain in a sadomasochistic dynamic. In its intensity, pain defines the self, but its logic leads to self-destruction as a final act of self-definition. Ambrosio acts out this logic, though he never really accepts it, and Dracula, for example, embraces the vision completely. If one attempts to define the self through pleasure, though, the patterns of domination and submission central to the masculine and feminine archetypes are erased. The experience of pleasure defines identity without heightened conflict and division; we become one with ourselves, and the alienation of self from Other is eased. The terrible, pervasive absence in the Gothic world is the absence of pleasure: the wasteland of the Gothic is a world in which cruelty, violence, and conflict are the only principles upon which the characters can act, only to destroy themselves.

Reproduction without pleasure brings forth only monsters and grotesques. The protagonists approach the act of reproduction as an act of violence or cruelty; when the Other has been brought forth, it remains resolutely and horrifically Other. Reproduction leads only to a renewed and intensified version of the conflicts within the self and between the self and the Other. Indeed, because the Other, like Frankenstein's creature, is an externalization of the conflicts of the creator, its appearance can only exaggerate internal tensions, not resolve them. Because of the absence of pleasure, the Gothic world becomes a horrific maze in which the protagonists pursue identities they cannot accept, even if they find them.

In the discussion of themes that follows, two problems arise. One is organizational. The Gothic fantasy is a complex tapestry, and we shall have difficulty separating the strands, for each archetype, each theme, each motif always transforms itself into its opposite. Incest begets violence, which leads back to incest; the theme of individual identity becomes that of the family; and the attempt to embrace a single archetype becomes a movement toward androgyny. I deal in this chapter with the problem of pleasure, the masculine and the feminine archetypes, then the incest motif, and finally, the problem of androgyny. These divisons violate the essential unity of the fantasy, but they are necessary if we are to understand clearly how it works.

The other problem requires a caution and a reminder at this point. Throughout this section, I use a vocabulary that is essentially psychological. I may seem to be discussing the fantasy as if it were a portrayal of the human psyche or a study in human psychology. We must, though, remember the nature of the genre. Its psychological archetypes, its patterns of masculine and feminine identity, are parodies of those of the romance tradition, patterns that have broken down as imaginative models for nineteenth- and twentieth-century society. The Gothic is not a vision of what human beings "really" are; it parodies failed, inadequate, out-moded conceptions of the self. The Gothic critique of the romance extends beyond parodying the archetypes of the self to an analysis of the entire nature of the relations between men and women in the nineteenth and twentieth centuries and the pervasive importance of gender in the social as well as the personal aspects of our lives. In the genre, stories about the self are also stories about the world in which the self exists.

The Problem of Pleasure

Through *Carmilla, Dr. Jekyll and Mr. Hyde,* and *The Picture of Dorian Gray,* we can focus more clearly on the problem of pleasure in the Gothic. In each of these tales of doubles, the division of the self occurs because of ambivalence or ambiguity about pleasure, particularly sexual pleasure. The pursuit of pleasure produces monsters in all three tales, and one can easily read each as a cautionary fable about the necessity of repression. This, certainly, is how Henry Jekyll interprets his own experiences, but it becomes a far less obvious conclusion under close scrutiny.

Carmilla

Le Fanu's *Carmilla* is a vampire story. The vampire and her victim, Laura, the narrator of the tale, are both women; the question of female sexuality and lesbianism is barely, if at all, glossed over.[2] Carmilla seeks out Laura, not, as Dracula does his victims, as prey, but as a lover. As she says to Laura,

'Dearest, your little heart is wounded; think me not cruel because I obey the irresistible law of my strength and weakness; if your dear heart is wounded, my wild heart bleeds with yours. In the rapture of my enormous humiliation I live in your warm life, and you shall die—die, sweetly, die—into mine. I cannot help it; as I draw near to you, you in your turn, will draw near to others, and learn the rapture of that cruelty which yet is love; so for a little while, seek to know no more of me and mine, but trust me with all your loving spirit.'

And when she had spoken such a rhapsody, she would press me more closely in her trembling embrace, and her lips in soft kisses gently glowed upon my cheek.

Her agitation and her language were unintelligible to me.

From these foolish embraces, which were not of very frequent occurence, I must allow, I used to wish to extricate myself; but my energies seemed to fail me. Her murmured words sounded like a lullaby in my ear and soothed my resistance into a trance, from which I only seemed to recover myself when she withdrew her arms.

In these mysterious moods I did not like her. I experienced a strange tumultuous excitement that was pleasurable, ever and anon, mingled with a vague sense of fear and distrust. I had no distinct thoughts about her while such scenes lasted, but I was conscious of a love growing into adoration, and also of abhorrence. I know this is paradox, but I can make no other attempt to explain the feeling.[3]

Strikingly, not only does Carmilla love Laura, but Laura responds positively, if hesitantly, to her advances. Her responses are the classic Gothic fusion of fear and desire to the object of enthrallment, which is both Other and a part of the self. As well, Carmilla's attitude toward Laura is not simply part of the repertoire of vampire tricks. Some of her victims she does regard as food—particularly peasants, for she is an aristocratic vampire—but she and Laura have a special affinity that began before they ever met. Laura had dream visions of Carmilla when she was a child. Though Laura never actively assents to Carmilla's advances when she is in human form, she is receptive when Carmilla comes to her at night, in her vampire form. Laura represses her memory of these moments, but this forgetfulness in effect allows Carmilla to continue her advances. Laura forgets, not because what occurs is horrible, though it is, but because she wants it to continue. Although she is a typically passive and respectable young Gothic heroine, Laura is also receptive to the unconventional love and sexuality offered to her by Carmilla.

Her attitude toward Carmilla contrasts sharply with that of her father and General Speilsdorf, the uncle of Carmilla's previous lover-victim. The men are, after a brief period of being charmed by the lovely and feminine Carmilla, horrified to discover what she really is and take arms to hunt her down. In their efforts, they are assisted by a local man named Vordenburg, whose ancestor had been Carmilla's would-be lover. The first Vordenburg had helped preserve Carmilla—in life, the Countess Mircalla Karnstein—from vampire hunters, but his descendant hunts her down, for he has become a professional vampire killer. Vordenburg suggests that Carmilla became a vampire because she committed suicide. Moreover, it seems likely that she killed herself because her sexual preference in life was the same as her sexual preference in death, and this was unacceptable in her world. Vordenburg's appearance not only allows LeFanu to fill in Carmilla's background but makes Vordenburg the instrument of delayed vengeance of the spurned male. The men in the story are determined to destroy Carmilla because she threatens their hegemony over women; the motif of the conspiracy of patriarchs versus the conspiracy of women that appears in *Uncle Silas* is even more striking in *Carmilla*.

Of course *Carmilla* is a vampire story, and overtly, Carmilla is dangerous: she identifies love and death as one, and she will kill Laura if she has the chance because she loves her. When Carmilla is dispatched, Laura is saved from a terrible fate. Even ten years later, as she writes the story, her hand "trembles." But, though she calls her recollections "horrible" and the events an "ordeal," in the next sentence, she describes her encounter with Carmilla as the time when her "passions" were "most wildly and terrible aroused." Each time Laura attempts to relate her experience in the terms that any virtuous young woman should, she fails. We have already seen the last passage of her narrative, which sounds this peculiar, nostalgic, erotic note of longing that runs through all her recollections of Carmilla.

> It was long before the terror of recent events subsided and tothis hour the image of Carmilla returns to memory with ambiguousalternations—sometimes the playful, languid girl; sometimesthe writhing fiend I saw in the churchyard; and often from areverie I have started, fancying I have heard the light footstepsof Carmilla at the drawing room door.

For Laura, Carmilla remains the image of someone and something attractive and desirable; not only a lover, but an image of herself, hidden beneath the passive, respectable daughter her father seeks to protect. Through Carmilla, Laura encounters a version of feminine identity not bound by the conventional concepts of women that she herself embodies. Carmilla is not an image of the evils of sexuality in women or the dangers of lesbianism, but rather an expression of the form that active, assertive feminine sexuality would have to take in a patriarchal society. Carmilla's tragedy is not that she is vampire or a lesbian, but that her society has defined her sexuality as monstrous. Thus she reveals herself in a form that expresses that imposed monstrousness, the vampire. When the men in the story hunt Carmilla down to protect Laura, she does indeed become "a writhing fiend"; she is what they expect, what they have made her. Still, the manifestation of Carmilla's sexuality—vampirism and the identification of love and death—is corrupt; it is the sadomasochism typical of masculine forms of identity and sexuality in the Gothic. Only the masculine archetype can express sexuality actively, so the patriarchal world, not only forces her nature upon Carmilla, but it is in fact the originator of such monstrousness.

Formally, the story suggests that Carmilla's attractive and affectionate side is really only a cover for a hideous reality; certainly Laura's father and General Speilsdorf regard this to be the case. But Laura recognizes the "ambiguous alternations" in Carmilla's complex identity. If Carmilla is monstrous, then, so too is Laura. But here what is horrible is not substance, but the forms imposed on female sexuality and pleasure by masculine society. Laura and Carmilla cannot, of course, live happily ever after, Carmilla, we must recall, is already dead. However, Laura's narrative is presented to us, in a brief prologue, as posthumous, and given the concluding paragraph, the story may suggest that Laura and Carmilla are joined in death as they could not be in life. And though Laura has not lived on in Carmilla, as Carmilla said she would, Carmilla has clearly lived on in Laura, as a memory, an object of fear, an object of desire, a source of fantasy—reverie, as Laura calls it.

To perceive Carmilla as we do through Laura's memories mutes what is horrible about her and allows us to see what is genuinely and truly attractive, to see very clearly the impact of those attractions upon Laura. The compelling suggestion that *Carmilla* makes is that feminine sexuality contains within it a powerful energy, not simply reproductive, but essentially pleasure giving. If this energy were not defined by the conventional view of female sexuality as monstrous, then clearly feminine identity would take on a very different shape than that embodied in either Laura or Carmilla.

Dr. Jekyll and Dorian Grey

Carmilla explores the relationship of pleasure and identity in relation to the limitations of conventional ideas about women. *Dr. Jekyll and*

Mr. Hyde and *The Picture of Dorian Grey* deal with the same issue in relation to masculine ideals of identity, though in both stories the protagonists seem attracted to the pursuit of pleasure in part because of the strength of the feminine archetypes in their make up. In both stories, the male protagonists, consciously and purposefully, divide themselves in order to assert their identities. They accept, paradoxically, fragmentation as the price of completeness. Jekyll is quite frank about this: he creates Hyde to indulge those secret impulses and desires that he must repress if he wishes to maintain his respectable social identity:

> I found it hard to reconcile my imperious desire to carry my head high, and wear a more than grave countenance before the public. Hence it came about that I concealed my pleasures. . . . I stood already committed to a profound duplicity of life [and] a morbid sense of shame.[4]

The creation of Hyde, the alternate identity through whom Jekyll can indulge his pursuit of pleasure as a voyeur, for he is fully conscious of everything Hyde does, is simply the logical extension of his own natural way of life, the way of life of any man who wishes to remain within the limitations of social respectability and still pursue the extremes of pleasure. Respectability, of course, is a feminine value in the Gothic; Hyde is the release of Jekyll's fully masculine identity, stunted, but powerful when unrestrained.

Dorian Grey initially seeks to avoid the loss of youth and beauty that comes with adult experience, wishing to remain forever at the moment of awakening he experiences while talking to Lord Henry in Basil Hallward's studio. He is attempting to avoid the dilemma that confronted Vathek. On one hand, he wishes, like Gulchenroz, to remain forever young and innocent—or at least apparently untouched, which Dorian, in his ignorance, thinks is the same thing. At the same time, through the mysterious power of the portrait, he will be able to enjoy the widest possible variety of pleasurable experiences—wholesome and otherwise—which would ordinarily be inaccessible or destructive to him. Dorian, of course, does not escape Vathek's trap, for by the end of the novel, he realizes that his avoidance of the consequences of his self-indulgence has rendered all pleasure boring. After a moment of feeling virtuous for declining to seduce a young farm girl, Dorian realizes that all sensations, virtuous or vicious, painful or pleasurable, are alike to him, for he cannot truly experience them. He finds himself confronted with the ultimate meaninglessness of attempts to build identity on conventional ideas of self, Other, and pleasure. Unbounded by reality, Dorian's self dissolves, all experience, all inner life, worthless, with only death as a release. In making even vice insipid, Dorian combines the fates of Gulchenroz and Vathek. He is as ignorant of true pleasure as a child but suffers the ennervating boredom of stunted adulthood.

Both *Jekyll and Hyde* and *Dorian Grey* express the impossibility of living with both a public identity and a private, self-defined identity based on pleasure. Conventional ideals seem to demand the accommodation, but the nature of those ideals make this self-division impossible. In accepting their fragmented identity in the form of an actual double, Jekyll and Dorian simply formalize the inadequate conceptions of pleasure and identity from which they are attempting to escape. Both Jekyll and Dorian express themselves and define their alternate identities through the egocentric sadism of the male protagonist of the Gothic. Hyde tramples a small child at the opening of Stevenson's story, and Dorian refuses any responsibility for his evil actions. As Jekyll establishes a voyeuristic relationship with Hyde, so too does Dorian with his debauched self. He ruins his friends and lovers, in part, to watch the spectacle of their ruin and to imagine the effects of his actions on the portrait. This voyeuristic attitude toward pleasure enforces the passive and restricted relationship of the self to pleasure and thus to its own identity. Pleasure becomes the province of the monstrous Other, the double, not of the "true" self. This simply deepens the monstrousness of both pleasure and Other, and thus the alienation of the self from its own identity.

As with *Carmilla*, both these stories tell a conventional tale: too much pleasure kills. Only repression and control can maintain the integrity of the self. But, as we have seen, the fragmentation and division of the self is not a result of the pursuit of pleasure, but a necessary condition of its pursuit, a condition originating in the divided self already embodied in the public identities of these characters. In *Dorian Grey*, Basil Hallward and Lord Henry are also divided men. Basil expresses his deepest feeling in his art, transforming emotions into objects—exactly the process that Dorian uses in his relationship with the portrait. Lord Henry's radical ideas constitute a purely verbal identity, sharply contrasting with his fundamentally conventional and socially acceptable behavior. In *Jekyll and Hyde*, Utterson the lawyer mortifies his own love of pleasure, drinking gin rather than the wine he prefers and avoiding the theater because he enjoys it. The dilemma in which Jekyll and Grey find themselves is not created by their excessive self-indulgence but forced upon them by a society that refuses to recognize or accept the place of pleasure in identity. For Jekyll in particular, the depth of this self-indulgence is directly proportionate to the social demand for repression. Pleasure is not the cause of the shattering and fracturing of identity; rather, the identity fractures because of insufficient pleasure or pleasure made monstrous.

In both novels the absence of women is striking. Typically, one might expect at least a nominally threatened female in a Gothic story. In *Dorian Grey,* Sybil Vane might appear to qualify, but her limited presence functions to impress upon us her, and any other woman's, essential absence in the rest of the story. In their search for pleasure, Henry Jekyll and Dorian Grey throw off the feminine world of respectability, and thus their pursuit takes on a purely masculine, sadistic form, finally transformed into the masochism of suicide. Their fragmented identities lead them to a fragmented form of pleasure, one that, like all masculine attempts at self-definition in the Gothic, involves denying and extirpating the feminine. Carmilla must realize her affectional nature through masculine sadism, for this is the only style of active sexuality available to her; in order to express their masculine identities in terms of pleasure, Hyde and Dorian become sadists. Once again, we see that masculine identity demands the repression of feminine identity, and that this act of repression controls, not only the forms of identity, but also the forms of pleasure. Both become monstrous, not from inner necessity, but from the intractable logic of the conventional world.

The failure of identity, the distortion of the relationship of self to Other that produces monsters, and the disintegration of the self into Gothic nothingness all turn on the deformation of pleasure, its conversion into pain, and its rejection as a means of self-definition. Attempts to reclaim the power of pleasure, in its paradigmatic form of sexuality, are subverted by fear, anxiety, and hostility. The quest for pleasure and selfhood are, in the Gothic fantasy, always transformed into a quest for pain that ends in self-destruction.

Manfred of Otranto

We have come across Manfred, ruler of Otranto, a number of times already in our discussion as the typical male Gothic protagonist. Manfred is also typical—is quite literally the prototype—of the Gothic patriarch struggling to establish his masculine identity. The two roles are, for Manfred, the same, for his struggle to preserve his individual identity is also a struggle to hold onto his patriarchal power, both as father and as prince of Otranto. In this struggle, Manfred confronts a crisis of inheritance. On the one hand, his inheritance of Otranto is illegitimate, for his grandfather Riccardo obtained the throne by murdering Alphonso the Good. On the other hand, his own line of succession has been broken by his son's mysterious death. Manfred's inability to pass his throne along threatens, not only his status as prince and patriarch, but, metaphorically, his personal identity. The illegitimacy of his rule is shadowed by Alphonso's curse; the failure of his line will mean the restoration of the legitimate line and the revelation that he is a fraud and a usurper. In order to hold together his own identity and Otranto, Manfred must become his own son, passing his corrupt inheritance on to himself as he fulfills both his own role and Conrad's.

Manfred's image of himself as an individual and as a ruler is tied to the masculine archetype's will to power. The sadism of the male protagonist is revealed, not simply as an accident of the Gothic spectacle, but rather as intrinsic to the masculine conception of identity, which defines the self by its ability to impose its will upon those around it. For Manfred, his family is both the instrument of his power and the symbol of his identity; his wife and children are tools and emblems. Because Matilda cannot extend the male line and is thus, unlike Conrad, an ineffective symbol of Manfred's identity, she is unimportant and her father ignores her. Because Hippolita cannot produce another male heir, she is useless, and Manfred will divorce her to marry Isabella, Conrad's intended. Manfred regards Isabella neither as a person nor even as a sexual object; she is just another human mechanism for the replication and maintenance of his identity and power.

In following the logic of the masculine pattern, Manfred appears to have completely lost his capacity for human feeling, and his relationship to his family becomes that of a workman to his tools. Even erotic impulses are transformed in order to support and extend Manfred's conception of himself and his power over his family and the state. Despite his attitude, Hippolita and Matilda remain deeply devoted to Manfred; they act in accordance with the feminine archetype, conceiving their identity in terms of virtuous subservience and loving respectability. The members of the royal house of Otranto seem perfectly matched, but in fact, Manfred is an uneasy patriarch. He relies upon the compliance of the women in his family to fulfill his will, and he must also depend on Isabella to marry him and bear him an heir. Everywhere he turns, the compliant female is essential to his goals; even as he dominates the women, he finds himself dependent upon them. In Isabella's case, the respectability so central to the feminine personality works against Manfred, for she regards marrying her dead fiance's father as incest and refuses him.

But Manfred finds himself in a peculiar relationship, not only to the female characters, but also to elements of his own nature. Walpole describes Manfred as "naturally humane," and he is repeatedly moved by sympathy and pity for his victims. "He was ashamed of his . . . inhuman treatment" of Hippolita, but he quickly hardened his heart against her, for he had villainy to perform.[5] When, as happens over and over in the novel, Manfred becomes hysterical in the face of opposition and difficulty, we are seeing the manifestation, not only of his anxiety about his quest to maintain his masculine power and identity, but of the repression of the sentimental, feminine aspects of his nature. The identity created through power and patriarchy is self-alienating and thus self-defeating. Manfred's rejection of his wife and daughter are really rejections of himself; his violence against Isabella and, finally, Matilda, whom he accidently stabs to death thinking she is Isabella, is also emblematic of his violent rejection of his own affective qualities. Each rejection, each act of violence that Manfred intends to affirm his identity in fact erodes and destroys it. At the end of the novel, Conrad and Matilda are both dead as a result of their father's quest for power, and in destroying his family, Manfred has destroyed himself. His quest is poisoned from the start because his power and identity are illegitimate. Alienated from the values of the feminine, the actions of the masculine personality are violent and chaotic. The principle of dominance fails because its logic is self-destructive. At the very end of the novel, Walpole addresses the question of whether a legitimate patriarchal identity can exist without destroying itself. Theodore is, after all, not the grandson of a usurper, but the conventional romance hero who by the end of the tale discovers his true identity and returns to his rightful place. Walpole has, of course, implied the irrelevance of this quest hero by focusing on Manfred, and we see that even though Theodore is restored to his throne and true identity, he is no better off than Manfred. He had fallen in love with Matilda and is inconsolable at her death. He eventually marries nevertheless: "After frequent discussion with Isabella, of his dear Matilda . . . he was persuaded he could know no happiness but in the society of one with

whom he could forever indulge the melancholy that had taken possession of his soul."[6] In Otranto, no one lives happily ever after, not
Theodore, and certainly not Isabella, forever indulging the melancholy of his soul. What in Manfred was manifested as hysteria in
Theodore appears as melancholy, but both states betray the masculine alienation from the feminine Other.

If the logic of masculine identity leads to the destruction of those
around it and finally to self-destruction, then the feminine identity
assents to this logic. We have already remarked on the extraordinary
passivity and the malleability of the women in *Otranto*. As she dies,
unwilling to rebuke her father herself, Matilda calls Father Jerome,
who has the temerity to criticize Manfred for murdering his
daughter, a "cruel man," who has "aggravated the woes of a parent."
Hippolita wants nothing more than to obey Manfred and disappear
from the face of the earth into a convent. Isabella, somewhat spunk-
ier than the other two, having little desire to marry Conrad and even
less to marry Manfred, is, despite her protests, overruled. When her
father, Frederic, appears, he cheerfully agrees to give her to Manfred
in exchange for Matilda, and she can do nothing about it. Hippolita
is even willing to consent to this absurd parody of incest, as fathers
exchange daughters and turn them into wives. The corruption of the
feminine lies in its complete powerlessness and its inability to generate any other value than adherance to respectable passivity.

Walpole expresses, in his portrayal of uniformly virtuous women,
a strange admiration for the feminine, but he thoroughly undercuts
that admiration by linking feminine goodness to ineffectuality and
victimization, often willingly assented to. He seems unaware of the
real alienation of the masculine identity, for he too conceives of
woman as inescapably Other. Powerless, the feminine has nothing of
substance to offer the masculine; hysterical or melancholy, the masculine personality betrays a sense of incompleteness but can only
attack and destroy the emblem of what it lacks. For Walpole, the
crisis of identity is a male problem, one without a solution. Women
have neither a problem nor a solution, they are merely the victims of
the patriarch run amok.

Manfred's Heirs

The heirs and reincarnations of Manfred are all troubled by the same
problem: no amount of power is ever enough power; no action can
ever generate the force to allow the protagonist to escape destruction. The male protagonist in the Gothic fantasy aspires—overtly, in

the cases of Wieland, Frankenstein, Melmoth, and Dracula—to the power of God, the original Father, the font of legitimacy and identity. However, as we saw in chapter 1, the Gothic world is marked by the absence of the numinous, of any principle or order or authority except those of metamorphosis and doubleness, which in effect are those of chaos and disorder. The absence of the Father creates a vacuum that can never be filled; once God is gone, he can never be created out of the merely human. The collapse of legitimation for their identity means that the male protagonists of the Gothic fantasy are pursuing a chimera, longing for a status they can never attain. Indeed, in attempting to affirm the masculine archetype and take on the power of ultimate authority, they become monstrous parodies of God, capable only of destruction and terror, never of true creation and love of creation, even when they are in fact creating themselves.

The Gothic fantasy's pervasive anxiety about legitimacy is the literary expression of the failure of the Divine Father as a source of authority. This sense of crisis also reflects the problems created by the breakdown of traditional social structures in postrevolutionary Europe and America. The failures and uncertainties that enveloped both religious and secular authority in the real world are localized in the Gothic fantasy, and given immediate and specific form in the failure of the family to establish and maintain a secure identity. This grounded the larger upheavals in the basic structure of modern society in a context that all readers could immediately understand, since the family was an essential part of their everyday lives. Thus the various "family" stories we find in the Gothic fantasy embody the links between the problems of personal identity and family relationships on the one hand and, on the other, the transformation of culture and society, the movement of history, in the nineteenth century. The genre in this way established the links between inner and external reality.

These connections also reflect the ambiguous attitude toward history embodied in the Gothic. On the one hand, the past is the place from which all evil and corruption flows, from the pollution that threatens Manfred's title, to the terrors that assail Vivaldi and Elena in *The Italian* and Roderick and Madeline in "The Fall of the House of Usher," to Count Dracula, rising from the grave to impose his dreadful inheritance upon England. As the examples suggest, aristocrats are very often at the center of the widening circles of the Gothic whirlpool. On the other hand, despite the failure of the past to provide continuity or authority, only in the past were these things possible. The Gothic fantasy articulates a nostalgia for the time before the breakdown of tradition. It is recalled in *Otranto* as the days before the rightful line was desposed. In "The Fall of the House of Usher," Roderick's poem "The Haunted Palace" recalls the glorious history of his family, before the curse of incest began to destroy them. In *Dracula,* the count tells Johnathan Harker of the period when his family—and presumably himself, when he was human—reigned as the rightful and legitimate rulers of Transylvania. Behind the images of a polluted and corrupt past lies the recollection of a more distant age. This golden or heroic past can hardly be recognized through the distorting terror of the intervening years.

The mixture of longing and repulsion that makes up the Gothic attitude toward the past is paralleled by its view of the possibilities of the present. While many Gothic protagonists are aristocrats, many others—Caleb Williams, Edgar Huntly, Robert Wringham, and Henry Jekyll—are not and seem to represent a somewhat generalized type of middle-class man. But whether aristocrat or bourgeoise, the male protagonists embody the values and ideals of the modern individualist. They are self-made men in the fullest, and sometimes most literal, sense of the term. Their visions of power and identity parody both the romantic faith in the power of individual imagination and the bourgeois faith in individual effort and energy, the "luck and pluck" of Horatio Alger. But, not only does aristocratic tradition fail to establish a proper basis for identity, but so do the middle-class and romantic alternatives. This accounts for the fact that if the male characters are not counts or dukes, they may very likely be scientists, the most radical type of the new nineteenth-century individualist. Thus, parallel to the vision of a corrupt past is the vision of a hopeless and absurd present. The failure of the past on the one hand "liberates" the protagonist from bondage to a dying tradition; on the other, it presents a challenge to which no one can rise: to create something out of nothing, to make an identity out of one's own power and nothing more. The Gothic protagonists confront a situation that might make them tragic heroes; but neither as aristocrat or individualist do they attain such status.

They are not heroic, or even tragic, characters, though the conventions of the romance hero and the Faustian archetypes lie behind them. The Gothic males pervert the heroic quest for identity and the tragic search for power because their conceptions of identity and power are fundamentally twisted. Yet some retain a certain heroic or tragic quality about them, even if it is ultimately undercut and dissipated. The one who comes closest to achieving this status is Melmoth in Maturin's *Melmoth the Wanderer*. We have already discussed him as a proto–existential rebel in search of a humanized universe; this and his love for Immalee make him the most truly heroic of the Gothic male protagonists. He is apparently capable of love, something usually impossible for male characters in the genre. But for Immalee, marrying him means joining him in his quest to transcend the power of God and reverse the meaning of salvation and damnation. Even as we recognize Melmoth's near-heroic stature, we also realize that his quest is perverse and that, for him, love has become equivalent to death. Marrying Immalee means bringing her under his power, into his kingdom of the undead. Though more benign than Dracula because he is capable of genuine human emotion, Melmoth cannot be heroic because his quest is corrupt.

No other Gothic male approaches the status of conventional hero as closely as Melmoth does, but a number of them are figures of great power and energy, whose force of personality makes them titanic, if not heroic, characters. Manfred of *Otranto*, Schedoni in *The Italian*, Ambrosio in *The Monk*, and Dracula all have this quality. They are daring men, risk takers whose reach for power is awesome, even though corrupt. These characters seem brothers to Milton's Satan in hell, the brooding, brilliant rebel commander. However, the qualities of the Gothic male range downward from this, and many are more like Satan as Toad in the Garden.

A number are pathetic or ridiculous, Robert Wringham of *The Private Memoirs and Confessions of a Justified Sinner* is perhaps the archetype. Hogg exploits the potential of the character for ironic comedy; in Wringham, he has created a villain so petty, stupid, and ridiculous that we can barely feel anything but contempt for him. He inspires none of the awe or fear of a Manfred, Melmoth, or Dracula. Nevertheless, he shows the usual characteristics of the Gothic male. He imagines himself the elect of God; indeed, he conceives of himself as superior to God, since he can be saved without obeying any of God's laws. He hates sensuality, claims to have freed himself from sexual desire, and under the prodding of Gil-Martin, the devil, undertakes the destruction of his family. This homicidal maniac might be portrayed as powerful and impressive, but he is simply petty and willful, childish in fact, and the reader can hardly wait for the devil to take him off to hell. Throughout the story, Wringham is the victim of his own ridiculous delusions and obtuseness. We can see so clearly that Gil-Martin is the devil, even while Wringham is babbling about him being Peter the Great, that we also see Wringham is caught in a trap that shouldn't have fooled a twelve year old. The Satanic egotism and ambition of Melmoth or Dracula are here reduced to neurotic stupidity. This embodiment of the masculine identity, utterly repressed and controlled, utterly obsessed with his power and superiority to God and man, is really only the world's greatest prig.

This weakness, the pathetic quality of the male trying to enact the masculine archetype, appears over and over in the genre. Henry Jekyll is the sneaking, cowardly voyeur worried about appearing respectable, while Edward Hyde is also ridiculous when he awakens in Jekyll's clothes, sizes too big for him, as if he were a child dressed up and playing at adulthood. Silas Ruthyn, the aging, perfumed dandy, is another example of the Gothic male reduced to contemptible proportions. Strikingly, this inadequacy infects even the titanic characters. Manfred's crisis is brought about by an absurdity, a giant helmet falls on his son, and he himself is repeatedly shown as hysterical. His attempt at vengeance—the murder of Isabella—goes grotesquely wrong when he kills instead Matilda, his daughter, perhaps the only person in the world who really loves him. Schedoni is finally outwitted by his own trickery, as his double, the suborned monk Nicolo, comes back to accuse him before the Inquisition. Ambrosio is often reduced to the status of panting voyeur, indulging in masturbatory fantasies about a picture of the Virgin Mary and, later, the image of Antonia in Matilda's mirror. Furthermore, he seems to need Matilda in order to break out of voyeurism into action. Finally, of course, he is ripped to shreds and taken off to hell right after signing his pact with the devil because he has forgotten to ask for a long life of sensual pleasure. Even Dracula has his pathetic moments, for example, when Harker realizes that the count is, not only the coachman who picked him up at the Borgo Pass, but also the servant who cooks his meals and makes his bed. This deception is, of course, also sinister, but it serves to show us the count in a much less magnificent light. Victor Frankenstein, "the new Prometheus," is both weak—he is always slipping into a coma at critical points in the story—and obtuse. He cannot figure out that the creature's promise "I will be with you on your wedding night" is a threat directed at Elizabeth, not at him, even though he has just finished destroying the creature's mate.

Despite the Gothic male's links to the quest hero and to Faust, to the Satan of the early books of *Paradise Lost,* he is always only a step or two away from being a toad, a prig, or a fool. His tendency to delude himself and get caught in his own delusion is a direct result of his repression of his feminine half. Blinded to half of his own identity, he cannot see himself or the world as they really are. Willful blindness is necessary if the protagonist is to seize the power and authority of the patriarch, but it also ensures that the goal can never be reached and that the quest for identity is really over before it even begins.

The ridiculous and absurd qualities of the Gothic male remind us that these characters are parodies, self-created parodies of their own masculine identity. In attempting to attain the God-like power of the completely masculine patriarch, they create versions of themselves that range from the monstrous to the pathetic and that are always grotesque distortions of what they think they are. In their search for genuine identity and true independence and power, they achieve the exact opposite. Indeed, as we look closely at them, we see that these characters are in many ways automatons whose will has been taken from them by the very style of identity that was meant to liberate them from external control.

Manfred, of course, does what he does because of the necessities imposed upon him by the curse on his grandfather. Ambrosio needs Matilda to direct and control his desires, and she leads him straight to the devil. Schedoni finds his own plots entangle him in snares that finally destroy him, and Victor Frankenstein becomes the victim of his own creature, following into the Arctic the trail his monster tauntingly leaves for him. Silas Ruthyn is in bondage to his opium addiction, and even Dracula is bound by those rules that shape and control the existence of vampires; by the end of the novel, he can do nothing more than lie inert in his coffin, hoping his servants can get him safely home. This automatonism, the surrender of the will even while the protagonist thinks he is asserting it, is an extension of the blindness and duplicity that results from the repression and rejection of the feminine. The will, like the self, is doubled, and in rejecting half his identity, the Gothic male also loses control of his own will. Matilda's manipulation and control of Ambrosio is perhaps the best example of how the feminine, nominally passive and submissive, comes to control the active, dominant male.

Charles Brockden Brown's *Wieland* and *Edgar Huntly* both explore the loss of will that goes along with the protagonist's embracing of the masculine archetype. Theodore Wieland has put aside his "inheritance," the strange religious mania that lead to his father's mysterious, almost supernatural, death. When Carwin the biolquist (ventriloquist) uses his powers to trick Wieland, the strain of religious mania is catalyzed. The dark, mysterious Carwin is the double of the calm, rational Theodore; though Carwin never speaks to him in God's name except to end his mania—and thus cause his suicide—Theodore's encounter with the double leads him to begin hearing voices of his own. These voices command him to murder his wife, children, and sister, that is, to extirpate the feminine, affective, and sexual from his own nature by destroying his family. While under the influence of the voices, Theodore is a cheerful madman, though he is perfectly aware of what he has done; when Carwin returns him to sanity, Theodore is so horrified at his actions he kills himself.

Theodore's identity is not simply doubled, but multiple; he has external doubles, Carwin and his sister Clara, to whom he has a typically Gothic incestuous attachment. He is also two people in one: the sane Wieland and the smiling maniac who gets murderous orders from God. The first Wieland lives comfortably in a world where his father's legacy, power and madness, have been put away; in effect he lives in a world without God, and this is a blessing. The second Wieland is in full possession of his inheritance, and the return of God to the world is also the return of the masculine archetype, the patriarch, in all his monstrous violence.

All this comes to Wieland unbidden and apparently undesired. The madness is activated from the outside and possesses him. While he acts out with ruthless and horrible completeness the dynamics of the masculine archetype asserting itself, he does so mechanically. His will is completely submissive to what he takes to be the will of God, though it is actually his own suppressed identity and inheritance speaking to him. The transformed Wieland passes, not only beyond the understanding of the other characters, but beyond his own as well; when he returns from madness, he is unable to understand, accept, and bear what he has done, and by killing himself, he becomes the last victim of the masculine archetype.

Edgar Huntly also awakens suddenly, without willing it, to his masculine identity, but not through inherited madness. He also encounters a double, his feminine self embodied in a male character, Clithero Edny. Edgar pursues Clithero, with whom he feels a deep affinity, into the forest, where the mad sleepwalker has retreated into a subhuman, animal existence. Edgar believes he can "sooth and comfort" Clithero and lead him back to normality; instead, he too takes to sleepwalking, and entering the forest during a trance, falls into a pit and awakens transformed. The separation of the masculine from feminine represented in Clithero and Edgar allows the masculine archetype to take possession of Edgar, creating a superman. Self-created and self-authorized, Edgar transcends the human and becomes the ultimate expression of masculine power. An eighteenth-century Tarzan, he swings through the forest conquering natural obstacles, wild animals, and savage Indians; twice he is metaphorically resurrected from the dead. Once the debilitated and debilitating feminine identity, Clithero, is sloughed off, what remains is pure, irresistible masculine power, "o'er leaping the bounds of time and space."

Edgar, however, finds his transformation completely bewildering. He has lost all contact with the conventional world: he does not know how he came to be in a pit in the forest, he does not know what day or time it is, nor is he exactly sure of where he is. Throughout the first-person account of his adventures, we sense that Edgar is alienated from the masculine identity that has, in effect, possessed him. He is both amazed at what he does and repelled by his acts of violence. Just as Theodore cannot reconcile his sane and insane selves, Edgar cannot accept his superhuman qualities. He is perfectly content to let his powers slip away and return to his conventional identity.

Brown treats the masculine archetype as a form of madness or possession, an incursion upon the identity that deforms and alienates the individual from himself. Both Theodore and Edgar become automatons in the grip of an identity more powerful than themselves, and in this, any heroic or tragic dimension is lost to them. They neither summon up nor actively assent to their transformation; Theodore is frightening but pitiful in his madness, and Edgar is almost comic in his incomprehension of what is happening to him. Embracing the masculine archetype—or, here, being embraced by it—creates a powerful illusion, which then dissolves into air, leaving only horror and confusion.

The male protagonists of the Gothic fantasy transform the heroic romance archetype and the Faustian tragic hero into an essentially pathetic character, self-blinded and duplicitous, a monstrous parody of the identity he attempts to assert, which is really no identity at all. They become their own victims in pursuit of masculine selfhood, and this renders them, not heroic, but absurd. Strikingly, though, they retain their capacity to generate fear. At the very end of *The Private Memoirs and Confessions of a Justified Sinner,* even Wringham can create some sense of terror as he is dragged down into the abyss. The Gothic protagonist does not pass into the comic, despite his absurd qualities, because these qualities are always expressed in conjunction with violence, directed both at other characters and at himself. The violence always ends in the downfall of the protagonist, who thus becomes an image of monstrous, mindless, self-destruction. As a parody, the Gothic fantasy destroys the patterns of identity of the romance hero and the Faust character, as well as its central male protagonist, leaving no stable conception of identity at all.

Virtuous Young Ladies: Women in the Gothic Fantasy

The feminine characters in the Gothic fantasy are always victims of masculine rage and violence; they are also models of virtue and propriety. Only Matilda in *The Monk* seems to combine at least some conventional feminine qualities with masculine power and strength. She seems, when she first appears, devoted to Ambrosio, and she is also a sexual being. But as her power over Ambrosio grows, her capacity for affective relationships disappears and her sexual relationship with him is transformed into that of dominator and dominated. When we find that she was sent by the devil to corrupt Ambrosio, we realize that her feminine qualities were all along simply a ruse and that she never was a "true" woman.

Characters such as Matilda and Isabella in *Otranto*, Antonio and Virginia in *The Monk*, and Elizabeth and Charlotte in *Frankenstein* set the pattern for the feminine personality in the Gothic. These virtuous, respectable women are the guardians of the family and the embodiment of love and purity. They represent unfallen innocence and appear to exist simply to serve as the prey of the rapacious and dangerous male characters who imprison, rape, and murder them. Their ineffectiveness as protectors of their families and of their own lives and virtue implicitly equates goodness with victimization, respectability with passivity. Given this vision of the feminine personality, though, the creator of the fantasy is faced with the fact that these characters can only be victims of the Gothic world or pass through it to return to the conventional world where their goodness is recognized and respected. They at first appear to have no necessary or logical connection to the world of the fantasy. Indeed, in early works in the genre, they seem to stand in the place of the missing quest hero as the emblem of a complete and whole personality.

However, the feminine characters in fact always assent to their fall into the Gothic abyss, though this is mainly through what they do not do, rather than by their active participation. In *Otranto*, Manfred's wife, Hippolita, tacitly consents to all his desires, including his desire to divorce her and marry Isabella, thus endorsing a marriage that is technically incestuous. In *The Monk*, Antonia is deeply attracted to Ambrosio; though she is unaware of the incestuous quality of that attraction, or even that it is in any way sexual, she too tacitly encourages and desires his advances. Both Charlotte and Elizabeth in *Frankenstein* pamper and indulge Victor, thus feeding the egotism that leads to his attempt to usurp the power of God.

Most often, the participation of the feminine personality in her own victimization stems from the equation of respectability with passive obedience to authority. This authority is often just the general social norms that prescribe appropriate feminine behavior, but heroines of the Gothic fantasy also have an almost irresistible urge to obey the commands of male authority figures. Certainly some of them do resist authority: Isabella refuses to marry Manfred when he demands it, though she seems doomed to give into her father's orders that she agree to the marriage, and Emily St. Aubert does refuse to sign her property over to Montoni. But the strongest resistance any feminine character can muster is refusal; they are incapable of initiating action or of active rebellion, at least as individuals. Thus they are drawn into the dynamic of opposition that is central to the Gothic definition of masculine and feminine identity. Whether they accede to male authority or passively resist it, they still acknowledge its control of the realm of action and its power to imprison those who refuse to obey.

The feminine personality obeys the voice of male authority because that voice represents power. Although it is fearful, if that voice is obeyed, the feminine self can align with and thus obtain power. It is purchased at a cost, though, the feminine is overpowered in the destructive battle between masculine and feminine archetypes. The fatal attraction of the powerless for the powerful is the central mechanism by which the feminine self is drawn into the Gothic world.

We shall begin our discussion by examining three works—*The Mysteries of Udolpho, Uncle Silas,* and *The Turn of the Screw*—that tell essentially the same story: a virtuous young heroine is imprisoned and tormented in a lonely place by the power of masculine authority. The first of these novels attempts to portray the feminine archetype as totally separate from the man who oppresses her and triumphant in asserting, not only the values of respectability, but its power as well. As we shall see, the story subverts its apparent system of values. In the other two novels, we shall see how later authors, Sheridan LeFanu and Henry James, developed the tensions and contradictions that underlie the feminine self, tensions Radcliffe attempts to avoid and repress.

Italian Love, Italian Vengeance: The Mysteries of Udolpho and The Italian

If *The Castle of Otranto* articulates the contradictions and instability of the masculine identity, *The Mysteries of Udolpho,* the chief Gothic inheritor of the sentimental tradition, is a hymn to the power and value of feminine identity. In this novel, the hero, Valancourt, is reduced to a cipher; at one point we are led to think that he has come to Udolpho to rescue Emily, but this is an illusion. In fact, he is off in Paris indulging himself, and he wll suffer for this later when Emily learns that he has not behaved well in her absence. For Walpole, the masculine identity, however self-destructive, occupies center stage; to some extent, he intended Manfred as a genuinely tragic figure. Radcliffe clearly intends that we see in Emily St. Aubert the model of feminine identity. Relentlessly respectable—in the history of the genre only Maud Ruthyn rivals her—her faults, sensibility, imagination, passion, are also her virtues, the emotional qualities that make her the sensitive, affective being she is. Her victimization is, not the test of her virtue, but actually the indicator of it. The degree of her suffering in Udolpho measures exactly her success as the feminine ideal.

Emily comes from a family that is positively Edenic. Her father is its central figure, but he has retired from life to a small house in the woods, where he lives idyllically with his wife, daughter, and beloved dog. He, like his daughter, is endowed with the virtues of sensibility, imagination, and passion, even though he has the wisdom to see that unless one controls such feeling one will feel only excessive pain. St. Aubert is thus also a feminine character, and the circle of warmth and affection he creates is broken only by his wife's, and then his own, death. Thereupon, Emily is thrust into the masculine world of Montoni and Udolpho. Montoni, who marries Emily's aunt and guardian for what he thinks is her fortune, carries both women off to his ruined castle of Udolpho, deep in the mountains, a cruel parody of the pastoral retreat in which Emily had lived with her parents. Montoni, in contrast to St. Aubert, is the archetypal patriarch; unlike Manfred, he is not naturally humane, and he has no scruples about terrorizing his wife and his niece. He regards both as property, a source of cash. He attempts to marry Emily off to one of his drinking companions and then to get her to sign over her estates to him. Otherwise, he ignores her. Like Manfred, he seems to have no sexual interest in women; all his energy is directed into his desire for power, for activity, which, as Radcliffe says, is the central impulse of his nature. Women are to him so completely objects that he does not perceive them as erotic beings or even, as Manfred does, as vessels of reproduction. This collapse of the erotic impulse in the patriarchal male is an aspect of the collapse of affect and the rejection of the feminine. Even lust affirms the connection of masculine to feminine and threatens the integrity of the masculine ideal.

For several hundred pages, we are treated to the horrors of the patriarchal family and Emily's torment. Montoni tortures and murders her aunt, and she herself seems headed for the same fate. But suddenly she escapes, simply walking out of Udolpho, never to return. The world of the castle and the horrors she has experienced simply fade into the past, like the hallucinations of "a distempered dream," as Radcliffe calls them. Radcliffe is unable to integrate the horrors and the dreadful suffering Emily has undergone into her character or her vision of the idealized family. Emily is already perfectly good when she goes to Udolpho; her goodness may be tested there, but she can learn nothing from the experience. Udolpho fades and is forgotten, after a series of adventures that, somewhat like Tom Sawyer's plans for Jim's escape in *Huckleberry Finn,* seem intended primarily to distract us from the fact that Emily's relationship to the Gothic world has never been resolved. That world does make one last appearance in the story of Madame Laurentini, the previous owner of Udolpho and also the murderer of the marchioness de Villeroi, Emily's other aunt, whom Emily had not known existed, since she died before Emily's birth. This final intrusion of Udolpho suggests that the Gothic world is not simply one spot, nor are Gothic villains always men. But Radcliffe does little with this, Emily returns to Valancourt, and they return together to the St. Aubert estate, determined to leave behind the terrors and fears of the outside world, reestablishing the circle of love and affection broken by the deaths of Madame and Monsieur St. Aubert.

However, in order to become worthy of this Eden, Valancourt has had to prove himself the equal of Emily's father. He has not, like the traditional hero, been able to prove himself by rescuing her from imprisonment. Rather, during his time in Paris, he has acquired a bad reputation and is accused, not only of being unchaste, but of having taken money from one of his lovers, of being a gigolo. Emily refuses to have anything to do with him, though she still loves him. The traditional male and female positions are reversed here. Valancourt is accused of the crimes that usually besmirch a woman's reputation, and Emily plays the role of the offended male lover who cannot marry a woman who has lost her virtue. Valancourt, who is vindicated of the charges—his worst sins are gambling and being seen in the wrong company—undergoes the loss of reputation and subsequent loss of his beloved that are usually the woman's lot. This experience of a peculiarly feminine victimization signals that he is ready to enter the charmed circle with Emily and begin a true family.

The Mysteries of Udolpho appears, then a celebration of the feminine ideal of the self and family, which in the course of the novel prove stronger than any depredations or threats. In passivity is strength, in respectability is identity. Yet despite this affirmation of traditional values, Radcliffe cannot fully bring off the feat. The affective, feminized family appears in the novel only as it is dying or as a hopeful dream, never as a fully realized fact. Further, Radcliffe has been forced to stage-manage Emily's escape from Udolpho and has not, as I have already argued, been able to explain how such contradictory worlds, such different families and different styles of identity can coexist.

If the patriarchal family and the masculine identity can, in *Udolpho,* simply be dismissed and the affective family and feminine identity affirmed by an act of will, Radcliffe finds this less easy to do in her last book, *The Italian.* Once again, in this novel, the hero and heroine are subject to terrorizing encounters, first with the evil monk, Schedoni, and second with the Inquisition. Both Elena and Vivaldi slip inexorably into the state of victimization that defines feminine identity in the Gothic; Vivaldi would like to be a hero but cannot. Both he and Elena are paralyzed by Schedoni's hocus-pocus and by the power of the Inquisition. Vivaldi's own family persecutes him; both the marchioness and marquis regard their son as a vehicle of family honor and dignity—as an extension of their own identities— and the marchioness actually falls in with Schedoni's plans to have Vivaldi murdered, rather than allow him to make a "degrading" marriage. In *The Italian,* no familial grace from which to fall exists; the masculinized, patriarchal world is everywhere. Elena is an orphan, but even her family history is stained with blood and violence, for Schedoni proves to be her uncle, the man who murdered her father and attempted to rape her mother. Schedoni believes for a moment that she must be his daughter, and even then, he thinks only of possibilities of using her to gain power and prestige for himself; suddenly he is more than happy to see her marry into the old and powerful family of Vivaldi.

Both Vivaldi and Schedoni are confronted by the Inquisition. Vivaldi takes on, like Valancourt, the feminine qualities of passive endurance and virtue. He cannot defeat the Inquisition, but he can bear himself patiently and trust that his truthful answers and fundamental goodness will allow him to escape. Vivaldi and Elena manage to slip through the net and make a happy marriage, apparently safe from the corrupted and impersonal power of the Inquisition and the evil schemes of both Schedoni and the marchioness, who kills herself when her husband discovers her part in the plot to have his son murdered. But in *The Italian*, Radcliffe has drawn the feminine and masculine identities, the affective and patriarchal worlds, much closer together than she did in *Udolpho*. The marriage of Vivaldi and Elena may establish a sort of Eden, but no such utopia existed previously in the novel. Further, the whole world has been shown as dominated by evil characters and, worse, by monstrous institutions. Though the conclusion of the novel suggests that Vivaldi and Elena triumph by and through the power of love, we can see that it exists only by the permission of the patriarchal world: that is, the marquis, a somewhat more benevolent parent than his wife, though the discovery of Elena's noble birth is certainly the only thing that makes him relent, and the Inquisition, whose power hangs over the happy couple even as they are freed.

The Italian and *The Mysteries of Udolpho* are feminist in the sense that they attempt to affirm feminine archetypes of family and identity. They are reactionary insofar as they define those archetypes according to criteria that make women victims, however virtuous and loving. In *The Italian*, which is an analysis of the effect of power on both the masculine and feminine personalities, Radcliffe come close to seeing that the affective nature is without power a hollow identity, a false ideal. Because the feminine and affective are defined as powerless, the characters who embrace these ideals embrace their own victimization. While the masculine and patriarchal can convert the feminine to its own use, the feminine and affective can achieve neither personal nor institutional power on its own. Thus, the feminine defines itself, not simply in opposition to the masculine, but as subordinate to the masculine, the masochistic extreme of the sadomasochistic dynamic.

Rewriting Udolpho: LeFanu

The implications of the feminine archetype are worked out more completely in two novels that are essentially rewritings of *The Mysteries of Udolpho*. Both LeFanu's Maud Ruthyn and Jame's nameless governess compare themselves to Radcliffe's heroines, and the plots of both novels follow the same contour as *Udolpho*, the young woman imprisoned by threatening men in a lonely country house. But in reworking *Udolpho*, LeFanu deepened and expanded the archetype that Radcliffe created, exploring the tensions and contradictions, the failure in the conception of the feminine that Radcliffe had tried to avoid confronting. LeFanu's approach to the feminine, both in *Uncle Silas* and *Carmilla* is affirmative, though he is very aware of the weaknesses of this personality as it appears in the Gothic fantasy, weaknesses rooted in its virtues.

Maud Ruthyn's retrospective, first-person narrative follows much the same general outline as Emily St. Aubert's: she lives happily with her father until he dies, then is sent away to the home of her uncle, who tries to murder her, is rescued and united with Lord Ilbury in a triumph of domestic bliss. The novel seems to portray the movement from the Edenic world into the Gothic world—into a confrontation with the patriarchal demon in the person of Silas—and then back to Eden. Lord Ilbury, though he appears in the novel only so often as necessary to make him a convincing candidate for husband, is clearly not a patriarchal monster. In confronting Silas, Maud faces the masculine identity at its most loathsome: her foster father is an aging, perfumed dandy, addicted to opium. He has squandered his own fortune and has lived under a cloud ever since Mr. Charke, a notorious gambler, was found dead at Bartram Haugh, his estate. Though Charke had died in a closed room, apparently by suicide, popular opinion has always held that Silas murdered him, which, in fact, is the case. This monster uses his opium dreams in part as the source of strange religious visions, and his depravity is glossed over by greasy professions of piety. Not only is he the image of personal corruption, combining the violence and religious mania that we have seen as part of the masculine identity in the Gothic, but he is literally a corrupt parent. He attempts to use Maud to replenish his fortune, first by trying to marry her off to his buffoon of a son, Dudley, and when this fails—the moron has contracted a drunken marriage to a tavern maid—he tries to murder her. He has also degraded his own children to satisfy his perverse egotism. Dudley is a boor because his father has made him one, while Milly, Silas's daughter, has been raised to possess all the social graces of a Devonshire milkmaid. Though good-hearted and energetic, her inability to function in polite society has made her a virtual prisoner in Bartram Haugh. Silas's treatment of his children has no function except to emphasize his power and control over them. Otherwise powerless, he has practiced a form of metamorphosis on his children and turned them into clownish images of his own corruption. Silas's psychic violence upon Dudley and Milly is counterpointed by the direct physical violence of Hawkins, his gamekeeper, factotum, and bully boy: when his daughter Meg defies him, he simply breaks her arm.

Maud is thrust into this environment, victimized by it, but comes out safely. Indeed, while in the Gothic world of Bartram Haugh, she displays some genuine power of her own: she reconciles Meg and Milly—previously they have taunted and fought each other—and manages to make Milly respectable enough to take her place in society, thus freeing her from her father's domination. These acts of "white magic," though, are offset by her inability to deal with Silas and his female counterpart, Madame Rougerrie, who has made an earlier appearance in the novel as Maud's governess at her father's home, Knollys. Madame, as she is called, is a bald-headed, brandy-swilling, mannish woman; she serves as Silas's female double, for she is as masculinized a character as any Gothic protagonist. Indeed, given Silas's habit of drenching himself with perfume and Madame's baldness, we can see in these two characters the perversion and subversion of feminine identity within a corrupt masculinity.

The central story of *Uncle Silas*, then, portrays very much the same conflict between masculine and feminine identities, between the affectional and patriarchal families, that we see in *Udolpho*. However, on closer examination, we see that though the dominant note of the novel is the victimization of the feminine by the masculine, underneath this runs a constant awareness of the feminine's self-victimization in the presence of the masculine. To fully understand this, we must backtrack to Maud's life with her father, Austin Ruthyn, at Knollys.

Austin is a virtual recluse, a silent, remote man, caught up in his Swedenborgian religion. His solitary life is punctuated by occasional forays, usually by checkbook, into the world of politics and society. Though he is thoroughly respectable and upright, he feels an affinity for Silas. He refuses to believe that Silas murdered Charke, and he makes his brother Maud's guardian as a final gesture of his faith in his, and his family's, honor. In his willingness to use Maud as a pledge to his brother, Austin Ruthyn shows, not only that he is an archetypal Victorian father—remote, powerful, austere—but that his sense of identity derives from masculine, not feminine, archetypes. His brother, his double, must be vindicated; to do so he makes his daughter a pawn and endangers her life. He regards Maud, to this extent, as property.

Maud not only accepts her father's attitude but embraces it. Though she recognizes his eccentricity, she is throughly convinced he loves her and that they share an unusually deep bond. Despite all the evidence to the contrary, she persists in this self-deception, and since the narrative is retrospective, she continues to believe it years after her father delivers her into the hands of her crazed and murderous uncle. The very fact that Austin Ruthyn would hire a governess like Madame Rougerrie for his daughter suggests a blind spot concerning women and the nature of the feminine. He accepts Madame, which neither Maud nor any of the women servants do, because she is so fully masculine in her style and manner. Perverse and odd as she is, Austin can see nothing strange in her. He fires her only when Maud discovers her rifling his desk. What she may do to Maud is of little interest to him; what she does to him gets her fired.

Maud is, in her way, as blind as her father. She cannot or will not perceive the paternal family structure for what it is, nor can she acknowledge the oppressive attitude of the masculine identity toward the feminine. Instead, she creates in her fantasies an affectional bond between father and daughter that does not exist. Austin Ruthyn is not, like his brother, a monster; he is never cruel to his daughter and has taken care to provide for her upbringing. But he has no emotional relationship with her at all, and in her upbringing, he has taken care to make her the perfect Victorian daughter, fully obedient to her father's will. Even after his death, his word is law for Maud, though, in talking to her cousin, Lady Monica and Dr. Bryerly, her father's spiritual advisor, she concedes that they are correct in asserting that what her father has done in signing her over to Silas is foolish and dangerous.

Maud is so willing to assent to the despotic control of Silas because she has projected her deep and intense desire to establish an affectional relationship with her father onto her uncle. A portrait of

Silas as a young man hangs at Knollys; Maud gazes at this picture and fantasizes. She sees a "singularly handsome young man, dark, slender, elegant," his face characterized by "masculine force . . . and a fire in the large shadowy eyes, which were very peculiar, and quite redeemed it from any suspicion of effeminacy."[7] On the surface, this is the adolescent crush of a young woman living in an isolated house with her remote, eccentric father on any available male image. But this crush has larger implications, for she becomes fixated on her uncle, even though her father refuses to speak of him, and on Silas she projects both filial and erotic fantasies. If she could establish a relationship with Silas, she would achieve both the father-daughter relationship she longs for and, at the same time, an erotic relationship. Incest would close the circle of her affectional world, and establish Maud firmly at the center of a family based fully on love. She would, of course, realize her own family responsibilities in this circle; she dreams of vindicating Silas of Charke's murder and "leading him before cheering crowds."

Maud is far too virtuous and proper a young lady for these incestuous fantasies to ever surface in any serious way. But we see in her the essential enthrallment of the feminine to the masculine, provoking the incestuous impulse. Though never realized in any overtly sexual way, this devotion to her father and her uncle is almost as destructive as literal incest, for it binds Maud to their will. The feminine identity is attracted to the masculine because of its remote and apparently indifferent power. The impulse to capture that power, to draw it into the circle of affectional relations, is irresistible, for power is the one thing the feminine identity lacks. Conditioned, as Maud has been by her father, to be submissive, the feminine is molded to the needs of the masculine and thus attempts to accept the masculine on its own terms, as the dominant identity in the relationship, to be the masochist to the masculine sadist. Maud's conception of herself depends on the power of paternal figures, and she defines love and affection as they would. This helps explain her obsessive propriety and her apparent belief, even in the face of Milly's situation, that respectable behavior is, not an aspect of environment or upbringing, but a genuine absolute. Her conception of respectability is the expression of her devotion and complete acceptance of her father's conception of her.

Despite this powerful analysis of the failure of the feminine identity and the affectional ideal, LeFanu does not despair of the possibility of their achieving power and thus liberation from the domination of the masculine and paternal. The salvation of the feminine lies in its ability to accept combination and mutuality; like the masculine identity, the feminine can seek salvation by becoming more itself; unlike the masculine identity, though, this alternative, at least in *Uncle Silas,* does not seem totally delusive.

Maud is saved from the power of her uncle by what is virtually a conspiracy of women: Lady Monica, Milly, and Meg, the gamekeeper's daughter, all aid Maud in sustaining herself and, literally, saving herself from Silas. Dr. Breyerly, too, is part of this group, for though he is a man, he is feminized, the opposite of Madame, the masculinized woman. Maud, throughout the story, insists on calling these people, her only true friends and allies, "odd" or "queer" or "eccentric." In fact, of course, their oddness is nothing compared to that of the Ruthyn brothers, but she never sees this. These characters conceive of their relations to each other in affectional terms, as a matter of helping and encouraging each other, never as dominating or controlling. Individually they are powerless, but collectively they accrue, through the course of the novel, considerable power and force. At the moment of Maud's rescue—managed by Meg and Lady Monica through the intermediary of Lord Ilbury—Silas, thinking he has trapped Maud, murders Madame. In dispatching his peculiar double, Silas in effect murders himself and symbolically ends the hegemony of fathers over daughters, of the masculine over the feminine.

Yet Maud is unable to learn from this experience of the power of relationships formed outside the patriarchal structure of the family, an escape from the pattern of domination and submission we shall see again in *Dracula.* At the end of the novel, she has lost to a great extent her connection with the women and men who saved her from Silas. Even though she is married to Lord Ilbury and herself a mother, the center, presumably, of an affectional family, she still longs for her final and best paternal lover, not now her father or uncle, but death itself. "Blessed are the dead that die in the Lord," she writes at the end of her narrative, and she asserts that "this world is a parable—the habitation of symbols—the phantoms of spiritual things immortal shown in mortal shape."[8] If we have seen any phantoms in mortal shape in the novel, they are Silas, whom Lady Monica described as "not quite human," and Madame. Maud may believe she can "talk to angels," but she has held far more conversations with demons. Her devotion to death and the world beyond death, is an enthrallment to the Gothic world, to the final masochistic submis-

sion. Death, the ultimate father figure, holds out to Maud the promise of love and happiness that remain unfulfilled in life. Couched in
religious terms, her vision is an expression of the masculine-shaped
feminine identity that, through her encounter with Silas, she seemed
to have thrown off. The problems of the self in search of identity
cannot be solved through the rigid adherence to the gender-deter-
mined ideals with which the characters begin, nor through incest,
nor through violence. Only the oblivion of death, the complete surrender of selfhood, can resolve the tensions and anxieties with which
Maud must live. Her inability to seize upon the life-saving circle of
friends who have helped her and who offer a pattern of relationships
outside the family structure—even though Lady Monica and Milly
are related to Maud, blood ties are less important to them than a
genuine affection—suggests the problem with this alternative. The
circle of friends can replace the family, the cause of problems and
contradictions, only at a moment of extreme crisis. It does not have a
necessity, the internal coherence, to endure after crisis, and so Maud
finds herself back where she began, searching for the love of the
father to whom she must submit and longing for death.

Another Turn of the Screw

Henry James's *The Turn of the Screw* is another view of *Udolpho,*
refracted through the lens of Charlotte Brontë's *Jane Eyre.*[9] As we
have already seen, one aspect of the story is the collapse of the detective hero back into the Gothic underworld. As an ambiguous detective, the governess is both the victim of the manifestation of evil,
whether from the ghosts or from within her own fantasies, and an
instrument in the victimization of Miles and Flora. No critic,
whether on the ghostly or psychopathic side of the controversy over
James's novella, can suggest that the governess succeeds in saving her
little charges. In the sense that she is the victim of her own actions,
and through those actions the victimizer of the children, she expresses the masculine side of the detective's nature. At the same time,
the her actions at Bly are an attempt to hold together—or, more
accurately, to create—an affectional family and to fill the role of Victorian wife and mother. The results of her behavior are ambiguous
precisely because she cannot resolve the contradictions in the two
roles she is seeking to play; she has not accepted the isolation and
exclusion that are the price for the detective's stable, integrated
identity.

The governess's inability to undertake in full the detective's role

and her consequent uncertainty in that role stem from her un-
willingness to accept his reactive function and his rejection of sexuality. One might, of course, point out that she is reactive, whether
she wants to be or not, and that sexual pleasure is something she is
terrified of anyway. But to take on the detective's part would require
that she accept overtly her own reactive situation and thus surrender
the fantasies of power she has as the uncle's agent. She would also
have to acknowledge her own sexuality, even if in doing go she
transformed erotic satisfaction into analytical pleasure. For the governess, the role of detective would mean, not only accepting its limitations, but also facing her own deep complicity with the Gothic
world.

The feminine-affectional aspect of her identity manifests itself early in the story: she is remarkably frank about her fantasies of love
with the distant uncle. As she walks on the grounds, just before she
sees Quint for the first time, she thinks:

> It was a pleasure at these moments to feel myself tranquil and
> justified; doubtless, perhaps, to reflect that by my discretion, my
> quiet good sense, and my general high propriety, I was giving
> pleasure—if he ever thought of it:—to the person to whose pres-
> sure I had responded. What I was doing was what he had earnestly
> hoped and directly asked of me, and that *I could*, after all, do it,
> proved a greater joy than I had expected. I daresay I fancied my-
> self, in short, a remarkable young woman and took comfort in the
> faith that this would more publicly appear.[10]

This passage shows all the signs of a young woman acting out the
conventional female role, in which she can define herself as remarkable because she pleases a man, a fact that is a source of joy for her.
The phrase "more publicly appear" is coy and surely contains the
suggestion that such joy and pleasure must lead to marriage. The
uncle, an older, more sophisticated man, is an employer and father-
figure as well as the object of erotic fantasies; the same pattern of
parental, economic, and erotic power that we have seen in Silas's
and Austin Ruthyn's relationships to Maud appears here. Since she
acts as the surrogate mother to the children he wishes to ignore—
business and pleasure keep him in London—why should she not
imagine that she might take on the other role open to women, the
role of wife? She defines herself as feminine—passive, virtuous, respectable—and by submitting to the uncle takes on some of his
power, manifesting it in a feminine style, establishing an affectional

family with Mrs. Grose, Miles, and Flora. She even describes her relationship to the children, particularly Miles, as "infatuation," echoing her attitude toward the uncle. Since the children are "his," they are extensions of him, and she carries her feelings and fantasies about him into her dealings with them. The governess is trapped in a complex set of roles she surely does not fully understand: wife-mother, submissive to the patriarchal male, the instrument of his power in the household, as she transforms that power into essentially affectional terms, and finally, the detective who roots out the horror and corruption behind the decorous facade.

Because the governess is enmeshed in a pattern of interaction that creates anxiety—How shall she fulfill her duties? How shall she balance out the various demands on her energy and love?—she is sensitive to the apparition of Quint and Jessel. I do not wish to make one more attempt to solve the problem of whether the ghosts are really there or not; they are a projection of the Other, and the Other in the Gothic is always the self as well. Simply by the fact that she can see them, the governess is implicated in their existence, and whether she has created, summoned, or discovered them, the events of the novel move as though the ghosts had objective reality. And what the ghosts are does have objective reality, for they are, not simply beings, but patterns of identity and relationship that exist outside any individual manifestations of those patterns.

The ghosts embody the sadomasochistic relationship of the masculine and feminine. Quint, rough and arrogant—"he wore the master's clothes"—dominates Miss Jessel, who was genteel and feminine. "She was a lady," as Mrs. Grose says. Quint, as fraud and victimizer, and Miss Jessel, his patient victim, embody the Gothic reality that underlies all relationships. Miss Jessel is banished from Bly, Eden, perhaps to die in childbirth, and Quint dies from "natural causes," but a vague suggestion of supernatural vengeance hangs about his death. They return to haunt the children because this pattern haunts all nineteenth-century fantasies; as they grow up, Miles and Flora will inevitably be caught in the roles that Quint and Jessel have acted out. Since the world of Gothic horror is the world of masculine and feminine conflict, the children, as they mature, will encounter this conflict, whether in its conventional or Gothic form.

The governess's situation at Bly and her battle with the ghosts dramatizes the contradictions of the nineteenth-century family. The patriarch is absent, having no emotional link to the world he rules. The governess, the mother, runs a world of women, in which Miles chafes under the restrictions placed on his masculine identity. The governess must prove herself to win the love of the uncle—though love is the one thing the Gothic male never has to offer—through the qualities of the respectable feminine self. At the same time, she periodically descends to playing with the children as though she herself were a child. They strive to please her, as she says, seek out ways of "diverting, entertaining and surprising her; reading out passages, telling her stories, acting her charades, pouncing out at her, in disguises, as animals and historical characters." Though she asserts that they were good at their studies, "they got their lessons better and better," the dominant image of the her relationship to them is an older sister, drawn into their play. She does this, not only because only a few years earlier she was a child herself, but because it relieves her of the burdens of her multiple roles. She returns to the affectional world to escape the "pressure" of the uncle's masculine identity upon her. The conventional images of husband and wife that the governess and uncle act out are paralleled in overtly Gothic terms in their doubles, Quint and Jessel. Quint and Jessel are the awful, revelatory parodies of the uncle and the governess.

The governess has difficulty confronting the ghosts because she denies that these terrifying creatures are in any way a version of herself, that they have any natural connection to her world or her life. For her, the Gothic world remains unimaginable, completely and inescapably Other. Her inability to acknowledge the presence of the self within the Other leads to the way, for instance, she regards Miles and Flora's beauty and good manners. At first this is evidence that the children are angelic; by the end of the story, their childish charm proves that they are demonic. The governess is infected with a Gothic sense of the transformative and metamorphic nature of things: the beautiful and angelic become the demonic and thus, paradoxically, the ugly. She is unable, though, to accept this. The children must be one or the other, good or evil, just as identity must be one or the other, masculine or feminine, even though this sort of attempt to create stability and certainty is doomed from the very start. The inadequacy of the governess's point of view is emphasized by the fact that the children are literally in a process of transformation, though a natural one, toward their initiation into adult knowledge, and adult identity. Quint and Jessel are parodies, not only of what the uncle and governess are, but of what Miles and Flora will become. The governess loves her small charges, their childlike life together, and their closed affectional circle. She wants simply to maintain this state. The fact that the children will attain sexual and imaginative maturity is an uneasy reminder of the sexual and imaginative maturity with which she herself is struggling. When the governess, eating dinner alone with Miles at the end of the story, describes them as like "a young married couple," she has clearly projected onto the boy her own fantasies about the uncle.

In fact, she has nothing to offer the children as they become adults. In the face of what she perceives as the Gothic abyss, the horror she identifies with adult identity, the governess has only the value of respectability to offer Miles and Flora. She holds fast to her superficial identification of goodness with the respectable; she is less concerned with what Miles did at school than with the fact that he has been sent home in disgrace. At first she cannot believe he has been expelled because he does not look as though he has done anything wrong, and she puts off finding out about what he has done as long as she can, unwilling to probe very deeply below the surface of things. We can see this identification of the good and the respectable most clearly in the her comments on Flora, when the little girl becomes hysterical after the second scene by the pond. For the governess, the proof of Flora's corruption lies in the fact that she has turned "hard and common, and almost ugly" and speaks "like a pert, vulgar, child of the streets." The beautiful angel suddenly turns into a real child; she upsets the lovely decorum of the family that the governess is desperately trying to preserve. Unable to accept the implications of her own experience, the governess equates the polite with the good, the evil with the rude, and thus strives to affirm the validity of her own style of feminine identity. As we have seen in such characters as Ambrosio, Wringham, and Manfred, the attempt to hang onto masculine ideals of identity thrusts the male protagonist further into the Gothic world, where the illusion of this identity dissipates and he is destroyed. Here we have the example of a female protagonist attempting to maintain her feminine identity and, in doing so, acting out the violence that is the affirmation of the Gothic world's hold on the individual. For the governess, as we have seen, this struggle does not lead to the adventurism, self-indulgence, or religious mania of the masculine protagonist, but takes the form of a determined and intransigent defense of conventional values, which are really the outward forms of those things they seem to stand against. The ghosts cannot be defeated by respectability, for they are the reality that underlies the respectable.

The final image of the story, Miles dead in the governess's arms, represents the victory of the Gothic over the conventional ideals of the nineteenth century. The governess is both the Madonna and the Mater Dolorosa, maternal nuturance and maternal grief. But was her attempt at nurturing Miles what killed him? She embraces him with what she thinks is love, but it is also the embrace of death in which all the tensions and polarities of the story are present: adult-child, male-female, good-evil, life-death, love-violence. As her world collapses upon the governess, these polarities merge into a single, ambiguous image. Who is the adult? The young boy who wants to grow up or the young woman who has just barely grown up herself? Can we distinguish between the love and the violence, between life and death itself? The ambiguity of the last scene is summed up in Miles's last words: "Peter Quint—you devil!" Does he address Quint or the governess? In the Gothic fantasy, it does not really matter, to address one is to address the other, for they are both part of the pattern of identity that has killed Miles. The failure of the governess lies, not in her imposition of her morbid sexual fixations on the children, but rather in her own need to hang onto the conventions by which she lives, to retain her feminine identity. Miles is sacrificed to the polarized image of the self that dominates all men and women in Gothic fantasy. Unable to create, even temporarily, the alternative family that saves Maud Ruthyn, the governess must be true to the only images of self, family, and identity she has, even though those ideals prove fatal. To solve the crime, to save her client, she would have had to surrender, not only her conception of herself, her purely feminine identity, but also the possibility of any connection to another person at all, whether that connection was affectional or sadistic. In *The Turn of the Screw,* the price that must be paid to understand and truly escape from the Gothic world is the isolation that turns enthrallment into analysis. That price is beyond the governess's ability to pay.

Incest

Incest is a staple of terror in the Gothic fantasy. Even stories that do not actually describe incest or that do not take the motif very seriously often use the possibility of it to intensify horror and create a more lurid spectacle. In Godwin's *Caleb Williams,* the relationship of Falkland's enemy, Tyrell, to Emily, his cousin and ward, is saturated with the suggestion of incestuous desire, if not incestuous activity, though this appears as no more than a titillating possibility. The genre of course had no monopoly on incest, particularly as a source of sensationalism. Throughout the eighteenth century, it was a part of more realistic fiction.[11] Moll Flanders unwittingly commits incest with her brother, and Tom Jones fears, for a few moments, that he has slept with his mother. Not only did works that have passed into the canon use the motif, but it was also an aspect of popular fiction, though the threat seems to have been more popular than the actuality and sibling incest, as opposed to parent-child incest, was by far the more common variety. The Gothic fantasy was not, in employing the motif, doing anything novel or particularly "Gothic," though the idea of incest is reasonably frightening. However, it acquires within the tradition a thematic resonance that makes it more than just a source of thrills.

In *Otranto,* Manfred attempts to avoid the curse placed upon his line by committing technical incest, marrying Conrad's fiancée. Since he never gets to marry Isabella and since she was never married to Conrad in the first place and is no blood relation to Manfred anyhow, the threat in this novel is almost absurd. But Manfred inaugurates the Gothic tradition of incest. One of its basic functions in the genre is, grotesquely, the preservation and revification of the family and the identity of the Gothic protagonist.

Incest is a violation of the family, the destruction of the arrangement that make the very concept of family meaningful; mothers and fathers are distinct from sons and daughters, brothers and sisters are not lovers. Incest transforms the stable pattern of relationships into a sexual free-for-all, in which fathers become husbands, sisters become wives, and each person is, potentially, any other person's lover. By distorting the family in this way, it corrupts the line of inheritance, destroys legitimacy, and, of course, respectability. It isolates each person and denies any standard against which identity can be defined. Yet at the same time, incest is a typically Gothic extension of the affectional-sentimental family, in which the members are bound together by ties of love, rather than ties of power. The attempt to transform emotional and spiritual relationships into sexual ones is, in fact, an attempt to extend and strengthen the family and the identity it supports, though obviously a perverse one. Further, it allows the male protagonist to establish a relationship to his female double, particularly his sister, and thus to resolve his relationship to the feminine Other. This resolution is, of course, delusive and usually provokes, not reconciliation, but rather the violence and mayhem we associate with the male in the Gothic fantasy. Though incest has its origins in the feminine and affectional qualities, the male protagonist usually attempts to initiate it; he, of course, is the only character who can initiate action, and the women can only be victims. They can neither overtly assent to incest and thus violate canons of respectability, nor can they resist effectively. Incest is, for the male protagonist, an expression of his repressed and alienated feminine qualities, not an aspect of his aggressive quest for power. It is his fullest experience of the erotic, and in this experience of sexuality, he comes as close as he can to a relationship not based completely on power. Incest is, of course, a corrupt and illusory solution to the division between masculine and feminine identity, but it begins in the search for a reconciliation.

The Monk

In *Otranto,* Manfred attempts and fails at a very technical type of incest. In *The Monk,* Ambrosio not only rapes his sister but murders her, after having strangled his mother. He does not at the time know Antonia is his sister or that Donna Elvira is his mother, but we have had it made clear to us through rather broad hints. Ambrosio's story is in part a tale of a shattered family reunited, not in love and affection, but in incest and violence. *The Monk* is a novel deeply concerned with the failure and breakdown of the family, in the stories of Agnes and Don Raymond as well as that of Ambrosio. On the simplest level, Ambrosio commits incest because he does not know who his sister is, or even that he has a sister. He has been raised in a monastery of which he has become the abbott, and he knows nothing of women or sexuality, let alone sisters and incest. When the story begins, he is a typical Gothic male, acting out the archetypal masculine identity.

He has the power, authority, and control men always seek in the Gothic fantasy; his power is even legitimately achieved. But the legitimacy of his position is the source of his dissatisfaction. However much pleasure he gets from gloating over his status and reputation, he is limited by the vows of poverty, obedience, and chastity. These restrictions chafe Ambrosio, particularly the those imposed by chastity. The most complete assertion of his power over himself and the world would be the satisfaction of his sensual and sexual desires while retaining his title and power as abbott.

Thus sensual gratification becomes for Ambrosio the road to his fulfilled identity, the assertion of his egocentric autonomy. He is therefore somewhat atypical of the Gothic male, though Vathek,

Henry Jekyll, Dorian Grey, and to a lesser extent, Dracula show a fascination with the sensual and sexual as a way of asserting masculine identity and power. But Ambrosio is also seeking out his own feminine half, repressed and hidden, just as his sister and mother have been lost to him. Thus his pursuit of power is also a pursuit of his own feminine nature; in exploring his sensuality, Ambrosio does not so much extend the power of his masculine self as he does discover his own feminine side. The drama of incest and murder in the novel is the drama of his unconscious quest for his own identity. In the act of incestuous rape, he attempts to dominate and control his feminine half; when this does not work, he must murder Antonia and, in doing so, destroys himself. The pursuit of sensuality becomes, for Ambrosio, an act of violence.

Before he meets Matilda, Ambrosio's only knowledge of sensuality comes through his own fantasies. In his cell in the monastery, he keeps a painting of a beautiful Madonna; he imagines pressing his lips to "the treasures of that snowy bosom" and twining her ringlets in his fingers. These fantasies reveal, not only Ambrosio's fascination with sensuality, women, and the feminine, but his connection of these with illegitimate power. His fantasy is both blasphemous and metaphorically incestuous. For Ambrosio, the painting of the Madonna is Mother, Lover, and image of the Divine: everything he needs to complete his stunted identity. As long as he remains a voyeur, gazing at a picture, he is safe from his own desires. But his fantasies are made real in his encounter with Matilda, the demon posing as a woman posing as a boy posing as a monk, who seduces Ambrosio and introduces him to the delights of the flesh. He finds that Matilda satisfies his lust with her inventiveness and enthusiasm, but he still lacks something, a "something" that he identifies as Antonia. In his pursuit of her, he is lead by stages from fantasy to voyeurism to action, ending finally in his destruction and damnation. He seeks to go beyond the merely human and the merely male to become a superman of sensuality, infinitely satisfying his infinite desires. Yet in trying to define himself in this way, he is lead back to his need for the feminine, for a woman. Intuitively his desire fixes on the virtuous Antonia, for of course, the woman who most fully completes Ambrosio is his double, his sister. Both Ambrosio and Antonia instinctively recognize the deep connection between them, but she is too innocent and he too lost in his sensual fantasies for them to establish a brother-sister relationship.

To assert his identity through sensual satisfaction and affirm his status as superman, Ambrosio must pursue women on purely masculine terms. He can enjoy Antonia only by force or through the power of magic; if he established an affectional relationship to her, he would regard her as something more than a tool of gratification, which would limit his power over her, and he would thus fall short of his ideal. Behind all the obvious barriers between them—he is, after all, a monk—lies the fact that Ambrosio needs these barriers, for they protect him from the choice between his power as abbott, as ascetic, and his power as superman-sensualist. Further, because his desires are illegitimate, his status as abbott makes their very existence, let alone their satisfaction, an act of self-definition. The conquest of the feminine Other becomes also the conquest by the masculine self of monkish limitations.

Ambrosio's acts of violence are not, of course, gratifying or revivifying. After his rape of Antonia, he feels "base and unmanly," and he realizes that "the very excess of his eagerness to possess Antonia now contributed to inspire him with disgust." The act by which he sought to confirm his manhood unmans him; the assertion of identity through sexual gratification leads to anxiety and disgust, the loss of identity. Ambrosio would, at this point, like to give it all up, but he cannot. The logic that lead to kidnap and rape now demands that he murder Antonia when her cries threaten to reveal his crimes. Exposure would rob him of both halves of his identity: he would no longer be "the holiest man in Madrid" nor could he pursue sensual gratification. His superman status is duplicitous in every sense of the word, for he must show himself able to conquer all aspects of the Other—whether the monastic or the feminine Other—as well as his own doubled identity. Thus he attempts to seize, not only masculine power, but the power of the feminine Other as well. Ambrosio, however, has no real understanding of the power of affect; he has never experienced it in the monastery and feels it only vaguely and briefly at the beginning of his relationship with Matilda and, later, when he first begins pursuing Antonia. Since the power of affect requires submission, it cannot coexist with masculine domination and violence and is quickly blotted out.

All of Ambrosio's actions and appetites reveal his desire to resolve his relationship to his own feminine identity. The combination of longing and disgust and violence he displays toward Matilda and Antonia reflects his feelings toward his warped and distorted feminine half. His desire to dominate and control his doubled identity as ascetic and sensualist is part of his desire to dominate his feminine nature.

Ambrosio first encounters Matilda as the young monk, Rosario. Though his feelings toward the "young man" suggest a homosexual attraction, they are more complex than that. His first feelings of desire are stirred by an image of himself. When Rosario throws back his cowl and becomes Matilda, he reveals the woman hidden within the monk, and this act mirrors what happens to Ambrosio in that moment. Matilda is Ambrosio's alter ego, the fusion of his masculine and sensual qualities; she is the active agent in all of his sexual adventures, and her appearance forces him out of the state of voyeurism. She not only leads him to the rape and murder of his conventional feminine double, his sister, but at the end of the book, she leads him to sell his soul to the grotesquely masculine devil—complete with horns and tail—who takes him off to his final destruction. This warped embodiment of feminine identity, the externalized image of Ambrosio's repressed self, takes him to the ultimate act of summission—he signs away his soul—and then to seven horrible days of torment because he forgets to ask the devil to ensure him a long life of sensual pleasure.

Ambrosio becomes so enmeshed in the Gothic logic of his own identity that he regards damnation as salvation, the ultimate transformation. In his confusion, the sensualist endures pain and suffering; the sadist becomes the masochist: "The eagles of the rock tore his flesh piecemeal, and dug out his eyeballs with their crooked beaks." Ambrosio bears all this and more for six days, until finally a flood washes away the "corse of the despairing monk." He never consciously embraces pain as the logical extension of his sadistic sensuality, but he has been moving to this position all along. Alienated from his feminine nature, which is either externalized and masculinized in Matilda or violated and destroyed in Antonia, his violent sexuality must turn inward upon his fragile and self-contradictory maleness. His pursuit of identity leads him to his feminine double as well as to his feminine self; he can, however, only rape and murder his sister, whom he refuses to recognize, and finally consign himself to damnation. His own sensuality was filled with violence; appropriately, his last experience is of violence as sensuality. In his death, Ambrosio lives out the logic of his own quest for identity and the destructive conflict within himself.

American Siblings: Brown and Poe

In *The Monk,* Lewis uses the incest motif primarily as an expression of the masculine archetype's attempts to control and dominate the feminine. Ambrosio pursues women and sensuality for the sake of his own power and authority; they remain for him a means rather than an end in themselves. Thus he cannot use incest as a path to reconciliation, but only as a tool of dominance. In Charles Brockden Brown's novels *Wieland* and *Edgar Huntly,* we see incest as a means to an essentially feminine end, the creation of a loving and closed family circle. Neither novel uses the motif literally, as *The Monk* and "The Fall of the House of Usher" do, though Theodore Wieland's attraction for his sister Clara—and hers for him—is strongly hinted at. In *Edgar Huntly,* the incest is purely metaphoric, but the effect is as destructive as if it were actual. In both novels, the family circle created by incest is strikingly attractive; masculine violence, ego-centrism, and the lust for power disappear and the world seems a calmer, gentler place for this. But this proves a delusion, because incest cannot banish the masculine only repress it. As a result, violence and the lust for power are even more destructive and terrifying when they finally manifest themselves.

In *Edgar Huntly,* the incest motif appears in the Clithero Edny subplot. Clithero's story is the foil and counterpoint to Edgar's; Edgar becomes a superman, the embodiment of the masculine archetype, as a result of his fascination with the mysterious Clithero, whose story reveals that he has taken on the qualities of the feminine archetype through his involvement with the family of Mrs. Lorimer.

Clithero, the son of a peasant family in Ireland, is taken in by Mrs. Lorimer, a widowed gentlewoman whom he comes to love as his mother and whom he finds intensely beautiful. He serves as the companion to her son—about whom we hear virtually nothing—and falls in love with Clarice, her niece, who looks exactly like her. Clarice is the daughter of Wiatte, Mrs. Lorimer's much loved, but criminal, brother, whom everyone believes to be dead. Clithero, thinking he can never aspire to marry Clarice, resolves to leave Mrs. Lorimer, but she makes him stay, telling him that she is happy for Clarice to marry him. There is great joy until Saresfield, Mrs. Lorimer's fiancé, discovers that Wiatte is alive and has returned to Dublin. Saresfield and Clithero decide that he would ruin Mrs. Lorimer's life—and probably deprive Clithero of Clarice—and so refuse to tell her that he has returned. Wiatte, lying in wait for Clithero, attempts to murder him, but Clithero shoots him in self-defense, not realizing who he is. Convinced that by murdering Wiatte has ruined Mrs. Lorimer's life, Clithero decides to murder her to spare her the pain his terrible deed will cause her. Just as he is about to plunge a dagger into the sleeping woman, Saresfield and Clarice rush in and disarm him. Mrs. Lorimer sinks to the floor in a faint when she hears her brother is dead, and Clithero, thinking she has died from shock over his deeds, flees to America. His guilt manifests itself first in sleep-walking and then in a retreat to an animal-like existence in the wilderness. Edgar Huntley, the narrator and main character of the story, feels a peculiar affinity for Clithero, and he imitates his sleep-walking and his plunge into the wilderness. However, Edgar becomes more, not less, than human as a consequence.

Clithero grows up in an affectional, matriarchal family, a haven from the rest of the world. His love for Mrs. Lorimer finds a convenient outlet in Clarice, and Clithero seems about to join himself fully and completely to this feminine world and identity, when the return of Wiatte threatens the fulfillment of his dreams. Wiatte, a wild and egocentric man, is the archetypal paternal male intruding into the feminine world. He challenges Clithero, not simply because he threatens his marriage to Clarice and the happiness of Mrs. Lorimer, but because he presents an image of masculine power and authority Clihero cannot accept, though it is an aspect of himself. In the act of violence whereby he rids himself, Mrs. Lorimer, and Clarice of Wiatte, his identity cracks. Rather than acting out the masculine pattern of identity like Manfred or Ambrosio, Clithero has aligned himself with the feminine. When forced to violence, he cannot accept the self it represents, and he goes mad. In killing Wiatte, Clithero has rejected the feminine mode for the first time. On the surface, his actions are easily defensible and probably good for everyone concerned—except Wiatte—but they force on him the alternative identity he has submerged for so long. The incestuous nature of the Lorimer family, with the adoptive son marrying the niece who is the image of mother, is quite respectably sublimated. As long as Clithero remains fully within that circle, his identity is stable. Once, however, he is awakened to his masculine side through his encounter with Wiatte, he begins to act out the violence and domination that lie beneath his exterior. Naturally, of course, he decides to kill Mrs. Lorimer, not to dominate or control her, but rather to spare her pain and suffering—from the purest of affectional motives.

Thus, in *Edgar Huntly*, the incestuous definition of identity through the feminine self and the affectional family leads to destruction as surely as does Ambrosio's aggressive assertion of the masculine. The mild and loving incest devised quite happily by Mrs. Lorimer breaks apart, not from its internal contradictions, but because it cannot stand pressure from the outside, cannot defend itself from the threat of masculine intrusion in the return of Wiatte. Clithero is unable to accept his own actions because his sense of identity does not allow for such actions at all, even in self-defense. He has broken the pattern of affectional victimization. His world has betrayed him and precipitated him into madness. Having destroyed an image of the masculine self—which for Clithero was the image of the Other, a threat to himself and everything and everyone he values—he finds that he has destroyed a part of himself. In obedience to the patterns of Gothic necessity, he seeks then to destroy the original source of his identity, Mrs. Lorimer. And believing he has done so, he collapses: he sleep walks, becoming a nightmare shadow of himself, and finally descends into the Gothic world completely, losing all trace of humanness as he hides in the forest, his symbolic mother who will embrace him in death.

We have already looked at *Wieland* as a tale of demonic possession and transformation, but it is also a story of incest. The undertone of Theodore's life before he hears the voice of God links his violent outbreak to an unstable reconciliation with his feminine self, but it also reveals the weakness of the feminine archetype when pushed to its incestuous extreme.

The Wielands live in a paradise, not unlike that inhabited by the St. Auberts, on the banks of the Schuykill River outside Philadelphia. Theodore and his wife, Catherine, her brother, Henry Pleyel, and Clara Wieland, Theodore's sister, form a happy foursome, though Henry and Clara do not marry until the end of the story. The group sits in the garden of Theodore's and Clara's house, reading Cicero and enjoying each other's company. The incestuous potential of this situation—two pairs of brother and sister—is deepened by Theodore and Clara's deep devotion to each other; throughout the novel, Clara appears a much more important person to Theodore than Catherine. This parentless community is seemingly free of the patterns of domination and submission that usually plague the characters of the Gothic fantasy. Theodore and, to a lesser extent, Henry appear to have embraced the feminine archetype, and the four live together in complete equality and mutual affection. Indeed, the fact that at first Clara and Henry are, not only not married, but not lovers—Henry has a fiancée in Germany—emphasizes that sexuality has been completely sublimated into sibling affection within the circle.

When Carwin, the bioloquist, enters the lives of these characters, he catalyzes Theodore's latent religious mania and torments Clara with his powers. He threatens her with rape and murder, invading her house and making her a prisoner of her own fear. In doing so, he acts out Theodore's own desires toward his sister, though Carwin remains in the safe position of voyeur. After Theodore has killed Catherine, he takes her bloody body and lays it in Clara's bed, symbolically identifiying wife and sister, sex and death. When he makes a second attempt to murder Clara, she tries to defend herself with the knife she keeps to protect herself from rape; Theodore commits suicide with this knife when he returns to sanity. Carwin's appearance and his obvious interest in Clara also catalyze Henry's interest in her, and though he is briefly deceived about her virtue, Carwin's competition makes him realize he loves her.

Carwin awakens the incestuous and violent impulses that are barely beneath the surface in Theodore, and he also force Clara into the conventional feminine role of victim. He claims to use his powers to test if Clara is "a woman capable of recollection in dangers, of warding off groundless panics, of discerning the true mode of proceedings and profiting by her resources"—in other words, if she is unlike Emily St. Aubert—for, as he says, such a woman would be "a prodigy" or perhaps, an androgyne. But Clara is no such prodigy, and Carwin's appearance, which forces Theodore to embrace the masculine archetype, forces Clara to embrace the feminine archetype that she had avoided through the "family" the Wielands and Pleyels had created in their Eden. Although Clara does not acknowledge this, it is made clear in her summing up of what has happened: "If Wieland had framed juster notions of moral duty; or I had been gifted with ordinary equanimity and foresight, the double-tongued deceiver would have been baffled and repelled." Clara falls back on conventional ideas of virtue and goodness; the fault lay in the fact that Wieland and Clara were simply not calm and rational enough. But the course of the story has shown us convincingly that "juster notions of moral duty," "foresight," and "equanimity" would have been of no use at all. Carwin did not make Theodore kill his family; he simply brought to the surface an impulse that was already there. Nor could Clara have prevented being terrorized by Carwin and his mysterious attacks on her through his power of throwing his voice.

The life the Wielands and Pleyels had adopted, with its roots in the incestuous impulse, was undermined by its own nature. Carwin's intrusion did not cause the horror but was merely the occasion for it.

Carwin enters the world of the Wielands in much the same way that the creature enters the world of the Frankensteins. Indeed, he bears a certain resemblance to the creature.

> His cheeks were pallid and lank, his eyes sunken, his forehead overshadowed by coarse straggling hairs, his teeth large and irregular, though sound and brilliantly white, and his chin discolored by a tetter. His skin was coarse grain, and sallow hue. Every feature was wide of beauty, and the outline of his face reminded you of an inverted cone.
>
> And yet his forehead, so far as shaggy locks would allow it to be seen, his eyes lustrously black, and possessing, in the midst of haggardness, a radiance inexpressibly serene and potent.[12]

He is both monstrous and ambiguous, ugly yet radiant, and not clearly masculine or feminine. If he is not quite an androgyne, he is still a grotesque human being. His actions are also an inversion of those of the detective; he is a voyeur who, through his unusual powers, creates terror rather than controls it. I would argue that Carwin can disrupt the world the Wielands have created because he is the image of what underlies the placid, rational calm of the Eden by the Schuykill. He is both Theodore and Pleyel's double in his relationship to Clara, and as Clara's mysterious persecutor he becomes the focus of all her anxieties and fears, her demon double. In this role, he calls out what is already there hiding under a surface of barely controlled incestuous desire.

The stories of incest in both *Edgar Huntly* and *Wieland* reveal the failure of the feminine archetype drawing in the bonds of family tighter and tighter, to create a stable and workable identity for its members. To follow out the incestuous impulse brings the characters closer to violence; the happy marriages of Clithero and Clarice, Clara and Pleyel, that would close the incestuous circle are prevented by the outbreak of masculine violence. Henry and Clara are finally free to marry at the end of *Wieland* only because, since Theodore and Catherine are dead, they are no longer metaphorically brother and sister.

The Fall of the House of Usher

The greatest Gothic fantasy using the incest motif is, of course, Poe's "The Fall of the House of Usher." The Ushers have consciously and literally attempted the experiment in the creation of identity that in

Brown's novels is metaphoric and subconscious. Here the horror is right on the surface, and we see clearly how the incestuous and violent impulse come together. Madeline returns from the crypt:

> There was blood upon her white robes and the evidence of some bitter struggle on every portion of her emaciated frame For a moment she remained trembling and reeling to and fro upon the threshold—then with a low moaning cry, fell heavily inward upon the person of her brother and in her violent and now final death-agonies, bore him to the floor a corpse, and victim to the terrors he had anticipated.[13]

The terrors he had anticipated were, of course, the embraces of his sister, and he does finally embrace her in a violent parody of sexual climax. The Ushers, an ancient and noble line, subvert both inheritance and respectability in their incestuous tradition; these two values are simply a fragile shell that contains the depravity at the center of the Usher identity. The literal fall of the house into the tarn mirrors the collapse of the outward emblems of wholeness into the final expression of the unity of sex and violence, Madeline and Roderick's deaths.

Even as the Ushers have become images of self-created horror, they present a delicate, "feminine" self. Wraithlike Madeline and hypersensitive Roderick, diseased and unable to function outside their mansion, suffer the last infirmities of sensibility, of the sentimental and affectional nature. They are so attuned to the world and each other that all sensations are painful. The Edenic retreat of the St. Auberts' and the illusory refuges of the Lorimers and Wielands have become a prison, the horrific reality of a family that in maintaining itself brings about its destruction. This prison is not kept by dangerous or vicious monsters, by a patriarchal villain. Here jailer and jailed are indistinguishable. Roderick and Madeline not only look like each other, they are as close to being each other as two people can be. Once again we see the grotesque parody of the affectional bond within the family. Roderick and Madeline are bound by the closest of ties; they see in each other both self and Other. The two poles have become so close that they are not really separable anymore. But this uncanny mirror image that is the self but not the self is really no identity at all. The curse of the Ushers has reduced both brother and sister to utter passivity. They have been poisoned at their source, morally and psychologically, of course, but physically as well. Roderick's hypersensitivity and Madeline's catalepsy are im-

ages, not simply of the dangers of inbreeding, but of the total collapse of the family as a source of identity.

In *The Monk* and *The Italian,* we could see beneath the patriarchal
surface a twisted version of the feminine self and the affectional family. Beneath the distortion of the affectional family of the Ushers, we
can glimpse the remains of patriarchal sadism. Clearly, in order to
preserve their line, the Usher women, like Madeline, have become
virtual prisoners in the house. But these women, whether they sub-
mitted willingly or not to the domination of their brothers, have had
their revenge, for they have enslaved their captors and thus come to
control the Usher men, who are made over into debilitated and corrupted versions of their sisters. Such power or energy as exist in the
family comes from Madeline, who has the strength to rise from the
crypt to kill, or simply return to, Roderick, who dies from fear and
shock at her reappearance. Since in women lies the power of reproduction by which the Ushers have taken control of their identity,
it is fitting that she should be the last Usher born—or really, re-
born—before the family dies forever.

Roderick tries to kill his sister, not because he hates and fears her,
though he does, but because he loves and desires her; she is himself
and the means by which he will perpetuate the Ushers and thus his
own identity. Anything he feels about her, he also feels about himself. He cannot endure the suffocating tradition that has given him a
cruel joke of an identity, so he tries to suffocate Madeline and end
the gruesome parody of family forever. Madeline's return from the
grave is, in fact, exactly what he wants. In attempting to kill her,
rather than make love to her, Roderick has replaced the terrifying
sexual relationship with a sadistic one, a pathetic assertion of masculine power. At the same time, his entombing of his sister is a masochistic act, for with his acute senses—or imagination, it hardly
matters—he has been buried with her for the whole week she has
lain in the tomb. The Ushers' grotesque attempt to harness the energy of sexuality, which embodies the collapse of the paternal and affectional family archetypes into each other, can now be replaced by
the pattern that is implicit in their relationship already—absolute
sadomasochism, each feeling completely the pain inflicted on the
other.

The Crisis of Androgyny

Neither power through violence, nor respectability, nor incest serves
the characters in the Gothic in their search for identity. In their

transformative and metamorphic world, the only answer that would appear to make sense is the synthesis of the masculine and feminine halves of the self into a single androgynous being.[14] The masculine and feminine parts of the self would then exist in harmony and balance, in a process of interchange. No identity would be wholly masculine or wholly feminine, whatever its sex. The conflict between self and Other would end, because the reconciliation of the two would be achieved when each was accepted as one half of a single whole.

The masculine and feminine in the Gothic fantasy are defined in such a way that this reconciliation and blending is impossible. Egotism cannot coexist with affect. The will for power conflicts with the will for virtue, because masculine power must be illegitimate, seized by the man himself, not handed on by external authority, while the feminine can submit only to legitimate authority, which acknowledges the limitations and boundaries of respectability. Further, the masculine and feminine archetypes are defined by their opposition; the idea of reconciliation and synthesis is antithetical to their very nature.

The Gothic fantasy thus dramatizes both the necessity and hopelessness of androgyny as an alternative to the deadly war within the self. The hopelessness lies in the ways the characters conceive of the masculine and feminine qualities and in their refusal to acknowledge their own doubled natures. They do not realize they need to become androgynous; rather, as they become lost in the underworld, they see the androgyne as monstrous and threatening, something essentially nonhuman. They perceive it this way because of their own warped conception of themselves; through the fractured lens of their identities, they can see only images of the grotesque. The androgyne fails in the Gothic fantasy because the nature of the masculine and feminine archetypes and the characters' attachment to those archetypes make any alternative a threat to the security of male and female identity.

The androgyne also frightens the characters because of their inability to accept the power of sexual pleasure. As long as identity is clearly masculine or feminine, fully separated in male and female, sexuality is simply a reproductive power. Owing to the inescapable conflict between men and women, pleasure is never a significant aspect of sexuality. Sex is really just a mode of violence, part of the dynamics of power. An androgynous being would, though, be able to enter into the sexual experience of a partner, would in fact share pleasure, rather than seek to dominate and control the Other through sexual violence, for no Other would exist. An androgynous archetype of identity would allow men and women to approach each other as equals; differences would be softened, not sharpened. Without the necessity of conflict, a relationship would be based on pleasure rather than the dynamic of sadomasochism, and the power of reproduction would be linked, not to violence, but enjoyment. However, the Gothic characters are too deeply attached to conventional conceptions to accept this. The prospect is simply too radical and threatening.

The protagonists thus maim themselves in order to save themselves from what they see as a monstrous state. This mutilation appears in the repression of such characters as Schedoni and Robert Wringham, who reject their feminine halves, and in the helpless respectability of Emily St. Aubert, Maud Ruthyn, and James's governess. All these characters are incomplete, blind to their own natures; self-deception is their mutilation. The governess never considers alternative interpretations of the ghosts, because they might implicate her in their appearance, nor will Maud accept that her attachment to her father, and then to Silas, is a virtual death wish. Schedoni, like Manfred before him, simply refuses to accept the fact that he has feelings, and Robert Wringham is so obsessed with his own goodness he cannot see evil when it is before his face or in his own actions.

Self-deception may allow a character to appear more or less intact. However, the closer one moves toward the state of androgyny, the more terribly mutilated one will be; in their struggle to escape monstrousness, the characters actually become more monstrous. Madeline and Roderick Usher are identical twins, the products of generations of incest. In their close connections, both physical and psychic, each approaches the state of androgyny, but they are both sick and enfeebled, unable to leave the house that is their tomb. Silas Ruthyn, sickly and perfumed, seems inhuman; and by the end of *Frankenstein,* Victor comes to look like the creature he pursues. When Henry Jekyll splits himself in two, his alter ego is a deformed being whom others perceive as monstrous, though Jekyll, at least at first, acknowledges his kinship to Hyde. Dorian Grey mutilates himself by inflicting his sins upon his portrait; finally he kills himself in an attempt to destroy the portrait completely and thus be rid of this dreadful image of himself. Whether the character remains a single being or splits into a pair, the impulse to self-mutilation is directly correlated to fear and anxiety about the dual nature of the self and the possibility of androgyny. The closer the character comes to acknowledging his or her doubled state, the more obvious and grotesque the self-mutilation.

However, the Gothic fantasy is not without functioning versions of the androgyne. The detective absorbs the qualities of both the masculine and feminine archetypes; in him, the will to dominate is reconciled to the will to submit. Though essentially egocentric, the detective defends respectable values; though essentially reactive, he nonetheless possesses power. However, he achieves reconciliation within the self at the price of isolation. The only complete identity in a world in which the mutilated self is the rule, the detective can never encounter another like himself. Isolated as he is, for the detective, the power of sexuality is confined to voyeurism. He can look and understand, but he cannot become involved. Sexual energy here does not become violence, but rather analysis. This analytic perspective denies the detective a full relationship with others. Watson can be Holmes's friend, but never his equal; Stapleton may be a foeman worthy of his steel, but he must be destroyed.

Another version of the androgyne that appears in the Gothic is the Catholic Church, particularly as represented by the Inquisition. A monstrous bureaucracy, it possesses the power to destroy even such a powerful man as Schedoni in *The Italian*. Although in many ways, it may seem a strange analogy, in understanding the ways in which the Inquisition embodies the qualities of the androgyne, we shall see more clearly how this figures looms over the other characters.

The Inquisition is able to blend and reconcile the powers and qualities of the masculine and feminine archetypes. It is capable of ruthless, violent action and yet, at the same time, of combination and community, the essential power of the feminine. The fusion of these two modes of power creates an institution that can obliterate human identity, and the characters in the Gothic fear above all the obliteration of male and female in the synthetic identity of the androgyne.

The masculine qualities of the Inquisition are quite clear: what could more fully embody maleness than an institution made up of men called "Father"? The system is completely patriarchal; authority is handed down from one generation to the next, guaranteeing legitimate power in a continuous line of descent. Its power is presumed to flow directly from the Divine Father, through the pope. The Inquisition achieves, in this sense, what all Gothic males seek: the power of self-creation and regeneration, the powers of God. But the Inquisition is also a communal organization, a family under the wing of Holy Mother Church. Each Inquisitor in novels such as *The Italian*, *Melmoth the Wanderer*, and *The Monk* has a title, but no name; identity is fully and completely submerged in the group. Equally important, the Inquisition's task is the enforcement of orthodoxy, an analogue to the feminine virtue of respectability. Orthodoxy refers mainly to matters of dogma and belief, while respectability implies first and foremost chastity, but both concepts mean the acceptance of conventional, socially sanctioned values. Departure from orthodox belief, like unchaste behavior, threatens the legitimate line of authority and power.

The Inquisition, then, is androgynous, at least metaphorically, because it synthesizes and reconciles the masculine and feminine archetypes. However, it also represents the terror of androgyny because synthesis comes at the price of both individual power and affect. The Inquisition admits no possibility for individual action, nor does it take into account individual feeling. The fusion of the archetypes is achieved by the complete destruction of individual identity. The true androgyne would unite masculine power with feminine affectiveness and thus liberate individual identity. The Inquisition destroys the identity by denying to the individual either power or affect. To become lost in its prisons is to become lost in the endless Gothic maze, where nothing human can exist. Thus, in some fantasies, the Gothic world itself is identified with the androgyne: each embodies a seemingly inhuman order in which the self is hopelessly lost and, finally, destroyed.

At the same time, we must also see that because of the vow of celibacy taken by nuns and priests, the Inquisition, the monastery, and the abbey are images of the repression and mutilation that the characters inflict upon themselves. In *The Monk*, when Agnes is punished so terribly for her pregnancy, and in *Melmoth the Wanderer*, when the lovers are imprisoned in the catacombs of the monastery and starved to death, we see that the Church's primary opposition is, not heresy, but sexuality. Thus, the apparent opposition of the Church as androgyne to male and female identity is false. The Church may be an oppressor, but it is not a true androgyne. It is a monstrous parody that the protagonists project out of their fears. The terrors of the Inquisition make the terrors of divided selfhood seem small; its unity is far worse than the characters' dividedness. In fact, though, the Inquisition and the characters it oppresses are aspects of the same anxiety about androgyny and sexuality that imprisons people in their identities.

The problem of the androgyne can be seen most clearly in texts in which the doubles are both men or both women. Ambrosio's pursuit of Matilda and then Antonia maintains the apparent division between masculine and feminine in male and female: Ambrosio can deal with his own feminine half by projecting it into the female Other who will become his victim. When the doubles are the same sex, the problem becomes acute because the appearance of division cannot be maintained. The doubles must, in effect, battle for the same space. If the typical dominator-dominated pattern is followed, then one of the pair must accept the role of the supressed archetype. If the doubles are to define a whole, one must embody the feminine, the other, the masculine archetype. We see this quite clearly in *Dr. Jekyll and Mr. Hyde,* for instance. Jekyll and Hyde are both men, though only Hyde seems to embody the masculine archetype; naturally he seeks to dominate Jekyll and control him. Jekyll, unwilling to accept the position of submission, attempts to fight off Hyde, but cannot do so. In the end, unable either to reconcile themselves in a single identity or to accept the dynamics of masculine-feminine sadomasochism, both Jekyll and Hyde must die. In attempting to externalize the part of himself he represses, Jekyll is confronted by the full implications of his own doubleness, which he cannot accept.

When the doubles are both female, the dynamic operates somewhat differently. In *Carmilla,* Laura never becomes fully conscious of Carmilla's vampirism and tries to repress her own attraction to her. But since affect and the submergence of the self in the Other is the natural impulse of the feminine, Laura has an easier time accommodating herself to Carmilla's love and thus to her own approaching death. In either *Dr. Jekyll and Mr. Hyde* or *Carmilla,* though, doubles of the same sex heighten and intensify the doubleness of the self, either the Other must be absorbed back into the self, which Jekyll cannot manage, or the self and Other must become identical, which Carmilla would achieve by killing Laura in a union of love and death.

We can examine more closely the ways in which characters battle against their doubled natures and the possibility of androgyny by looking at *Caleb Williams* and *Frankenstein*. In *Caleb Williams*, Williams and Falkland become doubles by accident, but their whole conflict turns on their attempts to escape the feminine role acknowledgment of their own feminine halves. In *Frankenstein,* Victor creates a monstrous twin who presents him with a horrific mirror of himself. In neither novel can the characters accept their own doubleness or potential for androgyny, and so they must end their crisis of self-confrontation in destruction.

Caleb Williams

William Godwin's *Caleb Williams* shows how violence against the feminine, which in *Otranto, Udolpho,* and *The Monk* was directed against women, is transformed into violence against the feminine half of the self. The antagonistic doubles of the novel, Falkland and Williams, are each obsessed with preserving their "name"—literally, their public reputation, but metaphorically, their masculine identity—for in their conflict each sees his feminine half made clear to him. Williams begins by lavishing on Falkland the devotion, even adoration, that daughters characteristically reserve for fathers in the Gothic; but when Williams discovers Falkland's guilt in the murder of Tyrell and the execution of the Hawkinses for that murder, Falkland cannot be secure unless he knows Williams is under his strict control. Thus he must force Williams into submission in order to protect his illegitimate good name. Williams cannot allow himself to be pressed into the role he would be willing to play of his own choice because it would destroy his conception of his identity as a man, with a "name" of his own. For Falkland, Williams's refusal to assume the submissive role challenges his conception of himself as a dominating, powerful male, thus forcing him into an essentially feminine position. Falkland must dominate Williams, and Williams must escape domination, if either of them is to retain their orientation to the masculine archetype and deny the feminine half of their identities. Thus Falkland projects his feminine half onto Williams, and he, in turn, repeatedly transforms his identity through disguises—Kit Williams, notorious thief and jailbreaker, an Irish begger, a Jewish writer, a goldsmith. Neither Falkland's relentless pursuit nor Williams's repeated metamorphoses can bring stability to this situation.

The doubling of the two men comes into focus when Williams discovers Falkland's secret guilt and Falkland realizes that Williams knows his secret: Williams knows Falkland is a murderer, and Falkland, that Williams is, in effect, a spy. Williams comes to his certain knowledge by breaking into a locked trunk, and thus he too is a criminal. The shame each feels at the exposure of his secret signals the surfacing of the feminine archetype in each man; while the purely masculine archetype demands power that is essentially illegitimate and illegal, the feminine demands legitimate authority as the basis for identity. Shame and guilt are emotions related to the feminine obsession with virtue and respectability; Falkland and Williams overtly manifest these feelings in masculine pride, concern for "name." In reality, what each learns about the other is, not simply that one is a murderer and one a spy and thief, but rather that each has a feminine side. Since the story is told from Williams's point of view, we are most fully aware of Falkland's attempt to displace his feminine half onto his double; but at the end of the novel, we realize that Falkland has always felt Williams posed the same threat to him. Falkland is sick and dying and is brought into the courtroom for his last confrontation with Williams a virtual corpse. His physical debilitation is the outward sign of the wasting away of his masculine self under the pressure of anxiety about his own feminine half being revealed, not to the world, which would know only of his crime, but to himself should he have to accept public shame and submit to legitimate authority.

Williams and Falkland undergo a strange reconciliation before Falkland's death. On seeing Falkland, Williams repents of having brought him to trial.

> I would submit to any imputation of cowardice, falsehood, and profligacy, rather than add to the weight of misfortune with which Mr. Falkland is overwhelmed. . . . No penitence, no anguish, can expiate the folly and cruelty of this last act I have perpetrated. Mr. Falkland is of a noble nature[15]

Falkland responds in kind.

> Williams, he said, you have conquered! I see too late the greatness and elevation of your mind. I confess that it is to my fault, not yours, that it is to the excess of jealousy that was ever in my bosom, that I owe my ruin.[16]

As they praise each other and blame themselves, the whole nightmare of pursuit and persecution seems to vanish. In this moment, the feminine emerges in both men: Falkland, now dying, can put aside the need to dominate, and Williams, who is no longer being forced into it, can accept his feminine half and reverts to the worship of Falkland, which was his natural impulse. However, the masculine archetype has collapsed, not because of the corrosive effects of the feminine archetype struggling to be expressed, but rather through the intolerable strain of repressing the feminine in the presence of the double who calls it forth. Falkland and Williams's inability to accept the fact of their doubled identity and their consequent need to repress the feminine half leads them to destroy each other. Each man begins by trying to hide his guilt for a crime. Falkland tries to repress Williams by imprisoning him, and Williams responds by transforming his identity, doing anything to escape being Caleb Williams, while at the same time always seeking to clear his name—that is, to return to being Caleb Williams on his own, masculine terms. Only after the masculine halves of the self have destroyed each other can the feminine emerge and be reconciled, but these maimed identities are equally inadequate. At the end of the novel, Falkland is dead and Williams, deprived of the double he regarded as a father, is bereft. He says, after his vindication "I have no character left which I wish to vindicate." Unable to accept their potential androgyny, these two characters survive by projecting the feminine self onto the Other; when the Other disappears, Caleb Williams finds he has no identity at all.

Their complex interchange of identities reveals, not only the presence of the feminine and masculine within a single self, but how these archetypes are in a dynamic relationship to each other. Falkland's masculinity calls forth Williams's feminine desire to submit, but when Falkland tries to force this state on Williams, Williams's resistance calls forth from him the feminine self that Falkland is so determined to repress. The relationship of doubles is, not a simple opposition of masculine and feminine, but a projection of that opposition within the self onto the double. The struggle with the Other for identity is an act of self-mutilation that springs from the desire to escape the androgyne implicit within the doubled self. Each of the doubles has both a masculine and feminine side; the conflict occurs when one of the pair tries to force the other to assume one role in the dynamic of identity in order to free himself from his own doubleness.

Frankenstein

Frankenstein is subtitled *The New Prometheus,* but it might easily be called *Men without Women.* Mary Shelley develops and refines the themes that her father laid out in *Caleb Williams.* Victor Frankenstein's assertion of his masculine identity and rejection of his feminine, affectional family becomes a confrontation with his own doubled nature and potential androgyny. Like Manfred, he tries to create his own identity outside legitimate channels, though rather than attempting to become his own son, Victor builds his offspring in the laboratory. The line of inheritance in *Frankenstein* is as weak and corrupt as in *Otranto,* if not more so, for Victor refuses to take the responsibility for his creation that Manfred actively pursues. Victor cannot sustain his masculine identity and power, and his creature wrecks upon his family the destruction Manfred brought upon his own. In doing so, the creature performs the violent acts that Victor wants but cannot acknowledge to himself. The restless desire to be rid of suffocating powerlessness, leads the masculine self, once "free" of the affectional and feminine, to confrontation with that side of its nature and, inevitably, to self-destruction.

The conflict between the masculine and the feminine is embodied in the opposition betwen male isolation and the feminine family. The three concentric rings of the novel all repeat this dynamic: Walton's rejection of his sister, Mrs. Saville and her family in England; Victor's rejection of his family, shortly after his mother's death, for six years at the university; and finally, the creature's rejection by the Delacy family. The dynamic is not, of course, quite the same in all instances: Walton and Victor have parallel experiences, while the creature reverses their pattern. Walton and Victor both leave behind the world of women in favor of those of men—the sea or the university—but the creature desperately wants to enter the world of women and the family. Strikingly, when he cannot do this, he forms a male community of two, himself and Victor, though Victor is an unwilling partner in this enterprise. The stories of all three men end in the icy polar wastes, identified as the scene of purely masculine activity—the search for power and fame—and finally the world of death.

The families in the novel all appear, at least at first, as attractive alternatives to arctic horror. The Frankensteins are close and loving, though this love is mainly showered on young Victor, who conceives of himself as the center of his family's life. Even more the quintessential feminine family are the Delacys, whom the creature watches through a chink in the wall. In his view, the Delacys are wonderfully happy, spending their whole lives loving and caring for one another. The family appears to be a safe haven, a refuge from the outside world. But these two families are literally refugees. The Delacys are outcasts, accepted neither by Christians nor Mulims, and the Frankensteins are a collection of strays. Caroline, Elizabeth, and Justine, who, though a servant, is like a member of the family, come from families that have broken up, primarily for economic reasons. The make-up of these families signals their essential weakness and the precarious place of the affectional ideal in the world. The creature yearns for a family only because he has never had one; based on their experiences, Victor and Walton both flee their families, though at the same time, each longs for that haven they have deprived themselves of, Walton by leaving it, and Victor by allowing the creature to destroy it.

The failure of the affectional family here lies in more than its weakness in relation to the external world. Its structure is fundamentally incestuous. Caroline, Victor's mother, is the Baron Frankenstein's former ward, and Elizabeth, Victor's intended bride, has been raised as his sister. Walton's family is really just his sister, and his attachment to her carries with it the hint of incest. The creature's plan for starting a family in the Andes also falls into this pattern; since Victor will have to build his mate, she will in effect be his sister. Thus, Victor allows his family to be murdered by the creature because in doing so the creature wipes out the image of an incestuous, powerless identity from which Victor desperately wishes to escape. Though Victor over and over professes his love for his family and for his friend Clerval, he does nothing to protect them; only after they are gone does he actively pursue the creature. Indeed, through what we can only see as an unconscious self-delusion, he refuses to recognize that the creature's threat, "I will be with you on your wedding night," is directed, not at him, but at Elizabeth. Victor should realize this, since the threat is made just after Victor has destroyed the creature's mate, but instead he allows the creature to take his place in the marriage bed with Elizabeth and murder her. This destroys Victor's family, but it also removes the suffocating threat of incest and ends forever the fear of being drawn back into that world where masculine identity is submerged in the affective chaos in which distinctions between mother, sister, daughter, husband, brother, and son are erased.

Victor builds his creature as an act of self-assertion, of identity making. By creating life in his laboratory, he achieves the power of God, and indeed, he states that he hopes his creature will worship him. He has also usurped the power of the feminine, for he has reproduced without a woman. He thus seizes power that should not be his and establishes his own patriarchal line. He at first seems a sharp contrast to the figures of male authority that appear in the novel; Delacy is blind and enfeebled, Baron Frankenstein is ineffectual and hardly present, and the two scientists Victor works with at the university are men of learning without power. But his power is soon undermined by what he has wrought. The creature he has built is Victor's family. Clearly his son, the creature is also his brother and his double, for what Victor makes, he is. As the creature comes to dominate Victor, taunting him with his superior strength, depriving him of his sister-bride on his wedding night, he becomes Victor's father figure. The night he brings the creature to life, Victor dreams first of Elizabeth, then of his dead mother in her shroud; he awakens to see the creature standing by him. The creature is in this way also identified with Victor's mother and sister-fiancée. All of Victor's family relationships—with Caroline, the baron, Elizabeth, with Clerval, his virtual brother—are contained in his relationship to his creature, who is not simply the projection of Victor's masculine identity but also of his feminine side. The relationship that Victor thought would magnify his masculine identity in fact renders it intensely unstable by forcing upon him its contradictions and tensions.

The creature, huge, powerful, ugly, is an even more extreme version of the superman we saw in *Edgar Huntly,* as well as a parody of Victor's dream of masculine power. Victor flees the creature because the externalized image of the masculine archetype terrifies him; he does not want to acknowledge that this is the image of what he aspires to. Insofar as the creature is the projection of Victor's masculine archetype and aspiration, his destruction of the Frankensteins reflects Victor's own desires and impulses. But the creature is not simply raw, untamed, masculine power; Victor in fact forces him to become this in order to avoid accepting his own responsibility. The creature has two sides to his nature: physically he is grotesquely masculine, but his sensibility is essentially feminine. He loves music, is easily moved by the scenes in the Delacy house, and wants nothing more than to be part of an affective circle of relationships. Rejected by both Victor and the Delacys because of his horrifying appearance, his feminine half withers, starved for affection. As the creature gradually becomes more and more masculine, Victor becomes more and more passive; whenever the creature does something terrible, Victor collapses into illness and delirium. He both avoids responsibility for the creature's acts, and shows himself to be the submissive partner of the pair.

Victor's responses are founded in his refusal to accept the fact of the creature's androgynous nature. Were he to accept the creature's capacity for affect, his feminine side, Victor would not only have to accept responsibility for his violence, the result of ill treatment, but he would also have to accept that his own masculine identity coexists with a feminine one, because the creature is Victor's double. Victor will play the passive role while the creature acts out the unconscious violence in Victor's attitude toward his family, but once that violence is complete, Victor attempts to seize again the masculine role and destroy what he has created. What Victor fights is, not simply a double who threatens his identity, but a double who reveals far too much about his own identity to him. The creature shows Victor the truth about his own nature; in seeking to destroy him, Victor is trying to destroy that truth, just as he allowed the creature to destroy the family that represented the externalization of his feminine half.

The creature, a completely unique being, becomes the nexus in which all of Victor's struggles with his own identity are made clear. The creature's androgyny challenges Victor, and he fails the first test: he can build the creature, but he cannot accept his connection to him. The creature's demands that Victor accept their relationship terrify him because they call upon the feminine, affective side of his nature, which he wants to escape. Victor's only response is to establish the pattern of sadomasochistic violence, first between the creature and the Frankensteins, then between the creature and himself. In order to preserve the illusion of his own exclusively masculine identity, Victor will die, for death is the only escape from the androgyny implied in the act of creation and the creature himself. Once he has forced the creature into conforming to the masculine archetype, Victor cannot then subdue and dominate him. He would rather they both die than put aside the masculine and come to the reconciliation that would synthesize the masculine and feminine halves in each.

Dracula: The Formulation of Myth

The tradition reaches its logical fulfillment at the end of the nineteenth century in *Dracula*. Bram Stoker attempts to resolve the central anxieties expressed in the genre, the twin fears of pleasure and androgyny. In *Dracula,* Stoker creates a pair of androgynes, Count Dracula and Mina Harker, and in doing so, seeks to liberate the desire for androgyny from the fear of sensual pleasure. In this strategy, Stoker fails; in fact, he renews the dynamics of the Gothic fantasy in such a way as to transform its parodic impulse into a mythologizing one. Dracula becomes the archetypal representative of the Gothic world, the primal creature of the Gothic abyss, and he is in himself complete and whole, a true alternative to human identity.

Though that alternative may be horrific, it is nontheless powerful, for Dracula escapes the fragmentation that the doubled human identity faces, even if he does so by embracing terror as a way of existence. In him, death becomes, not the end of the crisis of identity through the destruction of the self, but rather the monstrous gateway into a completely new kind of identity. Dracula's difference in kind, rather than simply in degree, from the humans in the story makes him a truly mythological figure.

Stoker's novel dramatizes the conflict between two communities, between, in effect, two species, competing for survival.[17] The community of the vampires stands as the single example in the tradition of beings who have settled fully and completely into the Gothic world. Dracula himself, as we have seen, has fully internalized the sadomasochistic aspects of masculine identity, as has his harem of female vampires. They live in an underworld in which the masculine and feminine have come together on terms dictated by the former, and the resolution of the dichotomies between the two patterns of identity is the creation of a whole world of monstrous androgynes. Because Dracula has recreated his three human lovers as vampires, he is not only their lover but their parent. Thus the motif of incest continues in the vampire world. In his obsession with blood and his horrific immortality, in Redfield's references to him as "the Master," Dracula shows that he is a parody of Christ. He has gone beyond seeking to hear God's voice or to become God, he now is God, the Savior, at least in his own realm. At the heart of that realm is the perversion of love, the transformation of the affective impulse into an act of destruction that is also a perversion of sexuality. Neither Dracula nor the female vampires have any particular sexual orientation: they will suck the blood from anyone, man, woman, or child. Their magnetic sexual attractiveness does not work on each other, only on humans, because the humans find in them, not only the call to death that lurks in the patterns of identity we have been exploring, but a resolution of the conflict between self and Other.

The vampire's transformation of love into sadism can best be seen early in the novel, in the scene in which female vampires lust after the blood of Jonathan Harker. Dracula forbids them their victim, and they reply, "You never love, no, you never love." He replies, "You know well I loved once." At first this appears to be a grotesquely pathetic moment, in which the vampires yearn for love as pale echoes of their lost human identities. In fact, though, the exchange is sinister and obscene when we realize that what the vampire means by "love" is literally the sucking of the victim's blood. Sexuality and love have become the act of feeding. Dracula has made literal the romantic trope that for the lover, love is food and drink. The vampires are androgynes, but their androgyny is an expression, not of increased sympathy and widened identity, but of an indifference to everyone but themselves. The androgyne grows out of the conceptions of masculine and feminine that dominate the real world and have their negative image in the Gothic fantasy. The Gothic gives back, not only the terrifying parody of male and female, but a monstrous vision of the androgyne that is their unacknowledged offspring. When Dracula stands over Mina, having forced her to drink his blood in a blasphemous sacrament, he calls her "my wine press," and the female vampires greedily suck the blood from a child that Dracula has broght them as a substitute for Harker. Conventional ideas of masculine and feminine identity can only form a parody of the androgyne.

In contrast, the humans who oppose Dracula are bound together by ties of love and friendship; their relationships are so spiritually uplifted in standard Victorian fashion that the modern reader may find them somewhat hard to take. This human group, a voluntary family opposed to Dracula's conscripted one, has no true patriarch; its roots are in the feminine ideal. Van Helsing does take some of the functions of the patriarch, for he knows more about vampires than do the rest, but his leadership rests on his particular knowledge and wisdom, not on his status as eldest male. All of the men who were Lucy's lovers, Seward, Holmwood, and Morris, are apparently adventurers, but they, too, subordinate themselves to the feminine ideal of the family. They do this in part because they worshiped Lucy and hold their own sacrifices of blood to her, through transfusions, sacred. In this attitude there is a genteel and benign paternalism, perceiving women as passive victims to be protected. The men attempt to place Mina Harker in this category, and had they succeeded, their community would have been a glossed-over version of traditional male hegemony over the feminine. But in fact, Mina becomes the most powerful figure in the group; if anyone dominates, it is she. By initially excluding her from the witch hunt for Dracula, the men in fact make her more vulnerable to his attacks. When they recognize this, they must take her into the circle as an equal, and Mina, with what Van Helsing calls her "man's brain and woman's heart," really plans the pursuit of Dracula; her courage far outstrips that of her male comrades', for she is in danger of losing her soul as well as her life. Mina is a far more attractive androgyne than Dracula, combining intelligence, decisiveness, and efficiency with tenderness. She can succeed in making her place in the band of male questors exactly because her presence converts them from would-be quest heroes to members of a true family. She serves as sister-mother-confessor to all, though wife to only Harker. As in *Uncle Silas,* the affectional "family" can absorb masculine power if the bonds of the real family don't interfere. Parents, and parent figures, die with remarkable frequency; the old solicitor who is like Harker's father, Lucy's mother, and Holmwood's father all die in the course of the novel. The voluntary family takes the place of the biological family.

Emancipation from the biological family relieves the characters of anxiety about the sexuality it embodies: the relationships of the vampires are coldly androgynous, and those of human family are purely spiritual. However, we must also note that Mina is the only female Gothic character who is not a virgin. The fact that she is a sexual being as well as a friend to the men suggests that some of her power stems from her ability to act on her own sexual desires. Lucy, who is a virgin when Dracula makes her his victim, is a target because of her repressed, though extremely sensual, nature. Her fantasies about marrying all three of her suitors and her sleepwalking betray an erotic restlessness on which Dracula seizes. Sensual but chaste, Lucy's sexuality has no outlet, no mode of expression. In Mina, the Gothic heroine has truly made the transition from girl to woman. She comes closest to a fully integrated and stable identity as any character in the genre, with the exception of Dracula himself, her monstrous, masculine enemy.

In the end, Mina and her companions succeed: Dracula is destroyed and the curse is lifted, not only from the humans, but as Mina asserts at the last moment when Dracula smiles, from the vampire himself. The novel has dramatized the conflict between two versions of identity, two versions of the family, and crystalized the themes of the Gothic fantasy in their most direct and powerful form. In Dracula, Stoker created a character who has become one of the dominate icons of the twentieth-century imagination. The count refuses to stay dead; he returns over and over in films, novels, and television, in literally hundreds of incarnations and revisions. We have taken the villain of *Dracula* and made him our own, made him, I would argue, one of our images of what we are. If *Dracula* is an attempt to solve the central issues of the Gothic on their own terms, it has the strange effect of transforming the genre from a parody to a myth. We accept Dracula as he sees himself, as a whole and powerful identity, not an aspect of our old and worn-out images, but a clear reflection of our true selves. Awful as he is, Dracula thus becomes an empowering vision of the self as Other, as Outsider. When a tradition like the Gothic stands in a parodic relationship to the world, our relationship to it must be analytical or escapist. But as we embrace it as a fable of identity, Dracula passes from fantasy, as does the whole genre, to myth, becoming a fiction that is also a "truth."

But if Dracula can pass into myth, become a new kind of self, why does his opponent fail to do so too? Mina fails because, though she is an androgyne, she does not resolve the problem of pleasure that is the other side of the crisis of the doubled self. Dracula has completely done away with pleasure; he simply redefines it as pain. Though monstrous, he is whole. His success is predicated on his total rejection of the power of pleasure as a means of synthesis and reconcilation. Thus, he is maimed but, at the same time, complete. Mina almost attains the full power of androgyny through her acceptance of pleasure, symbolized in her adult, female sexuality. But in her contact with Dracula we see the failure of her androgyny: Dracula's sadomasochistic sexuality can corrupt Mina, transform her into an "almost" vampire. When the Host touches her forehead, her flesh is seared, for she is, by her own words, "unclean." Yet why should Dracula be able to make the woman who is his equal unclean, while she is unable to transform him at all? She speaks to the men of the necessity of doing what they do to the count out of love, and yet she still must rely on violence, the stake through the heart, to defeat him. Had Mina fully integrated the power of sexuality as pleasure in herself, Dracula could never have corrupted her. Sexual pleasure, except when confined to marriage, remains intrinsically unclean for Mina, and for Stoker. Thus Stoker's heroic androgyne cannot use the most powerful weapon available to her as a defense against the count—the secure knowledge of the purity of her own sexuality—and must rely on traditional masculine violence to do the work of "love."

Stoker's spiritualizing of Mina marks his failure to confront and accept the implications of his own dialectic, one androgyne formed from pain, another from pleasure. Finally, in the last words of the novel, when we see Mina through Jonathan's eyes, she has fallen back into the role of Mother; he sees her now, seven years later, as the woman men defended, not the woman who led men in her own defense. Thus, unlike the count, she is forced back into the unresolved, unacknowledged doubleness that is the usual state of characters in the Gothic. The myth of *Dracula*, then, becomes a myth of the power of pain.

The very fact that it can be used to express this mythology of pain suggests that perhaps the problem with the figure of the androgyne goes deeper than the specific problems of the novel. Stoker's inability to resolve the problem of sexuality and pleasure in relation to individual identity is surely the reason why Mina cannot act directly against Dracula, why she cannot cure him but must kill him. Both Mina and Dracula fail as androgynes because they reflect the corrupted visions of masculine and feminine identity upon which they are based, Dracula in his own nature, Mina in the inescapable images of woman as passive, spiritual Mother that surround her. But can any androgynous vision of identity truly offer a conception of self to which real men and women might adhere? The very idea of the androgyne seems rooted in the notion of differences between masculine and feminine; these two poles must exist before they can be reconciled. We must recall that the Gothic fantasy does not present a critique of the conception of masculine and feminine qualities, but rather of the distortion of those qualities and the definition of the relationship between the two poles of identity as sadomasochistic. This critique is rooted in the cultural values and necessities of the nineteenth and twentieth centuries, not in an eternal vision of an abstract, ideal identity.

Perhaps, then, the androgyne is, not an alternative vision of identity at all, but an idealization, a fantasy that sharpens and focuses our sense of what is wrong with our perceptions of masculine and feminine. The pursuit of the androgyne, in this sense, is indeed the pursuit of an illusion, an illusion that transforms itself into something monstrous. But if the characters in the Gothic fantasy always encounter this monster, in our experience of their encounter, we can obtain a new sense of what the ideals of masculine and feminine might mean and what their relation to living men and women might be. Because men and women cannot escape the biological fact of difference, the androgyne must remain a creature of the imagination, like the unicorn. Dracula's success in transforming himself from man into monster is directly proportional to his achievement of monstrous androgyny; and paradoxically, Mina's failure to retain her androgynous state may point toward the real, rather than the fantasy, alternative to horror. If her reversion to Mother is unsatisfying, particularly for a modern audience, we may take it as a sign that she remains an actual woman, a living human being, not a creature out of nightmare or fantasy. The vision of androgyny that leads Van Helsing to say Mina has a man's brain and a woman's heart is still distorted; these words of praise reveal a deep attachment to the deadly opposition that has made Dracula what he is. Just as he was wrong to think Mina could be kept out of the battle, Van Helsing is wrong about the real nature of her best qualities: it should be, not man's brain, woman's heart, but woman's brain and woman's heart that make Mina who she is. We may also hope for a man's heart to go with a man's brain in some new image of male identity.

3

The Gothic in the Twentieth Century

The Gothic fantasy casts its shadows into the twentieth century; its twilight deepens and surrounds us still. Strikingly, the cast of characters in the twentieth-century fantasy depends heavily on the classic novels of the nineteenth. Dracula, Frankenstein and his creature, Dr. Jekyll and Mr. Hyde, the Ushers and Poe's other madmen and victims, James's governess retain their hold over our imagination and are still the staples of the tradition in both film and fiction. Even more important, the structure and themes of the genre have changed little. The Gothic fantasy remains a fable of failed identity because modern culture has yet to resolve the relationship within the identity into either the archetypal conceptions of masculine and feminine that we have inherited from earlier eras or the alternative archetype of the androgyne. Some of the apparatus and trappings of the fable have changed, partly because film offers a new medium with new technical resources and partly because the treatment of the its themes and dynamics is more explicit now. Nevertheless, the essential continuity of the tradition will become clear in my discussion of five important films: *King Kong, The Cat People, Halloween, Psycho,* and *Vertigo.*[1] Individual works in the twentieth, as in the nineteenth, century offer varying interpretations of the genre, but my point here is, not to explore variations among Gothic fantasies, but to show the persistance of the genre's basic forms and themes in our own era.

The Films

The first of the great twentieth-century horror classics is *King Kong* (1933). The film is both a classic and a curiosity; in its time its special effects—that is, its visual qualities as a spectacle—were unsurpassed. Today, more modern technology has made them seem simply quaint to many audiences, just as the Bleeding Nun and Wandering Jew of *The Monk* now strike us as silly and stagey. But despite our distance from the technical mechanisms of its spectacle, *King Kong* remains a compelling film, the vitality of which is only slightly diminished by its various imitators and descendents from *The Son of Kong* to *Godzilla versus Mothera*.

Kong embodies specific racist fantasies and fears, as well as a strange sort of attraction to the primitive, but above all, he embodies the masculine archetype. He is a "king and a god," according to Carl Denham, the man who captures him, a king and god who devours the brides served up to him by the weak and savage humans who have walled him away but fear and worship him. Kong lives and rules in a world of violent chaos and conflict, a truly demonized jungle swamp, but one in which this giant image of masculine power is perfectly content. The violence of his world matches the violence of his nature. But once he encounters the feminine in the person of Anne Darrow, he is doomed, for he must pursue this beautiful blonde Other to whom he is ridiculously attracted. It is important to see that Kong is ridiculous; despite his size and power, he is really an overgrown monkey, repeatedly given to "monkeyshines" and silly gestures of puzzlement and curiosity. Because of his size and power, these childish gestures are not cute, as they might be with a real monkey, but truly ludicrous. Kong thus fulfills the prescription for the Gothic male—he is violent, godlike, egocentric, and silly—whose encounter with the feminine Other proves fatal to him. Of course, by transforming the Gothic protagonist into this huge monkey, the producers of the film have come close to producing a parody of what is already a parody. Kong is impossibly monstrous and impossibly ridiculous at the same time; his attraction to Anne—which is explicity sexual, as we see in the scene in which he strips off her clothes—is both horrific and a bad joke. *King Kong* exploits the capacity of the Gothic for self-parody, though this does not undercut the force of terror in the film.

Though Kong is the image of the masculine self in its purest and most extreme form in the film, he has a masculine double in Jack Driscoll, first mate of Denham's ship and Anne's eventual lover. Jack is the prototypical American hero. Strong, silent, rather wooden and stupid, he begins hostile to the idea of a woman invading the man's world of his ship but ends up enthralled by Anne. At one point, after he has declared his feelings for her, Anne says, "Why

Jack, you hate women." Jack replies, "Yeah, but you ain't women."
Jack literally competes with Kong for Anne, for it is he who rescues
her from Kong's lair. Kong and Jack are twins, strong, inarticulate,
and dumb. The film exploits this doubling in ways that are at once
comic and pathetic. When Kong is displayed in New York, Jack ac-
companies Anne to the premiere dressed in the tuxedo Denham has
bought him—his "monkey suit." Moments later, Kong is revealed as
equally uncomfortable, but he is in chains, his arms and legs man-
acled in such a way as to suggest Christ on the cross. Jack "wins"
Anne from Kong, not because he is more powerful—more heroic,
more masculine—but for exactly the opposite reason. Jack submits
to the limits of civilization—he puts on his monkey suit—which
Kong cannot. Jack is able to submit to Anne and become "respectable" while Kong must possess the feminine Other only on his wild,
primitive terms. Anne must be his doll, his toy, submitting to the
terror of his picking her up and carrying her around like a thing.

Strikingly, though, as an audience we are less pleased that Jack
and Anne get together in a typical romance fashion than we are sor-
ry—even moved—at Kong's death. The giant ape is a much more
powerful reflection of the masculine identity than Jack because he is
so extreme in his monstrousness and his ridiculousness. Kong reflects more fully than any other character in the genre the terrible
naiveté, the innocence, that underlies this conception of masculine
identity. When he tries to function in the modern world, he seems at
first to triumph; his wild, animal power, raw and lawless desire,
sweeps away everything in his path. He destroys the onrushing ele-
vated train just as he destroyed the giant snake on his island, and the
large buildings of New York prove no problem for him. But when
he climbs the Empire State Building, Kong is dwarfed by modern
technology and then destroyed by the airplanes. On his island, behind the wall—in some vague, lost, unremembered age—Kong
truly was a king and god. But in New York, he is a sideshow attraction, "a show to gratify your curiosity" says Denham to his audience,
in a ludicrous spectacle. Kong can generate a nostalgic melancholy
for the primal masculine identity in part because his captor, Carl
Denham, is really a far more troubling, even sinister, version of the
masculine self.

Denham begins the film by announcing that he is "looking for a
girl," and he finds her in Anne Darrow, who is out of work and
virtually starving. Denham treats her to a meal and offers her a job;
when she begins to refuse, he assures her, in slightly aggrieved tones,
that she has nothing to fear from him. He is "strictly business" and

has "no funny business" on his mind. More than Jack, or even Kong, Denham is interested in a woman as a prop and property. Desexualized, he is after "money, adventure, fame" and "the thrill of a lifetime," which he promises to share with Anne. Later, on the ship, he films her in a scene in which she is supposed to react to a sight of horror. She of course has no idea of what she is reacting to; she is simply following Denham's instructions as her director. Nor, in fact, is it clear that he really knows what he expects her to see. But in the moment of directing this scene, Denham in effects stands in for Kong and dominates Anne in a way exactly parallel to the way Kong will. But Denham does this, not from any desire for Anne, but simply as a means to wealth and adventure. Like many Gothic males, Denham has rejected his own sexuality in the pursuit of power. In him, we see the masculine self in a truly modern guise; he is a bizarre combination of capitalist, adolescent, and artist, endlessly pursuing the excitement that will also make him a millionaire. Denham survives the whole encounter with Kong oddly untouched. At the end of the film, Kong is dead, Anne has been terrorized, and Jack domesticated, but Denham is left to moralize "twas beauty killed the beast." Apparently, he is genuinely immune from the fatal attraction to the abyss and the encounter with his own doubled self, for he seemingly has no double in Anne, unlike Jack and Kong. He is masculine identity truly purged of its feminine double, but he is thus maimed and dehumanized. Denham, in effect, has Kong and Jack to act out the crisis of the masculine self confronted with its feminine double, and as one is tamed and the other killed, he is left free of his initial imperative: "I'm looking for a girl."

Denham is an extension of the image of modern man we have seen in Dracula. His existence is defined by his desire for thrills and fame and by his safety in the position of voyeur; as a film director he is preeminently a watcher and observer. Though he tells the New York crowd that Kong has been brought to them "to gratify your curiosity," it seems all the action in the film has been arranged for Denham himself. The monstrous and ludicrous love triangle of Kong, Jack, and Anne has enacted the Gothic drama of identity for Denham, while he takes a hand only when absolutely necessary. Although at the end of the film he has not become a millionaire, he has had fame, adventure, and "the thrill of a lifetime." Through his three surrogates, he has entered the underworld—located first on Kong's island, later in the urban jungle of New York—and survived untouched.

Denham is in some ways more of a monster than Dracula, for he is so dehumanized that he has completely escaped the whole crisis of human identity. For Denham, everything reduces to money or thrills, a spectacle that he creates and enjoys though it leads to death, terror, and destruction for virtually all around him. Nor do we have any sense that he will be punished for what has happened; the deaths of the sailors and the destruction on the island are clearly long forgotten, and the policeman who stands beside Denham as he speaks the film's last lines makes no move to arrest him, while the crowd looks in awe upon the celebrity. His immunity comes, not only from his mutilated nature, but also from his position as entertainer. It reflects the fact that society accepts the price demanded for his spectacular "entertainments." Further, his society also accepts his triad of values: money, adventure, and fame. He is thus, paradoxically, a figure of complete and utter respectability, for his values and those of his society coincide exactly. The drama of masculine and feminine identity acted out between Kong and Anne is something it converts into entertainment, though such "funny business" leads to terror and death. In *King Kong*, we are allowed to watch society become enthralled to the Gothic spectacle and use that spectacle as a source of thrills before mouthing a conventional moral: "Twas beauty killed the beast." In the terms of our examination, the feminine destroys the masculine at the price, though Denham does not add this, of its own terrorization and imprisonment. In the characterization of Denham, the film lays bare a version of masculine identity that is able to escape from the crisis of identity. At once childish and greedy, Denham and his audience have so totally repressed their own dual natures—and their own sexuality, displaced into mindless thrill-seeking—that the spectacle of Kong and Anne remains utterly alien to them. But as the audience of the film, as opposed to the audience in the film, we can see that the truly human drama here has been the frightening, ridiculous, and pathetic spectacle of Kong and Anne confronting each other in the heart of the Gothic darkness.

King Kong focuses on the masculine half of the Gothic dynamic. *The Cat People* (1943) and *Halloween* (1976) develop the Gothic dynamics from the perspective of the feminine identity. Both films center on a young woman attempting to come to grips with her own sexuality and identity; Irena in *The Cat People* is finally destroyed by her confrontation with her masculine doubles, and Laurie in *Halloween* is terrorized. Irena's confrontation with the masculine half of her own identity is initiated by her awakened sexuality. She has three masculine doubles in the film: two are men, her husband,

Oliver "Ollie" Reed, and her psychiatrist, Dr. Judd. The third double is the black panther into which she is transformed by sexual desire and strong emotion.

Irena fears her doubled metamorphic nature because she believes it derives from ancient witches, evil beings who had to be wiped out by King John of Serbia; she keeps a statue of King John, a panther impaled upon his sword, in her apartment to remind her that she must control the evil within her. This evil is associated in her mind with passion and sexual desire, both of which she consciously attempts to supress. However, she is also deeply enthralled—in the positive sense—by her cat nature and spends hours at the zoo, looking particularly at the panthers and drawing pictures of them in her notebooks. At the zoo, she meets Ollie Reed—everyone in the film except Irena calls him by this silly diminuative—who is a clean-cut American romance hero. He is strangely attracted to Irena and marries her soon after meeting her. Terrified of the violent and aggressive nature of her own sexuality—in Gothic terms, the masculine half of her identity—Irena refuses to consummate the marriage. Ollie does not seem terribly upset by this, but he does insist she see a psychiatrist. The doctor, of course, does not believe that she can actually transform herself into a panther, and he talks to her about guilt and complexes. Irena tells him he has no understanding of the soul, only of the mind. The doctor, who carries the wonderful phallic symbol of a swordcane, is deeply attracted to her, for she awakens in him the sexual desire that seems completely missing in Ollie.

Ollie grows disturbed by Irena's strangeness and turns to his old pal Alice for comfort. Alice is "a swell egg" who really understands Ollie and knows what love is: "Just me and you and let the rest of the world go by." Ollie tells Alice that he has had a "swell life" and that until he met Irena, he has "just never been unhappy before." She seems to accept this statement without surprise, even though to the audience it conjures up the image of an existence so bland as to be positively unlivable. Ollie and Alice meet frequently to discuss his problems with Irena; his favorite food is apple pie, which he has whenever he eats dinner with Alice. If I have made Ollie and Alice sound like parodies of the American version of the happy couple of the romance, it is because this is precisely what they are. We have virtually no sympathy for them or their treatment of Irena, whom they start to ignore so they can get on with their own return to normalcy. When Ollie decides to get rid of Irena, who still loves him, perhaps because he is such an image of what she still regards as normal, he hypocritically tells her that he will give her a divorce, though he is the one who really wants to break up the marriage.

Aroused to jealousy by Ollie's attraction to Alice, Irena actually does turn into a panther and stalks Alice; once Alice escapes by getting onto a bus, and Irena, to assuage her bloodlust, must kill a zoo animal. She returns home, shaken and guilty, and we see her hunched in the bath, weeping, trying to wash away the blood she has spilled. But the second time Irena pursues Alice, she is content to terrorize her and seems to have no intention of killing her. Finally, in her cat form, she confronts Ollie and Alice; Ollie makes a crude cross with a pair of T-squares and Irena returns to human form. By this time, it has become clear that Irena can feel sexual desire, anger, jealousy, cruelty, and still not harm anyone; she is in control of her doubled identity. Ollie's rejection of her does not lead her to kill, and she seems to have achieved a balance between her masculine and feminine sides. However, when she returns to their apartment, Dr. Judd is waiting for her, and he tries to rape her. She defends herself by turning into a panther and kills the doctor, and deciding that her doubled nature is too great a danger and burden, she goes to the zoo and opens the panther's cage: the beast leaps on her and kills her and then is run over by a passing car as it tries to escape the zoo grounds. Ollie and Alice arrive together. Looking at Irena dead on the ground, Ollie says, "She never lied to us." They recognize that what Irena said—and was—was all true, but they turn their backs on her and walk away.

Irena is clearly a victim, not of her own doubled nature, but of the value systems and attitudes of the society in which she lives. In her cat form, she is monstrous, but the danger of the cat stems from her conviction that passionate feeling, any emotions that a respectable woman should not have—sexual desire, aggression, jealousy—are evil and that she is evil for having them. Ultimately, Irena cannot successfully adjust to her doubled nature because the masculine doubles that might define the other half of her identity are inadequate. In the terms we have developed, Irena is destroyed because she is enthralled: she is at once horrified and attracted to her own Otherness as imaged in the panther she metamorphoses into. She cannot reconcile herself to this Otherness because Ollie and Dr. Judd, who could become alternative images of Otherness for her and thus release her desires from her fears, both fail her. Ollie is a romance hero, whose only "desire," if we can call it that, is for a normality so bland that it seems identical with utter boredom. Dr. Judd is a classic

Gothic male: intelligent, egocentric, and finally, in his attraction to Irena, self-destructive. Irena is thus left with the conventional social evaluation of her nature, which condemns her. Without support, her momentary confidence in her ability to reconcile the two halves of her identity collapses, and she accepts the Gothic female's last, best lover, death.

In *Halloween,* Laurie is a twentieth-century version of the virtuous heroine; her ancestors are Emily St. Aubert, Maud Ruthyn, and particularly, the governess of *The Turn of the Screw.* Laurie is a straight-A student who doesn't date and who barely knows how to smoke a joint: in the scene in which she smokes pot with her friend Annie, she hacks and coughs whenever she inhales. Most important, though, Laurie spends most of her free time as a babysitter, and through the role of "governess," she is firmly linked to the heroine of James's novella. The film makes clear that Laurie genuinely likes the children she cares for, but it also makes clear that she uses her babysitting as a way of staying a child herself. The roles of child and mother are comfortable for her, but the thought of being a young woman—which, as we see in her friends Annie and Linda, means being sexually active—is clearly threatening to her. She does have sexual feelings; after smoking the joint, she confesses to Annie that she would like to go out with Ben Traemer. Annie arranges for Ben to take Laurie to the prom, but when she tells her about this, Laurie is horrified and insists that she will not go with him.

The masculine archetype in the film is embodied in Michael, who, when he was seven years old, murdered his sister on Halloween night, immediately after she had sex with her boyfriend. The murder is a typically Gothic moment of sexualized violence with an undertone of incest. The fact that Michael is a child both adds to the horror of what he does and serves as a perfect symbol of the fundamental infantilism of the masculine archetype. Michael is locked up in a mental hospital for fourteen years, but he escapes on Halloween to complete his murderous work. He systematically murders Laurie's friends and then, in the final twenty minutes of the film, comes after her.

Laurie, the model of virtuousness, seems completely at one with the values of the small-town America in which the action of the film takes place. This world of peaceful respectability, though, is simply a facade, for the teenagers in the town live by the pursuit of their own desire for pleasure. Laurie resists the lure of pleasure, and we might assume that, just as her virtue protects her from her own sexuality and the temptation of Ben Traemer, it will shield her from Michael, whose victims all seem to be sexually liberated. I would argue, though, that her very "goodness" draws Michael to her, for she is the purest—in every sense of the word—version of the feminine identity he can find and is thus his natural double. If he kills her, he will end the threat the feminine archetype poses for the masculine. In the sequel to *Halloween, Halloween II,* which continues the story of this night, we discover that Laurie is, in fact, Michael's other, long-lost, sister. Though this is not revealed in the first film, nor is the knowledge necessary for any analysis of it, it reveals how fully Michael and Laurie's story enacts the dynamics of the Gothic tradition.

Michael does not succeed in killing Laurie, but she is completely terrorized by his attack, which shakes her faith in the protective power of respectability. Indeed, the terror is multiplied, because twice she thinks she has killed him and saved herself and the children she is babysitting, and twice he rises to continue his pursuit of her. Laurie is saved by the intervention of Dr. Loomis, the psychiatrist who has been in charge of Michael's case at the hospital. Loomis has been hunting his escaped patient, for his encounters with Michael have converted him to the belief that Michael is a monster, "pure evil," the embodiment of death. Throughout the film, Loomis's behavior is erratic and twitchy; his look into the Gothic abyss through Michael has made him half crazy himself. He is searching for Michael, not to return him to the hospital, but to kill him. When at last he catches up with him, he pumps six shots into his patient, knocking him out a second-story window to save Laurie.

Laurie asks Loomis if Michael was the bogeyman, as the children have called him, for she has no other name for the terror she has experienced, and he replies "As a matter of fact, it was." But the children have not simply named the terror for her, they also have told her, "You can't kill the bogeyman." When Loomis looks out the window, Michael is gone. Neither respectability, repression, psychiatry, or finally, violence can dispose of the terror of the masculine archetype unleashed. The central difference between *Halloween* and other examples of the genre lies in its refusal to accept any moralizing statement at the close of the film. Michael is still loose, and Laurie is terrorized, and the terror cannot be confined by any conventional authority or values.

We can further trace the continuity of the tradition in one of the central twentieth-century Gothic texts, Alfred Hitchcock's *Psycho*. Hitchcock renews the dynamics of the genre by placing them in a modern context, though his story is the same one the Gothic fantasy always tells. The film dramatizes the collapse of two identities, Marion Crane and Norman Bates. Marion, at the beginning of the film, is deeply troubled and guilty about her affair with Sam Loomis; like any Gothic heroine, she yearns for respectability and fantasizes about Sam coming to the house for Sunday dinner, where her sister could serve as chaperone and witness to the propriety of the relationship. Unlike her nineteenth-century counterparts, Marion does have an active sexual life, but her shame at her illicit affair reveals that though she behaves differently from Emily St. Aubert and Maud Ruthyn, she feels and thinks in much the same way. To fulfill her dream of becoming a wife in her own home, she steals forty thousand dollars entrusted to her by her boss, thinking that if she can pay off Sam's debts, they will live happily ever after. In stealing the money, she attempts to obtain power over her own life through illegitimate means and, paradoxically, through that illegitimate power to gain legitimacy. The theft expresses the masculine archetype's egocentric need for power, even if Marion's ultimate end is feminine respectability; this act of masculine assertion plunges her into the abyss. She is now caught between two archetypal impulses: the will for virtue (marry Sam and live happily ever after) and the will for power (seize control of your identity by defying moral and social laws). Marion's guilt, as in Falkland and Williams, is a sign of the feminine archetype's presence; it overwhelms her, and she becomes paranoid, particularly menaced by a threatening figure of male authority, the policeman who wakes her up after she has spent the night sleeping in her car by the side of the road.

Marion drives on into the night and into the Bates Motel, just a few miles short of Sam and happiness. Her encounter with Norman Bates convinces her she must do the right thing and go back to the conventional world, even if it means giving herself up to the police. But she has wandered too far into the Gothic underworld and can't escape. Norman is shy, gentle, awkward, and even more trapped than Marion; he is simultaneously desperate for her company and anxious about her presence, attracted to her and afraid of her. He watches her undress to take a shower in a typically Gothic moment of voyeurism, but rather than becoming sexually roused, he is transformed into his murderous and violent Mother, his other self, who slashes Marion to death in the shower. Norman is a classic maimed androgyne; his feminine self is manifested in his "real" male identity as shy, proper—he cannot even say the word "bathroom"—gentle

Norman Bates, while the masculine archetype is embodied in Mother. This reversal of traditional archetypal and sexual correlation keeps him from recognizing his own doubled nature; he holds conversations with Mother, not realizing his actual mother is dead, and he does not understand that the slasher in the dress and wig is really himself. Watching Marion undress brings into focus the tension between Norman's sexuality and his doubled identity; his murder of Marion in the guise of Mother transforms sexuality into violence and circumvents the potentially explosive revelation of his ambiguous and twisted nature.

His identity and crime is uncovered—literally, as Sam rips the wig and dress off him in the fruit cellar—by Sam and Lila, Marion's sister who has come searching for her. These two are completely conventional romance characters: Sam is a strong, masculine hero and Lila is a sweet, if spunky, blonde. They are immediately attracted to each other and at the film's end, it seems clear that they will marry. As far as Sam is concerned, Marion and Lila are virtually interchangeable, and Lila seems perfectly willing to simply become Marion's replacement. Sam and Lila are even less interesting than Theodore, Matilda, and Isabella in *The Castle of Otranto*, whom they somewhat resemble, for as perfect romance types, they are empty and dull. The happy ending of the film is equally unsatisfying. Despite the presence of these "normal" characters and the apparent restoration of order, our sympathy is always with Norman, pathetic and monstrous as he is, and his situation is really the true conclusion of the film. The next to last scene is of Norman, sitting in his jail cell; on the soundtrack, we hear Mother's voice, cackling and babbling about how she wouldn't hurt a fly. A shot of Norman staring insanely at a fly dissolves into a shot of the car with Marion's body being hauled out of the swamp where he had hidden it. We are left, not with images of marriage and wholeness, but with a vision of death and disintegration.

Hitchcock uses the subversive dynamics of the Gothic, not only in his portrayal of Sam and Lila, but by his use of the detective and the detective's modern brother, the psychiatrist. Arbogast, the detective, thinks he is hot on Marion's trail but, unable to understand Norman, merely succeeds in arousing his fears that Mother will be discovered—that his own doubled nature will be revealed. So Norman puts on his dress, wig, and other identity and murders him. Hitchcock easily disposes of the detective as incapable of unraveling Norman's psyche; Arbogast, poor fool, thinks he is merely searching for a missing secretary and the missing money. In the third to last scene, Hitchcock also disposes of the character who ought to be able to solve the mysteries of Norman's mind, the psychiatrist, the detective of the subconscious. Dr. Richmond offers an explanation of Norman's behavior that seems to satisfy Sam, Lila, and the assembled town officials. In fact, he doesn't explain anything—he simply describes what Norman has done. Hitchcock chose to cast Simon Oakland as the psychiatrist; Oakland looks more like a linebacker or a dockworker, and he yells his lines at the top of his voice, waving his arms and wagging his finger in the faces of his audience. The performance completely strips the character of any authority, and the psychiatrist becomes an object of parody, as ridiculous and inadequate as Sam, Lila, and Arbogast.

Hitchcock's parody of the psychiatrist functions in much the same way as that character in *The Cat People* and *Halloween*. In these two films, the psychiatrist is either an evil figure or has been converted to a belief in the supernatural and thus, like Simon Oakland's psychiatrist, cannot offer any real analysis of what has happened in the course of the story. All three films escape becoming psychoanalytic tracts or allegories by incorporating that point of view, just as nineteenth-century Gothic fantasies subverted conventional Christian wisdom and moralism by making them part of the story. Through this use of the psychiatrist figure, the genre in the twentieth century retains its subversive, parodic relationship to orthodox cultural values and assumptions.

The genre's parody of the images of romance heroism generated in the twentieth century can also be seen clearly in Hitchcock's *Vertigo* (1958). In *Vertigo,* the very possibility of identity disintegrates. The movie reveals the instability of feminine and masculine identity, and the ineffectiveness of the detective, the psychiatrist, and the lover. John Ferguson is a less comic parody than Arbogast and Dr. Richmond in *Psycho* because he is the central character in the film. Like the governess in *The Turn of the Screw,* Ferguson tries to function as a detective, but his own unanalyzed obsessions and fears make him a party to the very crime he wishes to prevent.

Ferguson suffers from vertigo; his weakness, which he did not know he had, causes the death of a fellow policeman during a rooftop chase that opens the film. Though it is by no means clear that Ferguson could have saved the other man, he feels deeply guilty about his weakness and failure and has retired from the force to do nothing in particular. Ferguson has literally looked down into the abyss and become "unbalanced." Our sense of his inner weakness is reinforced by the fact that throughout the film he is known by a variety of names. To some characters he is Mr. Ferguson, to some he is John, to some Scottie, and to Midge, his friend and one-time fiancée, he is Johnny. The lack of a single name reflects Ferguson's own uncertainty about who he is. He will respond to any name anyone chooses to call him.

When Ferguson goes to see his old college aquaintance Gavin Elster, he hears Elster's wife, Madeleine, is behaving strangely and may be going insane. Elster wants him to follow her and keep an eye on her and to establish exactly what is going on. Ferguson discovers that Madeleine may be insane, or she may be possessed by the spirit of her grandmother, who committed suicide after her lover abandoned her. He is drawn into the case and tries to be both detective and psychiatrist, seeking to cure Madeleine by making her face her fears. He loses interest in curing himself, and, in trying to save her seems to forget his own weaknesses and fears. He also falls in love with Madeleine, who is an erotic image of someone even more vulnerable and haunted than he by a past disaster. In his various roles—detective-voyeur, psychiatrist, lover—he has projected both his fears and desires onto Madeleine, who serves as his feminine double. She is both an object of desire and a victim, and these two qualities are mutually reinforcing.

Ferguson's attempt to move from the role of detective to psychiatrist to lover fails. Madeleine apparently acts out her fate by hurling herself from a mission bell tower, leaving open the question of whether she was insane or possessed. Devastated by his second failure to save another from the abyss, he collapses in a severe depression and is hospitalized. Midge, who loves him, decides that their relationship is over. Previously, she has been content to play mother to Johnny—she even says "Mother's here" when trying to comfort him in the hospital—but she realizes that she can no longer help him by providing him with a mother-sister to whom he can come when things go badly. As always in the genre, the affective, feminized pattern of relationships is shown as powerless. When he gets out of the hospital, Ferguson can do nothing but revist the places he associates with Madeleine, for he is completely enthralled by her image, which is really, of course, a projection of his own identity.

Madeleine is, in fact, an illusion, a woman who does not exist. Ferguson never met the real Madeleine Elster, but rather a woman whom Elster persuaded to imitate his wife as part of a plot to kill her.

When Ferguson sees Judy Barton on the street, he is struck by her "resemblance" to the Madeleine he knew; he introduces himself and asks her out. Quickly, though, he begins to try to make her over into Madeleine, with no regard for her own wants or desires, unable to accept that Judy Barton is a real person. When he asks her to dye her hair to match Madeleine's, he says, "It can't matter to you." The psychiatrist-lover slowly is transformed into the patriarchal male, re-making women to suit his own desires and fantasies. When, in the process of tenderly recreating Madeleine, he reverts momentarily to his role as detective and discovers that Elster and Judy had conspired in the murder, he turns into an enraged monster, whose only desire is to punish Judy, not for her crime, but for denying him his fantasy lover. He takes her out to the mission and drags her to the top of the bell tower, suddenly cured of his vertigo. It seems possible that he will, in fact, throw her from the tower. Our sympathy is with Judy, for she reveals that she was deceived and threatened by Elster, who of course remade her just as Ferguson has, and she really loves Ferguson. Exactly what Ferguson's intentions are remain unclear, though he does not really seem to want to kill Judy. However, we never find out because, startled by the appearance of a nun who has come up to find out what is happening, the terrified Judy leaps from the bell tower, acting out the fate of the real Madeleine, becoming one with her in death.

Ferguson is left alone once again. He has failed in all his roles throughout the film: policeman, detective, psychiatrist, lover, and even in the role of patriarchal male, for he cannot protect Judy, as she asks just before she panics and jumps, from her guilt and fear. He could not, for he could not protect himself from his own guilt and fear. The film ends with Ferguson looking down at the body of his dead lover, staring wide-eyed into the abyss a third time. He faces again the fact of his own helplessness in a world in which horror is the only constant. No self is stable. Who is Madeleine Elster if she is really Judy Barton, and who is Judy Barton if she can become Madeleine Elster? Which John Ferguson is the real one? Johnny? Scottie? The detective? the lover? the sadist? At best, identity is a momentary projection of desire.

Vertigo tells again the story of the collapse of identity in the dominated-dominator relation of feminine to masculine, man to woman. Further, the film renews the Gothic's refusal to offer a heroic figure who might serve in an empowering social myth. No role is adequate to the demands of effective action because each role is poisoned at its root, in the divison of masculine and feminine into oppositions. The fusion of roles that Collins managed in *The Woman in White* and *The Moonstone* here dissolves once more. Like the governess in *The Turn of the Screw,* who "dispossesses" Miles, Ferguson has enacted a grotesque justice. He has discovered the murder he inadvertantly aided in and oversees the punishment of one of the murderers. But Judy is least reponsible for Madeleine's murder; she has simply been a pawn in Elster and Ferguson's plots from the beginning. She and Madeleine are the victims, doubles of each other, while Elster and Ferguson are their doubled oppressors. Ferguson's involvement in what happens is a result, not of his immorality, as is Elster's, but rather of his entrapment in the dynamics of victim and victimizer.

In returning the detective story to its Gothic origins, Hitchcock adds a brilliant stroke. He provides the analytical explanation of what has really happened before the end of the film, when Judy reveals the deception and murder in a letter to Ferguson she chooses not to send, in the hope that he will really fall in love with her. The narrative that underlies the bizarre and inexplicable events of the film is straightened out for us, but as we see Ferguson repeating the transformation of Judy into Madeleine, duplicating in his quest for love what Elster did as a means to murder, we see that that knowledge does not solve the mystery. When Ferguson realizes what we have known for a number of minutes, it simply drives him to a new level of madness and obsession. The cyclical pattern of *Vertigo,* always concluding with the fall into the abyss, exposes and destroys the last illusion by which the detective lives: knowing the truth, creating narrative through the scientific use of imagination, cannot liberate the self. The final image of Ferguson, again frozen in his confrontation with the Gothic, means that the genre has recaptured its progeny one more time, returning the detective and the audience to enthrallment to fear and desire.

Thus I would argue that though the Gothic story—a fable of disintegrating identity in a chaotic world of transformation and metamorphosis—has not changed, its audience and the orthodoxies of that audience have. Its world of sexual repression, incest, violence, doubled identities, and monsters is very familiar to us today; indeed, modern audiences think themselves liberated in comparison to their Victorian forebearers. Not only do we have what we like to think of as a more easy aquaintance with its content, but we also have a scientific vocabulary that explains—or perhaps tries to explain away—what we see in the Gothic fantasy. Clearly it is quite easy for people to read modern fantasies as simplified dramatizations of one of the great modern myths of identity. One of the commonplace analyses of the Gothic is that it reveals "the dark side" of human nature, a dark side whose existence has been analyzed and conceptualized in modern psychology, particularly in the theories of Freudian psychoanalysis. Thus, now, just as in the nineteenth century, the genre can be read as supporting the wisdom of an orthodox point of view of human nature and human value. Freudian theories of the mind, of course, have nowhere near the widespread popular appeal and influence of Christian values and ideals in the nineteenth century; but in our more pluralistic culture, in which it has become hard to discern any clearly dominant fable of identity, the Freudian vision is one very significant mythology. The Gothic turns Freudian orthodoxy back into an aesthetic construction, an aspect of fantasy, thus subverting it. While it might appear to "support" this vision of selfhood, in fact, its coupling of Freudian archetypes and patterns with tales of the supernatural implies that both are equally aspects of imagination.

The difference between the relationship of the modern Gothic fantasy to orthodox Freudianism and, by implication, to scientific ways of understanding the world and the relationship of nineteenth-century fantasies to traditional Christian values lies in two factors. First, Christianity accepts the existence and power of the supernatural, which science does not. Thus, in some sense, the nineteenth-century Gothic, with its evocation of the supernatural and irrational, was on common ground with the dominate orthodoxy of the time, though it mapped out that ground in a radically different way. In the twentieth century, when scientific and rationalist values seem dominant, the supernatural aspects of the Gothic appear more alien than ever. Thus we have either films like *The Cat People* or *Halloween,* which reassert the reality of the supernatural in the face of psychoanalytic knowledge and in explicit defiance of orthodox assumptions about the way the world is, or films like *Psycho* or even more strikingly, *Vertigo,* in which all events seem fully rationalized and scientifically explicable but yet defy such treatment.

The second, and more important, difference lies in the fact that Christianity preceded the Gothic fantasy, but the Gothic fantasy preceded Freudian psychoanalytic theories. Indeed, I would argue that the fantasies of the nineteenth century helped create the imaginative and cultural climate that led to the formulation of such modern mythologies as Freudian psychology and literary modernism. This fact of historical precedence and the pluralistic nature of modern culture make the relationship of the genre to Freudianism somewhat ambiguous. Through Freud's work and literary modernism, the Gothic vision was, as I shall argue, transformed into a mythology, a genuine vision of what the world and the self are, rather than simply a parody of values that had worn out their usefulness in a new era. Thus, the twentieth-century Gothic is engaged in a peculiar kind of shadow boxing. Some of the orthodoxies it parodies are, in many ways, serious versions of its own world, myths made from the dynamics and themes of the fantasy itself. The parodying of these modern mythologies is also, paradoxically, part of the popularization of their vision. The modern Gothic is thus in the unusual position of undermining its own offspring and, in doing so, spreading the orthodoxy it subverts.

We may wonder why this relationship continues. After all, the outworn nineteenth-century conventions and values, particularly the extraordinary tendency to sexual repression, seem to have evaporated. Why would fully articulated mythologies based on the Gothic fantasy continue to provoke and sustain new fantasies? First, though the shape of anxiety and fear has changed, these emotions are not gone, nor have their sources changed. To have dealt with nineteenth-century anxiety about identity and sexuality does not mean we have come to terms with these problems; I do not think we can argue that we have solved the problems of identity and sexuality all that much better than the people of the last century. Second, those modern mythologies for which the Gothic fantasy prepared the way do not fully resolve the its implied critique of either romance mythologies of identity or the transcendent power of the imagination. Indeed, as we shall see in the next two sections, modernism and Freudianism "resolve" the genre's parodic relationship to the world by reviving the romance mythology and accepting the Gothic vision of horror as an accurate description of reality rather than as a critique of specific ideas about reality that have failed.

The Gothic and Modernism

In discussing the relationship between the Gothic fantasy and modernism we are dealing with the ways in which the motifs, dynamics, and themes of a popular genre are transformed and used by a much broader and complex cultural movement. Many strains of modernism remain relatively uninfluenced by the Gothic tradition, and I do not wish to claim any direct link between the two. Nevertheless, the

Gothic fantasy introduced a number of themes, ideas, and images that the modernists took over; it helped prepare the way for modernism and provided some of the tools with which the modernists worked. Ironically, its greatest influence shows in the modernist attempts to revive the romance quest hero, the figure that had disappeared in the Gothic parody of the romance's fable of identity. Specifically, we will examine this influence in a discussion of Conrad's *Heart of Darkness,* a work that defines the Romance quest pattern in much modernist fiction, such as *The Good Soldier, The Great Gatsby,* and *Absalom, Absalom.* Conrad's novella, published in *Blackwood's Magazine* in 1899, is the clearest link between the Gothic and modernism, a link symbolized by the fact that *Blackwood's* had been an important force in the popularization of the Gothic fantasy.

Before turning to *Heart of Darkness,* though, we will examine some of the more general connections between the Gothic fantasy and modernism.[2] The sensibility of both reflects an essentially apocalyptic vision. The disintegration of the house of Usher, the massacre of Victor Frankenstein's family, the threatened devastation of England by Dracula and his army of vampires are all examples of this in the Gothic. The sense of horror that seizes such characters as Emily St. Aubert and Clara Wieland is a precursor of the awareness of final disaster and destruction that informs many modernist works. The distinction between the two lies in the fact that the Gothic fantasy tends to focus on the movement toward collapse, the moment when the house of Usher disintegrates into the dark tarn in which it is mirrored, while the modernist sensibility seems more postapocalyptic, as when Jake Barnes looks about the ruins of a dead and empty civilization. This distinction is not a hard and fast one, however, perhaps because for a truly apocalyptic sensibility, the terrible moment is always now. Both traditions are colored by a sense of crisis, of breakdown and collapse. The tension that calls the Gothic into being at the beginning of the nineteenth century also marks the creation of modernism at the beginning of the twentieth despite the fact that the Gothic reflects the anxieties of the middle class, and modernism is a movement formed around artists and intellectuals.

Both genres are founded on a feeling of isolation; in each the protagonists are alone, cut off from a communal reality that might offer support for individual identity. Victor Frankenstein is modern in part because he breaks away from his family and works in isolation; from Manfred through Dracula Gothic protagonists must live in terms of their own will and desire. They become self-created men. In the modernist tradition, Jay Gatsby is a self-created being, a "son of God." Modernist protagonists, such as the various voices in "The Waste Land," have found that traditional values fail them; in "Usher," we see also see a failure of tradition, albeit a perverse one.

The isolation of the Gothic and modernist protagonist is enforced, not only by the failure of communal and traditional value systems, but by the breakdown of conventional concepts of causality and the idea of wholeness of personality and character. The doubled and divided characters of the Gothic fantasy reflect the break-down of conventional notions of what constitutes a self. This same disintegration appears, more realistically, in the modernist fascination with states of consciousness and in characters such as Edward Ashburham and Jay Gatsby, who appear to be one thing and are another.The Gothic use of dreamscapes, nightmares, and hallucinations as models for its narrative also anticipates some of the modernist experiments in storytelling. "The Waste Land" certainly duplicates the effect of a nightmare, as do sections of *Absalom, Absalom*, "Death in Venice," and "The Metamorphosis." The subjective worlds of *Mrs. Dalloway* and *To the Lighthouse*, as well as *Ulysses*, refine and develop the Gothic experiments with states of consciousness and the relationship of consciousness to reality.

These parallels in the use of dreams and the exploration of states of subjectivity bring us to another link between the Gothic and modernism, and that is the rejection of realism. Neither tradition makes any pretense of its fictionality, and in fact, each exploits its freedom from surface realism to fracture time sequence and narrative form. The enfolded stories that make up *Frankenstein* and the various points of view in Hogg's *Memoirs* and Stevenson's *Jekyll and Hyde* are similar to the multiple consciousnesses of Woolf's novels and the fragmentation of narrative structure in *The Secret Agent* and *The Great Gatsby*. The genres also share the quality of spectacle; modernist texts are spectacles, not only in the presentation of the strange and bizarre, as in "The Waste Land" and *Light in August*, but also in the sense that they are displays of literary pyrotechnics, as in *Ulysses*. The notion of spectacle is not confined to popular literature in the nineteenth century—in music, both Berlioz and Wagner come to mind—but the Gothic spectacle, like the modernist, is an aspect of the self-proclaimed fictiveness of the tradition. In contrast, realist spectacle, the panoramas of *Middlemarch* and *War and Peace*, was intended to enhance the text's realism by broadening its scope.

Perhaps the relation between the Gothic fantasy and the modernist movement can best be brought into focus by their common conception of the wasteland. The Arctic desert in which Frankenstein and his creature die, the ruined castles and haunted houses of Otranto and Udolpho, the Abbey of St. Clare in *The Monk*, the house of Usher, Bartram Haugh in *Uncle Silas*, Bly in *The Turn of the Screw*, Castle Dracula and the barren moors surrounding Baskerville Hall— the Gothic is full of images of ruins and blasted landscapes. As in Eliot's work, these wastelands serve as metaphors for the mental state of the protagonists. The chaotic world of the Gothic fantasy is an anticipation of the empty landscape of the grimmest versions of the modernist vision. In *Gatsby*, Nick Carraway describes the world to which Gatsby awakens after he finally loses Daisy as "material without being real," and that description fits the chaotic horror of the Gothic world as well.

The two traditions, then, share a number of motifs and archetypes. These parallels of method and sensibility do not, though, define the essential cultural link between the Gothic and the modernist movement. The two use very similar materials and techniques in radically different ways. Both create a world apart from conventional reality, liberated from conventional ideals and restrictions. But where the Gothic vision is parodic, the modernist uses Gothic materials as the basis of a new mythology, as a vision of what reality is actually like. The modernists shared with the romantics a belief in the transcendent power of imagination, but when they looked into the heart of reality they found, not joy and liberation, but horror.

The transformation of parody into cosmology is part of the adaptation of elements of a popular genre to an elite literary movement. The readers of the Gothic fantasy did not want an alternative vision of reality, not from their art; they wanted entertainment and release, at the least, and at the most, a gradual definition of the tensions that led to their need for escape. Whatever the problems that gave rise to the Gothic, their solution would exist in reality, not in art. Art would entertain and confirm conventional wisdom, though the genre also managed to convey to its audience information about what was wrong with their pleasure and their wisdom. The Gothic fantasy was, not a call to revolution, but at best a gesture of revolt, a momentary break with the values and attitudes of everyday life. By comparison with the modernist writers, the authors of Gothic fantasies dared relatively little; but because the genre never rejected, or claimed to transcend, the culture that had generated it, it possessed a greater, though more diffuse and admittedly ambiguous, capacity for social and political impact than the later tradition.

Modernist writers were not in any sense popular; the Gothic writers were rooted in the real world because their fiction had to enter the marketplace and compete for an audience's attention and money. They could not escape from their culture and made no claim to do so. Modernist writers, though, resolutely placed themselves outside the commerical world in which art was exchanged as a product and, indeed, glorified this fact. The list of works that were either privately printed or banned, or both, or that suffered a great deal of difficulty in obtaining a commercial publisher is, not only long, but from the modernists' point of view, an indicator of the vitality and importance of their art. They saw their alienation as unbridgeable. The connection with the conventional world signaled by the popularity of the Gothic fantasy—which, I would argue, is what vitalized and sustained the genre—represented for the modernists imaginative enervation and corruption. For them, the work of art was a sacramental, revolutionary act: art could transform the world. The transformation that this uncontaminated art would effect, though, was essentially a move backward, to predemocratic, precapitalist world; this is the note sounded over and over in Pound, Eliot, Hemingway, Yeats, Faulkner, Woolf, and Lawrence. The sacramental power of art, which transcended through imagination the abyss of reality, would transform the self, renew myth as a way of understanding the world, and in the process, rid culture of the corrupting influence of middle-class "art."

Modernism was a literary movement meant for a society that existed only in the minds of its creators; modernist works imagine a world very different from the capitalist, industrial, middle-class, urban world in which they actually existed. Indeed, the mythologizing of the Gothic into a vision of reality allowed modernist writers to define themselves in opposition to a hopelessly irredeemable world of horror, which they identified as modern Western culture. The power of art was, modernists hoped, such that its creation for the alternative, nonexistent society might in fact call that society into being. This society and its attendant culture, created out of transcendent imagination, would then replace the abyss. In its insistence on the self-redeeming power of imagination and the validity of a mythological cosmos that existed as a purely imaginary reality outside social and cultural conditions, the modernist movement cut itself off from significant political impact. From the modernist point of view, all political change could be accomplished imaginatively, without the aid of what one normally might think of as political activity. As the Gothic fantasy remained within the culture that produced it and made no claims for a transcendent vision, it placed the act of imagination, fantasy, firmly within the social and cultural context from which it sprang and thus established its potential political significance and power.

Paradoxically, the mythologization of the Gothic fantasy in modernism and Freudianism became the basis upon which the modernists and Freudians attempted to revive the empowering fable of the romance quest hero, the very figure that the Gothic had revealed as impossible to imagine in contemporary culture. The modernists' attempt to restore the quest hero is an indication of their orientation to a time and culture other than their own, a world located, for them, in the past: the premodern world in which the romance myth was a fully integrated vision of identity. In their nostalgia, the modernists tried to restore that which the Gothic attempted to reject. Of course, their uses of the quest hero are complex, and often ambiguous and ironic; it would be foolish to characterize their works as simply nostalgia, without relevance of modern imaginative needs and demands. However, it seems that modernist heroes are most compelling when, like the Gothic protagonists, they express ironically their own irrelevance and failure.

In the Gothic fantasy, no heroic character was possible; the characters who aspired to that status destroyed themselves or created monsters. Only the detective achieved any success in attaining heroic status, and he too fails to achieve a full resolution of the fragmented self that lies at the center of the genre. In our discussion of *Heart of Darkness*, we will examine the paradigmatic transformation of the Gothic fantasy into modernism, and the ways in which the modernist sensibility uses the detective and the dynamics of voyeurism and enthrallment to recreate the heroic male identity that the Gothic parodies.

Heart of Darkness

In *Heart of Darkness*, Conrad makes some minor allusions to the Gothic tradition, but much more important than these are the ways in which the novel uses the paradigms and dynamics of the genre. Marlowe's journey into the jungle is a descent into the Gothic world, a world where conventional values and ideals are suspended or irrele-

vant in the face of mystery, isolation, and suspense. Marlowe feels
the pull of the jungle and acknowledges his temptation to "go over
the side for a bit of a dance." He both fears and desires the temptation and becomes enthralled to Kurtz, the man who has gone all the
way over the side, into the heart of the abyss. Marlowe and Kurtz are
doubles, but Conrad varies from the traditional pattern in not making them mirror images of one another. Kurtz has entered the underworld on his quest for godhood, and he thus corresponds to the
usual paradigms of masculine identity that we find in the Gothic
fantasy. But for Marlowe, the quest is only metaphorical, and despite
his enthrallment to the figure of Kurtz, he retains some of the analytical distance we have come to associate with the detective. Thus in
Heart of Darkness, we have two protagonists, Marlowe and Kurtz;
this division of the focus of the novel is also a departure from the
Gothic tradition, which allows for only one protagonist and his double, who are locked in deadly struggle. Marlowe and Kurtz never
struggle, for Marlowe is content to remain in the position of voyeur
throughout the novel, never giving in to the temptations and possibilities of the Gothic. He is in this sense—with his devotion to
duty, his adherence to conventional values, his respect for the chief
accountant, who has retained all the trappings of civilization in the
face of the jungle, and for the cannibals on his steamer who restrain
themselves from eating human flesh—an essentially feminine figure.
Yet at the same time, he does not come under the domination of
Kurtz as has the Harlequin. Kurtz is the traditional masculine
Gothic protagonist, who becomes a monstrous parody of his own
spiritual and intellectual ambitions in his pursuit of power and his
identity. He is enthralled to the Gothic vision and to his own nature,
because as he has found they are the same thing. But Marlowe escapes this fate by accepting a feminized identity. Able to respond to
his situation passively, he becomes the investigator of Kurtz's bizarre
life and death, and he produces, like any good detective, a narrative,
a story that organizes the inexplicable experiences of the Gothic
world for those who have never been through it. As a voyeur and
detective, Marlowe is allowed to participate in Kurtz's disintegrating
quest and to emerge safe on the other side of the chasm in which
Kurtz saw the horror.

Yet Marlowe does not escape untainted by his experience, for despite his feminized identity, he, like Kurtz, cannot really accept the
feminine. Kurtz has the choice between two women, the Intended,
his European fiancée, and his African mistress, who holds out her

arms to him as he leaves. This double image of woman, one respectable, the other wild, divides feminine identity, a division Marlowe
accepts and believes in. Kurtz's fiancée is pure and innocent, according to Marlowe, a spiritual being who, like all women, is "out of it"
and must be kept so. Nevertheless the Intended, her purity symbolized by the whiteness of her face in the dark room where Marlowe meets her, is by that same whiteness connected to the corruption of the city in which she lives, "the whited sepulchre." In her, we
see the image of feminine purity united with the image of death and
corruption. In Kurtz's African mistress, we see the image of woman
as a part of the Gothic world, as a sensual and sexual being. She is
separated from the Intended by the gulf of the Gothic abyss. But
when Marlowe, trying to soothe the Intended, tells her that Kurtz's
last words, "The horror, the horror," were her name, he inadver-
tently makes the link between her and the world that he wants to
believe she is "out of."

In order to preserve the illusion of feminine exclusion from the
Gothic world, Marlowe tells a lie, even though he admits he hates
lies, for they have about them the "taint of mortality." The lie is
necessary, not for the preservation of the Intended's innocence, but
his own: insofar as he has internalized aspects of feminine identity,
he needs to protect that identity from contact with the horror of the
Gothic world. In lying to the Intended about Kurtz, he preserves her
illusions, but even more important, his own, about both women and
himself. Despite his evident acceptance of the fact that he is not "out
of it," Marlowe needs to retain some degree of distance from
Kurtz—the barriers of feminine identity, of the voyeur and the detective—to keep himself from seeing fully his doubled relationship
to him. In Marlowe, we see an attempt to make the artist an image of
the androgyne, with a double in the wasteland, but able still to return from that terrible place to tell the story and, in telling it, to
convert fear into pleasure, chaos into order, anxiety into closure.

Yet Conrad's revision of the dynamics of enthrallment and his creation of a narrator who appears to resolve the tensions of the Gothic
is undercut, not only by Marlowe's inability to accept his full complicity in the Gothic world, but also by the attitude toward that
world reflected in the story. Conrad makes overt the critique of conventional values and attitudes that is the underlying theme and structure of the genre; indeed, he expands upon this, for he calls into
question the whole of Western civilization. As Marlowe travels up-
river, all Western mores are revealed to be artificial, accidental cre-

ations of time and place with no intrinsic value or meaning. At worst, they are excuses to plunder and pillage the "uncivilized" Africans. At best, the values of Western civilization become, as they do for Marlowe and the chief accountant, empty rituals that form absurd but usable barriers against the horror that lies all around them.

Conrad's indictment of European civilization, though similar to that found in the Gothic fantasy, is more extreme, for he does not see the "jungle" as the outgrowth of specific cultural anxieties or tensions, but as the primal reality underlying all the artifices of civilization. The Gothic world is, not an impalpable nothingness taking its shape from the culture that dominates it, but rather the substructure of all cultures, whether European or African. The conflict between European and African cultures is, in fact, what makes possible the discovery of the single world that exists beneath them and what makes possible Kurtz's quest and destruction. In the conflict between the two cultures, their artificial nature is revealed and Kurtz is given the opportunity to act out his fantasies, living among the Africans and writing his essay for European consumption.

Conrad, of course, sees civilization as a necessary lie; without it, we would all, like Kurtz, find ourselves going over the side, free of all restraint but the outermost circle of our own fears and desires, a freedom that renders the self monstrous. When Kurtz, writing from the heart of the horror, scrawls "Exterminate all the brutes" in the margin of his essay, he may intend it to apply only to the Africans, but in fact it must apply to himself and to all human beings, for no one in the novel is a greater brute than he. Like Dracula, Kurtz is finally borne off into the darkness by his own monstrous egotism. Civilization is really only an elaborate series of barriers against that horror.

Yet despite this extreme and desperate defense of the value of respectability and repression, Marlowe, who sees the collapse of European values on the one hand and the collapse of the self without them on the other, recognizes that he has only a "choice of nightmares." Once the artificiality of civilization has been revealed, it can no longer provide a bridge across the abyss. For Conrad, the nightmares are true, two faces of a single, horrible reality. Though all conceptions of reality other than the horror are lies, only lies can form an alternative to horror. Marlowe's position as voyeur, detective, and narrator is thus shown to be hopeless but necessary. To create narrative is to create order, but to assert the existence of any real order is to lie. The values of the conventional world have collapsed, and the romance quest for identity has failed, and all that is left are lies, stories that have about them the taint of mortality.

In his revision of the Gothic fantasy into modernist myth, Conrad has moved the artist to the center of his vision, but the artist is still caught in the trap that ensnared the detective, his Gothic analogue. Marlowe says, "We live as we dream, alone," and in saying this he accepts the inescapableness of the passive, voyeuristic identity he has created for himself. Out of the doubled quest for identity in *Heart of Darkness,* Marlowe's peculiarly circumspect and oblique search for Kurtz, comes the figure of the solitary dreamer, the artist whose only power is the power of lies.

The figure of the artist as passive observer is a common one. Earlier examples of such figures certainly exist: Miles Coverdale in *The Blithedale Romance* and, in many ways, Ishmael in *Moby Dick* are two examples. However, the pattern seems pervasive in modernist fiction: Van Aschenbach observes Tadzsu, John Dowl observes Edward Ashburnham, Quentin Compson observes Thomas Sutpen, and Nick Carraway observes Jay Gatsby. In *The Sun Also Rises,* Jake Barnes also falls into this category, as he watches Robert Cohn and Pedro Romero. Of course, Marlowe and Kurtz also fit this paradigm. The exact relationship of observer and observed varies from book to book, but in all instances we can apply the characteristic Gothic pattern of enthrallment to each of these pairs. With the exception of the protagonists of *Death in Venice,* which constitutes a peculiar variation, each of these pairs has as the voyeur a passive male and as the observed, an active, aggressive male, one who is acting out variations of the conventional ideal of masculine identity, the ideal of the quest hero. Some heroes, like Ashburnham and Cohn, prove to be hollow echoes of the ideal; Romero, in contrast, almost seems equal to the demands of the tradition, even if he is also irrelevant to Jake and the modern world.

Each observer looks on with mixed feelings, variations on the Gothic combination of fear and desire; perhaps Quentin Compson's attitude toward Sutpen and Marlowe's toward Kurtz come closest to this particular formulation. Carraway's response to Gatsby seems to be amazement and moral disgust, or "unaffected scorn," as he calls it. The observer becomes the double of the man he observes, and the act of voyeurism becomes an act of self-definition, as the observer participates in the doomed quest of the hero from a safe distance. Each of the observers struggles to achieve analytical distance from the one he observes through the process of storytelling and thus to

escape his enthrallment to the Other. Each of these pairs of characters embodies a single identity, masculine and feminine, imaginative
and active; in this way, the novels offer images of the integration of
the feminine with the masculine, suggesting once again the fundamentally androgynous nature of the artist and his status as whole
identity in worlds of fragmented characters.

This process, is on the one hand, an attempt to redefine male identity in terms that put an end to the self-destructive pattern of the
Gothic male and the observed characters in each of the novels. But at
the same time, since the feminized observer must define himself, find
his story, through his contact with the traditionally masculine protagonist, the modernist use of the dynamic is also a revival and re-
suscitation of the patriarchal male. Kurtz, Gatsby, and Sutpen are
nothing if not would-be patriarchs. The observers who record their
lives come to see them as greater than other men, and their stories
become the observers' stories. The feminine self remains dependent
on the masculine self for definition and form, for the story the narrator tells is, finally, an act of hero-worship. Stable, whole identity is
really impossible; one can act or one can imagine, but not both. The
narrators achieve a kind of pale, reflected existence, which takes what
light it has from the dying fires of the hero, immolated on the altar of
his masculine identity. There are no stories about the feminine identity in this strain of modernism—this is obviously not true, for instance, of Virginia Woolf—for the only real stories are the tales of
the masculine quest hero. Yet the attitude toward the hero is equivocal: none of the narrators truly embraces without question the image of the patriarch, and the masculine identity is shown over and
over again to be self-destructive, even if gloriously so. The circle of
enthrallment is never quite closed, and the elevation of imaginative
energy over the physical energy of the observed character gives to the
narrator some degree of power and control. As storyteller, he is the
final creator of the observed character's life, the one who gives real
meaning to it.

In looking at the ways in which certain strains of modernism adapt
Gothic dynamics and themes, we see that they are looking at the
romance tradition through the lens of the Gothic, redefining the
world in its terms and rebuilding the quest hero through the modifi-
cations of its paradigms. Insofar as modernism is concerned with the
recovery and reestablishment of myth, this is natural and necessary,
for the Gothic fantasy was in fact a demand for new, empowering
myths of identity. But insofar as the modernists revived the myths

that the earlier tradition parodied, they rejected its imperative to explore other paths and possibilities.

The Science of Fear: Sigmund Freud Meets Dracula

No discussion of the Gothic can avoid discussing Freud; one of the most obvious ways of thinking about the genre is to read it in terms of Freud's system.[3] Its monsters become the id, the dynamics of sadomasochism the result of Oedipal anxieties, and the self-destructive impulses of the protagonists the expression of the death instinct. We cannot pretend that the striking parallels between Freud's thought and the Gothic fantasy do not exist. The world of the fantasy, operating through transformation, metamorphosis, and symbol, is narrative that appears to be a dream; its dynamics correspond exactly to Freud's descriptions of the nature of the dreamwork in *The Interpretation of Dreams*. For Freud, dreams are the expression of wishes unacknowledged in waking life; the Gothic fantasy is the expression of the fears and desires created, but unacknowledged, by conventional culture. Like a dream, it reveals the inner life of the individual. The likeness of the analyst to the detective is almost too well known to be mentioned. In 1913, Theodore Reik actually suggested to Freud that his methods were like those of Sherlock Holmes, though Freud himself was somewhat leery of the comparison.[4] We are drawn irresistibly by the apparent links between the Gothic tradition and Freud. Indeed, Freud wrote an essay on horror literature, "On the Uncanny"; he was aware of the Gothic, as he was obviously aware of Holmes, though perhaps his contact with the tradition lay more through German than English sources.

What, though, are we to make of these correspondences? We may take the approach of the orthodox Freudian and assume that the connections are inevitable; since Freud described accurately and scientifically the nature of psychic activity, the Gothic fantasy, insofar as it seeks to deal with states of mind and aspects of consciousness, anticipates the truths that Freud discovered at the beginning of the twentieth century. This view, of course, ends discussion of the Gothic as a literary, or cultural, phenomenon. Since all art would consequently reflect these basic truths, one major objection—other than those one might have to the assumption that what Freud said constitutes objective truth—lies in the fact that we must explain the development of a popular genre in England and America that seems to anticipate so much of Freud so explicitly. The particularly compel-

ling appearance of a link between Freud and the Gothic in fact suggests that something other than the natural correspondence of
literature to life is involved here. Further, it is somewhat difficult to
imagine the eighteen-year-old Monk Lewis simply stumbling onto
the deep truths of the human psyche based on his enthusiastic reading of *The Castle of Otranto* and *The Mysteries of Udolpho*.

Another explanation might simply call the parallels fortuitous.
Whether what Freud says is true or not, as a hermeneutical system,
his vision fits the Gothic fantasy, allowing the critic to convert its
imaginative dynamic into Freud's intellectual dynamic, making the
Gothic into an allegory. This approach is certainly possible, but by
begging the question of Freud's truth value, it also begs the question
of the exact nature and meaning of his relationship to the Gothic.
The problem remains, Why do these two visions, one a popular literary genre, the other the scientific-philosophical theories of a Vien-
nese Jewish doctor, correspond so well? If we discard on the one
hand the assumption that Freud is telling us the whole truth and
nothing but the truth and, on the other, an attitude of pragmatism,
we are left with two possibilities. First, direct influence, which given
the chronology, must mean the influence of the Gothic on Freud,
and second, the possibility that the two have a common, or at least
related, origin. The first seems highly unlikely. If we cannot imagine
Monk Lewis stumbling upon psychoanalysis, it is equally unlikely
that Freud was led to his theories by a close reading of *The Monk* or
any collection of Gothic texts. However, the second possibility is,
not only the only one left, but also the most probable.

In discussing Freud in relation to the Gothic, or in relation to
anything, we are always faced with the fact that his thought is very
complex and difficult, occasionally contradictory, and that he was
constantly revising his ideas. At the beginning of his career, he as-
serted that hysteria was not a typically feminine disorder; by the end
of his life, he has reversed this view. He was, despite his genius,
capable of producing such nonsense as *Moses and Monotheism*.
Though he always claimed to be a scientist, he was also an artist and
a philosopher, and there are as many views of what he actually was
and what he really meant as there are readers of his works. The de-
bate over whether he should be regarded primarily as a scientist or a
humanist still goes on today. Thus, any discussion of his relationship
to the Gothic must be somewhat tentative, for there are perhaps as
many versions of Freud as there are versions of modernism. Our
purpose is, not be to answer through this discussion what Freud is

about, but to suggest some of his continuities with the nineteenth-century world in which he was born and raised (Freud was born in 1856), and how, by comparing the dynamics and functions of the Gothic with the dynamics and functions of certain aspects of his system, we can better understand some of the implications of what the most influential thinker of the twentieth century had to say. Further, by comparing his vision to the fantasy, we may be able to see more clearly why Freud, whose ideas are radical, unconventional, and fly in the face of many middle-class assumptions, has become so influential an intellectual figure. His popularity and power is, as I shall show, founded on much the same basis as the popularity and power of the Gothic.

The Gothic is not a crude anticipation of Freudianism, nor its unacknowledged father. Rather, the two are cousins, responses to the problems of selfhood and identity, sexuality and pleasure, fear and anxiety as they manifest themselves in the nineteenth and early twentieth centuries. The Gothic arises out of the immediate needs of the reading public to escape from conventional life and articulate and define the turbulence of their psychic existence. We may see Freud as the intellectual counterpart of this process. Thomas Kuhn has suggested that scientific revolutions occur when previously usable scientific theories begin to break down, to generate more problems than they can solve, demanding new paradigms to explain new phenomena.[5] Freud stands as a major figure in the revolution that changed the Western conception of the inner life of the individual. Four hundred years before him, human beings had souls, and this concept defined their inner lives. By 1900, he had redefined the inner life in terms of the psyche: a purely secular, biologically based conception. The distinction between the two explanations is by no means absolute; to wrestle with temptation is to resist pleasure principle, and though Freud does not believe in life after death, he does use the German word for soul in discussing the psyche.

The Gothic was part of this process of revising—or, from one point of view, creating—this new conception of inner life. It, of course, never became a rigorous intellectual system that seeks to explain itself, as did Lockean, Hartleyan, or Freudian psychology. But it articulated the need for such a system, serving as a cultural signal of the fear and anxiety that sought escape and therapy in its fantasies. It is linked to the Freudian synthesis in two other important ways. I would argue first that it acclimatized the culture to the types of ideas Freud was to present as truth by presenting them as fiction. Freud was acceptable to the early twentieth century, particularly in England and America, exactly because the imaginative way had been prepared by the Gothic fantasy.

One of the most important aspects of this process is the use of the dream/nightmare narrative characteristic of the Gothic. In their subversion of traditional linear narrative structures and their substitution of transformation and metamorphosis for clearly defined cause-and-effect, the fantasies help prepare people for the ways in which Freud reads and makes sense of the dream work. The dream work thus becomes a recognizable genre, a type of text, neither a visitation from the gods nor the result of poor digestion. The rhetoric of the Gothic easily leads its readers to take everything in the fantasy symbolically, and the impulse to do so is almost irresistible. The imaginative pull of the genre comes in part from our sense that what we see there represents something in ourselves. It leaves this something more or less open, but it teaches its readers and its culture to respond to the images of the dream or fantasy symbolically. For Freud, of course, neither dreams nor literary texts are simply symbolic; they are also allegories of the archetypal struggle between id, ego, and superego. As his work developed, Freud became more and more convinced, not only of the specific content of the dream work's symbols for the individual patient, but that its symbols were in fact general, common to all dreamers. In this sense, he returns the world of Gothic fantasy to its origins, to the myths of identity of the romance tradition. If, as we have said, the fantasy is in part the romance fable broken and deprived of its vision, Freud is, in fact, restoring the pieces to wholeness.

Second, the Gothic fantasy prepares the way for Freud's vision, not only through teaching people to accept and read the dream work, but by affirming the existence and importance of fantasy, or psychic life, itself. Insofar as it is a rejection of romantic or religious fables of the self, a world drawn not from external systems or myths but growing out of the dynamics and necessities of the writers' and readers' private lives, the Gothic makes public the fact of inner existence. Characters in romances before the eighteenth century have relatively little of what we could call inner lives. Characters in realistic fiction have fairly complex ones—that, of course, is one of our criteria for judging a character successful in a novel—but they tend to be defined in relation to the external world, at least in the nineteenth century. The Gothic not only derives from, and affirms, the inner life of the individual, but it investigates the dynamics of that inner life, those phenomena we call states of mind and modes of consciousness. These are not explained systematically in the fantasy, but when Freud begins to offer a systematic analysis, the Gothic has helped prepare people for what he is talking about. Of course, it is hardly the only product of nineteenth-century culture and imagination that serves this function; Wagner's operas do much the same thing: *Tristan and Isolde, The Ring,* and *Parsifal* are about nothing if not states of mind. At the same time, we also see in these operas a certain Gothicness of tone and mood.

We have been discussing essentially formal connections between the Gothic fantasy and Freudianism, but clearly there are substantive, or thematic, links as well. Both Freud and the Gothic focused on the nature of human identity; both located the arena in which that drama of selfhood was played out as the family, and both saw it as a drama of struggle between masculine and feminine, a struggle for control of sexual energy. Freud's goal was to liberate the self from the crippling constraints of this struggle, which he calls neurosis, by giving the patient a genuine understanding of the sources of his dysfunction. The dynamics of the Oedipal conflict parallel the dynamics of the conflict between masculine and feminine modes of identity in the Gothic novel. Both patterns unite fear and desire, fusing sexuality and violence. Indeed, Freud follows out some of the most radical implications of the Gothic in his assertion of the fundamental bisexuality of all people and the dangers of conventional moral ideals:

> We may thus well raise the question whether our "civilized" sexual morality is worth the sacrifice which it imposes upon us, the more so if we are still so insufficiently purged of hedonism as to include a certain degree of individual happiness among the aims of our cultural development. It is certainly not the physician's business to come forward with proposals for reform, but it seemed to me that, by pointing out what significance the injurious results of our sexual morality, enumerated by von Ehrenfels, have in connection with our increase of modern nervousness, I could supplement the account he gives of them, and could thus support the urgency of such reform.[6]

This is Freud at his most radical, at least from a social point of view, rejecting the standards and traditions of the nineteenth century about both sexuality and pleasure and, in his ideas about bisexuality, its conceptions of masculine and feminine identity.

But at the same time that his vision seems to affirm some of the implied radicalism of the Gothic, we can also see that he carries with him a number of assumptions and attitudes that affirm much of what the genre ultimately subverts. In part, as with the modernists we have discussed, this was inevitable; Freud was seeking to create a positive, empowering analytical vision of the human psyche and he could not content himself with the indefinite gestures of revolt in which the Gothic writers could indulge. In searching for positive values, he inevitably attempted to adapt and use the values of the nineteenth century, with its "civilized" sexual morality, even while rejecting important aspects of those values.

Throughout his career, he was caught in a powerful process of pull and counterpull. On the one hand, his vision of human life is deeply deterministic; we are defined by what happens in childhood, before we fully control our lives, and those events are shaped by psycho-biological forces that control the lives of all human beings. On the other hand, Freud clearly believed in the power of the human mind and will. The mind could, if the individual was courageous and firm enough, know itself, and individuals could thus achieve analytical distance and some degree of control over their lives. These two views coexist uneasily at best. The very process of psychoanalysis, particu-larly the self-analysis that was the precondition for Freud's develop-ment of his theories, is an epistemological nightmare. Within a determinist vision of psychic reality, Freud attempts to clear a priv-ileged place where the analyst and patient may somehow stand out-side the dynamics of the mind and achieve understanding untouched by Heisenberg's principle of uncertainty, that analysis of a system is a modification and thus, in part, creates the system.

Freud, like the modernists, had accepted the Gothic vision as ex-pressing the dynamics of the inner life, not, however, as an ex-pression of a particular historical moment and its ideals of identity and pleasure, but as an expression of reality. The dynamics of psychic conflict were inescapable. Repression and sublimation were abso-lutely necessary, though their form might be varied to reduce anxiety and neurosis. For Freud, as for so many nineteenth-century thinkers, civilization and the preservation of any true identity were based on control of sexuality, of libido, and the sublimation of what he calls the pleasure principle. He saw this as a tragic situation, but a neces-sary one. His view of inner life and sexuality was similar to the Gothic (although we have no evidence that his views were really derived from Gothic fiction) because the other great pull and counterpull in his work is a fascination with the erotic combined with disgust. He seems to have viewed the subject of his work—not his patients, but his theories about the substance of their psychic lives—with the combination of fear and desire that virtually constitutes a state of enthrallment. Freud's prudishness has frequently been noted, and scattered throughout his writings are expressions of antipathy to sexuality: he uses such words as "dirt," "disgust," and "revulsion" when discussing certain aspects of sexuality.

> Anyone who in the face of this text [recognizing that heterosexual activity is always an expression of an incest fantasy] subjects himself to serious self-examination will indubitably find that at the bottom of his heart he too regards the sexual act as something degrading, which soils and contaminates not only the body.[7]

This is the condition of anyone who is "free and happy in love"! Freud also writes:

> The genitals themselves have not undergone the development of the rest of the human form in the direction of beauty; they have retained their animal cast; and so, even today, love, too, is in essence as animal as it ever was.[8]

Animal, degrading, soiling, contaminating: this is Freud at his most negative about sexuality, and he is echoing the attitudes toward pleasure that fill the Gothic fantasy, except that Freud's attitudes are not parodies of conventional ideas but his actual views on the subject. The impulse to liberate the individual from confining and restrictive patterns of sexual behavior was combined with a feeling that this must be done of horrible necessity, not because the liberation of sexuality and pleasure was good in itself. The popularized versions of Freud that appeared in the 1920s often suggested that he advocated acting on all sexual impulses to maintain psychic well-being. This could not be more wrong. Rather, he wished to substitute good repression for bad. The wishes that come from the id come like "demons from hell."[9]

Freud also affirmed as truth the death instinct that grips all Gothic protagonists from Manfred to Dracula. This theory, developed in *Beyond the Pleasure Principle* and returned to in *Ego and Id*, accepts death as "the real remedy," as Stanley Edgar Hyman titles his last section on Freud in *The Tangled Bank*. Since the Gothic protagonist could find no way to resolve the crisis of identity and accept the energy of pleasure embodied in sexuality, death—the final loss of

identity, the ultimate act of masochism—became the "solution" to
the struggle within the self. This, too, was the only solution for
Freud. At various points in his career, he was tremendously op-
timistic about the potential of psychoanalysis: "Psychoanalysis is the
instrument destined for the progressive conquest of the id. . . . "Our
medical practice will reach a degree of precision and success which is
not to be had in all the medical specialities." But in "Thoughts for
the Times on War and Death," he says, "If you would endure life, be
prepared for death."[10] When he came in his later years to regard
analysis as an interminable process, for analyst as well as patient, he
was accepting that the only conclusion to the tragic struggle to
strenthen the self—the ego—was death. Surely Freud's horrendous
battle with cancer must have affected his views in this regard, but he
did integrate his vision of the death wish into his system of thought,
whatever its origin. He would have read Gothic novels as cautionary
tales, and he would have accepted the caution as, on the whole, a
sound one.

Freud's attitudes toward sexuality, pleasure, and repression are all
aspects of one of his most admirable traits, his deep and abiding
respect for civilization in its highest forms. But at the same time that
he universalized what in the Gothic had been a description of a cul-
turally produced anxiety, so, too, within broad limits, did he identify
civilization with the world around him. His thought was fundamentally mythic in orientation.[11] He turned away from the world of
history, and in doing so, he sought to generate a reality outside of
time, conceptions of nature and civilization, of the inner life and its
outer relationship to the world, that would offer stability and perma-
nence, even if a grave and tragic kind. His tendency to accept what
was as inevitable, to identify in individual cases a necessity expressing eternal forces deterministically shaped, can be seen in his treatment of Dora. In this case history, Freud almost, but not quite,
advises his young patient to join what Philip Rieff calls the "loveless
ménage" of her father and his friends, Herr and Frau K.[12] In this, we
see Freud on the one hand advising his patient to accept reality and
learn to live with it—sound advice, surely—but also his tendency to
define reality as a situation that is, as Reiff says, really a cultural
problem, not an expression of the patient's psychic condition.

Perhaps the most important aspect of the value systems and ideals
that the Gothic undermined but Freud accepted was the traditional
distinction between male and female identity. Even though he recog-

nized the reality of women's sexuality and acknowledged a bisexual component in all human personality, including the feminine aspects of his own identity, his fundamental attitude toward women embodied the conventional patriarchal view:

> I cannot escape the notion (though I hesitate to give it expression) that for women the level of what is ethically normal is different from what it is in men. The superego is never so inexorable, so impersonal, so independent of its emotional origins as we require it to be in a man. Character-traits which critics of every epoch have brought up against women—that they show less sense of justice than men, that they are less ready to submit to the great necessities of life, that they are more often influenced in their judgements by feelings of affection or hostility—all these would be amply accounted for by the modification in the formation of their superego which we have already inferred [the dominance of jealousy— stemming from penis envy—in the emotional life of women]. We must not allow ourselves to be deflected from such conclusions by the denials of the feminists, who are anxious to force us to regard the two sexes as completely equal in position and worth; but we shall, of course, willingly agree that the majority of men are also far behind the masculine ideal, and that all human individuals, as a result of their bisexual disposition and cross inheritance, combine in themselves both masculine and feminine characteristics, so that pure masculinity and femininity remain theoretical constructions of uncertain content.[13]

The concluding comments appear to undermine most of what Freud has said at the beginning; if masculine and feminine patterns of identity are thoroughly mixed in real individuals and exist in a pure form only as abstract constructs, how could one ever know what was masculine or feminine in origin? The concession is in the realm of theory, but the substance refers to reality, whatever problems this may cause. His argument confirms the archetype of the affective feminine identity, though here hostility is as much a part of the emotional life of the woman as love or tenderness; this is feminine identity stripped of its sentimental trappings. Further, Freud sees the particular psychodynamics of women as dependent on their relation to men and the masculine archetype. What they are is conditioned, at least in part, by what they aren't. Even though he strips away some of the passivity and respectability from the feminine archetype, the dynamics remain the same as we have seen in the Gothic. What was in the fantasy monstrous, though, now becomes the substance of reality. Freud did not need the Gothic to come to this view of the relation between masculine and feminine identity, but by putting his view in relation to the genre, we see how fully conventional he was in his radicalism.

Freud's acceptance of the conventional vision of feminine identity is the necessary complement to his attempt to recreate and revive the masculine identity that the Gothic had demolished. The Gothic provided archetypes for his new vision of masculine identity: the detective, the voyeur, and as with the mondernists, the narrator. Freud's conception of the psychoanalyst and his patient is fundamentally the patriarchal-feminine dynamic all over again.

> The physician should be impenetrable to the patient, and, like a mirror, reflect nothing but what is shown to him.[14]

Such a relationship describes exactly the relationship we have seen in *Uncle Silas* between Austin Ruthyn and Maud.

> I cannot recommend my colleagues emphatically enough to take as a model in psychoanalytic treatment the surgeon who puts aside his own feelings, including that of human sympathy, and concentrates his mind on one single purpose, that of performing the operation as skillfully as possible.

> The justification for this coldness in feeling in the analyst is that it is the condition which brings the greatest advantage to both persons involved, insuring a needful protection for the physician's emotional life and the greatest measure of aid for the patient that is possible at the present time.[15]

We need not question the sincerity of Freud's concluding remarks to see that he has insisted that the psychoanalytic relationship be a struggle for power—he acknowledges his fondness for such struggle in his account of Dora's treatment—not an affective exchange. Like the father who exercises power by the withdrawal of affection, the analyst's role embodies essentially masculine, patriarchal characteristics. At the same time, however, he is a passive observer, a watcher, a voyeur. Emotions are his events. If the process of psychoanalysis involves transference on the part of the patient, clearly similar to the dynamics of enthrallment, so too does the analyst depend, like the voyeur, on his patients for imaginative and intellectual stimulation. They, like Kurtz, embark on the quest into what Freud calls "the underworld" of the unconscious; like Marlowe, the analyst re-

mains at a distance, creating out of his quest for the source of sick-
ness a fable of identity.

Freud was not unaware of the Gothic aspects of the psychoanalytic
process. In his essay "On the Uncanny"—by which Freud means the
effect that we have been calling Gothic—he writes, "Indeed, I
should not be surprised to hear that psychoanalysis, which is concerned with laying bare these hidden forces of the unconscious has
become to many people uncanny for that very reason."[16] He does
not seem completely displeased by this possibility.

Freud's reestablishment of the masculine identity and, hence, of
the quest hero in the figure of the analyst is one way of absorbing the
implications of the Gothic. Indeed, the argument of Hyman's discussion in *The Tangled Bank* reveals both that Freud's theories almost
always had their roots in his own processes of self-analysis and that
he shows, over and over in his language and his metaphors, that he
conceives of psychoanalysis and his own endeavors as a quest of
which he is the hero, "the dragon slayer," as Hyman puts it. Insofar
as Freud's theories are formalizations of his self-analysis, his relationships to his patients become analogous to the Gothic protagonist's relation to his double. Freud, from his masculine role as
analyst, can explore himself through the exploration of the double,
who is formally in the position of the feminine self, needing to be
dominated by the analyst even while resisting him. Indeed, resistance, a phenomenon that Freud was always aware of even when
we might not always agree it was there, is a muted version of the
conflict that makes the sadomasochistic relationship in the Gothic
possible.

Again, we need not question Freud's intentions or his personal
integrity to see in his work the rebuilding of patterns that quite surely were part of the problems he wished to solve rather than components of the solution. His work, both as a writer and theorist and as
an analyst, is a search for a workable definition of masculine identity
and a satisfactory relation between the masculine and feminine, both
between men and women and within the self, and also between the
self and sexuality, or the pleasure principle. In creating this synthesis,
he expands upon both the Gothic tradition and the conventional
tradition from which it was an escape. He was clearly seeking to clear
away what he saw as the most destructive and crippling traps of
conventional ideals. In doing so, he seems to have combined acceptance of those values with acceptance of the Gothic world as a genu-

ine description of psychic reality. Whether he got this description directly from the fantasies or not is less important than the fact of the correspondence, which, as we have seen, gave his vision a much greater degree of familiarity and accessibility than it might otherwise have had.

Freud reinvented the masculine ideal of the quest hero, the figure of the analyst and by implication himself, as the center of this revived mythology. Thus he clearly extended and strengthened the Gothic synthesis of the detective, emphasizing the masculine rather than the feminine components of that figure, both in the analyst's overt paternalism and in Freud's own emphasis on the "scientific" use of imagination. Though one can hardly suggest that Freud was unimaginative or that the powers of imagination did not play a tremendous part in the creation of his vision, he was always at pains to identify himself as a scientist. Sometimes he envisioned himself as an explorer or an archaeologist, but throughout his work runs the insistence on the scientific validity of what he is doing. The assertion comes over and over in *The Interpretation of Dreams;* and in *Beyond the Pleasure Principle,* for instance, Freud develops his argument about the death instinct in terms of a peculiar discussion of one-celled animals, the whole function of which seems to be to establish the biological, and therefore scientifically verifiable, truth of his argument.

Thus Freud resolves the detective, the voyeur, and narrator, the quest hero, and the patriarch—all the roles that he takes up and uses—into one larger role, that of the scientist. He seizes for his vision the prestige of science and scientific activity. He asserts that what he says is true, not in a metaphorical or mythic sense, nor, as in the Gothic, in a parodic sense, but literally true, just as the roundness of the earth or the heliocentric solar system is true. Unlike the Gothic, which hung suspended among ideals of the truth, whether scientific, religious, or literary, Freud commits himself without reserve to a material vision of the world, even if the inner life of the self in that world can be described in terms suitable to the Gothic fantasy rather than conventional scientific notation. This commitment to being scientific, to affirming a particular way of looking at the world, is part of Freud's power in our society. Though one may regard his vision as art or philosophy or myth or even as a type of autobiography, it makes claims to the power and prestige of science.

Freud thus creates the science of fear, and by this he confines fear and anxiety, the strange and mysterious dreams and impulses, the peculiar types of behavior that surface in our lives, firmly within the physical world. The Gothic world had been an indescribable nothingness, given shape and form by our particular terrors and fears, but finally beyond our understanding. Freud insisted that, mysterious and dark though it might be, the inner life was ultimately intelligible, if one was brave enough and honest enough with oneself. By insisting that he could explain the inner world, he assured his patients and followers that suspense and terror could be eliminated. If what was left was not completely satisfactory, it was nonetheless a liberation from superstition and fear, an escape from anxiety. Thus psychoanalysis, like the Gothic, performed a therapeutic function, but in such a way—at least theoretically, when Freud was most confident—that could bring about a genuine end to the process of analysis. But as we have seen, to liberate his patients from the mysterious fears and desires that controlled the shape of their lives, Freud had to create a deterministic universe around a small free space. He relieved people of a good deal of responsibility for their psychic lives, recognizing that "wishing is not doing," in order to allow them to take some control of the rest of their inner existence through the process of analysis.

The important differences between the nature of the Gothic's therapeutic functions and those of psychoanalysis lie in the fluidity of the Gothic vision and its faith in the powers of imagination and pleasure. The Gothic novel defined dynamics of identity and pleasure that were not eternal and fixed, that were extensions of the culture in which they existed. Thus, unlike Freud's vision, which by necessity drew around itself a closed circle, the fantasy opened up possibilities; it articulated fear and anxiety and, in doing so, clarified their nature and their source. However, it did not complete the circle by offering a cure. What the Gothic did offer was the fantasy itself, the transforming power of imagination, or as Coleridge would say, fancy. While fancy could not literally remake the world, it could redefine and recombine what was already there, creating new forms. Analysis, whether by the detective or the psychoanalyst, showed one what was there and how to live with the truth. Fantasy, by parodying what one took to be true, could liberate one from bondage to conventional truth, though by itself it could do no more than provide an uncertain alternative.

In part, then, Freud's achievement is to take the power of fantasy and ally it to the power of science, to unite fantasy and reality in one coherent system that would define the place where the individual was free and identity could be established, if not unbound, at least uncrippled. By tying as he did aspects of fantasy to the power of scientific analysis, Freud was compelled to lose one element of fantasy, and the element he gave up was the value of pleasure. Pleasure remained for him dangerous and essentially unclean, an aspect of our animal existence. We can, at this point, hardly diminish the significance of his achievement or the magnitude of what he attempted. But we can surely recognize that his vision of the self, in which id and superego battle for control of the ego, in which our fears and desires come as dreams and cripple us with neurosis, is hardly a liberation from the patterns of identity we have seen worked out in the Gothic. Though it is perhaps a stage in that process, the central problem in Freud's vision of identity lies in his own enthrallment to his fears and desires about pleasure and in his willingness to embrace the death instinct as a final remedy.

Epilogue

We have looked at the form of the Gothic fantasy, we have examined its central themes, attempted to explain its relation to its own cultural moment and to see how it contributes to and shapes aspects of twentieth-century culture. In exploring the Gothic tradition, we have been examining how a culture articulates its own identity, how it sends messages to itself in its popular literature and fantasies, and how, even in its attempts to escape itself, it confronts its own basic reality. Perhaps one of the fundamental insights we have gained is the power and flexibility of popular literature and popular culture. Though certainly the Gothic sends mixed signals to its readers, we have seen in the genre a very complex and important interpretation of conventional values and ideals. It is not a sterile or dead literary form, a simple escape, but a very vital and complex part of the imaginative life of both the nineteenth and twentieth centuries.

The study of the Gothic illuminates the unbroken connections between our imaginative life and our economic, social, and political life. The genre grows out of the conventional ideas about families, about the definitions of male and female identity that dominated the nineteenth century and continue to affect our own ideas today. As a type of "fancy," it shows us how our imaginations, our escapes, our dreams, are influenced and formed by our place in history; indeed, an understanding of the Gothic shows us that our dreams are forms of information about our relation to the real world.

To a great extent, discussions of the Gothic that emphasize it as a revelation of the unconscious, as an apprehension of the numinous, as a mythology of our "dark side," miss this fundamental point about

191

the historicity of the imagination. Writers who view the genre as reflecting eternal aspects of human consciousness tend to agree with Freud that "dark, unfeeling, unloving powers determine human destiny." One need not deny that dark powers exist to see that whatever bondage we may be held in by them, however they may confine and cripple us, is a function of the moment in which we live. We have seen how the Gothic reveals that the monsters of fantasy come, not from deep within our minds, but from the forms of identity and selfhood shaped by our conventional reality. The Gothic heroine is in bondage to her society's conception of feminine identity, and the Gothic hero tears himself to bits in pursuit of an unattainable ideal of masculinity. The tradition does not offer a vision of imaginative transcendence, nor does it suggest that imagination is capable of the power of transcendence. The Gothic imagination returns us to where we started with no final resolution, for resolutions lie, not in the imagination, but in the world in which the imagination functions.

Both Freud and the modernist writers we have discussed strove to establish a vision that would liberate the twentieth century from the dark powers of the nineteenth. Yet as we have seen, in their attempt to create an empowering mythology, they are caught half way between escape from those dark powers and their affirmation. The search for transcendence itself creates mythologies that attempt to freeze what is part of the movement of history, and so even in their most revolutionary gestures, we see Freud and the modernists reviving the ideals of the nineteenth century, accepting the Gothic critique and parody as a description of reality.

In addition to the vital interrelationship of the imagination with the real world central to understanding the Gothic, the genre offers us another, equally important insight. This is the inescapable and essential value of pleasure in the definition of human identity. We know the Gothic world is a terrible place because nowhere in it is there room for real pleasure; we enjoy the Gothic novel because through it we find a way of transforming pain and suffering into pleasure. To recognize and accept pleasure as a fundamental aspect of our human life is not to ignore or escape the reality of pain, nor to refuse to see its place in our sense of identity. But the Gothic, in its continual transformation of images of suffering into pleasure, its portrayal of the dead end of suffering and the terrors of the pleasure impulse deformed into monstrousness, affirms that the most vital human impulse is the search for pleasure in its fullest and most imaginative forms. The continuing vitality of the Gothic tradition, its extraordinary hold on us, grows from its revelation, through the images of pain, death, and disintegration, of the possibilities of pleasure, life, and wholeness.

Notes

Introduction

1. For a discussion of the "Gothicness" of such works, see Elizabeth MacAndrews, *The Gothic Tradition in Fiction* (New York: Columbia Press, 1979), and Robert Keily, *The Romantic Novel in England* (Cambridge: Harvard Press, 1972), on *Wuthering Heights*. Leslie Fiedler, in *Love and Death in the American Novel* (New York: Dell, 1966), argues, not only for the Gothicness of Melville, but of virtually all of American literature. Judith Wilt, *Ghosts of the Gothic: Austen, Eliot, and Lawrence* (Princeton: Princeton Press, 1981), discusses the relationship to the genre of three writers not usually associated with it. Lowry Nelson, "Night Thoughts on the Gothic Novel," *Yale Review*, 52 (1963): 236–57, argues that *Moby Dick* and *Wuthering Heights* are the logical culmination of the tradition. Robert Hume, "Gothic versus Romantic: A Re-evaluation of the Gothic Novel," *PMLA* 84 (1969): 282–90, argues the same sort of connections between the Gothic and *Moby Dick*, *Wuthering Heights*, and *Sanctuary*. I do not contend that these texts have nothing in common with the genre; on the contrary, they are clearly imbued with its sensibility. But in many ways they do not fit the pattern at all, containing many non-Gothic elements. To call them Gothic is simply to expand the term to a point where it is no longer useful; ambiguity, a conflict between good and evil, even fear and terror, do not make a novel Gothic. The similarity between the Gothic novels and these texts stems from the fact that they were addressing similar imaginative and cultural issues and coming up with similar responses. The genre became influential because writers like Brontë and Melville were dealing with the same issues it did, not because Brontë and Melville found their issues in its fantasies.

2. My understanding of popular literature and the operations and functions of formula and convention in popular fiction has been shaped by John Cawelti, *Adventure, Mystery, and Romance* (Chicago: of Chicago Press, 1975), and Northrup Frye, *The Secular Scripture* (Cambridge: Harvard Press, 1976). On the sociology of popular literature, see Herbert J. Gans, *Popular and High Culture: An Analysis and Evaluation of Taste* (New York: Basic Books, 1975); Leo Lowenthal, *Literature,*

Popular Culture, and Society (Palo Alto: Pacific Books, 1961); Levin L. Schucking, *The Sociology of Literary Taste,* trans. Brian Battershaw (1931; Chicago: of Chicago Press, 1974); and Russell Nye, *The Unembarrassed Muse* (New York: Dial, 1970).

3. On the development of the reading public in the late eighteenth and nineteenth centuries, see Richard Altick, *The English Common Reader* (Chicago: of Chicago Press, 1957). J. M. S. Tompkins, *The Popular Novel in England, 1770–1800* (1932; reprinted., Lincoln: of Nebraska Press, 1961), deals with the early Gothic novel and its public. Ian Watt, *The Rise of the Novel* (Berkeley: of California Press, 1957) deals with the rise of realism and its relation to the rise of the middle class reading public in the eighteenth century. The rise of Gothic fiction in the 1790's and beyond is the growth of middle class fantasy, which parallels the rise of realism which Watt discusses.

4. Frye conceives of romance less as a genre, in the sense that the Gothic constitutes a genre, than as a body of mythology and a set of conventions out of which other literary works and genres are created. While his discussion of the romance is provocative and defines many of the conventions and patterns that appear in all fantasy literature, his view is essentially ahistorical. Though he does allow for variation in the embodiment of the romance mythology, he does not see that mythology itself undergoing significant transformations based on the historical era in which any given version of it exists. The archetypes of the romance come from prescientific, preurban, pretechnological cultures; in the eighteenth century, as culture became scientific, urban, and technological, the romance could not retain either its old form or its old significance. Popular genres such as the Gothic and science fiction cease to be romances in Frye's sense of the term, though they continue to exploit the conventions and patterns of the tradition. At the same time, romance as romance does not fully disappear, and so forms such as the Gothic not only use its conventions and formulas but also rely on the reader's expectations about how more traditional forms of the Romance work for the full force of their effect. As Frye seems to suggest at one point, the romance tradition is integrated into the realistic tradition, thus allying two forms against which the Gothic reacts.

5. For a discussion of these motifs in the romance, see Frye, *Secular Scripture,* pp. 97–126.

6. For a discussion of the vampire that focuses on its use as metaphor in both Gothic and canonical literature, see James Twitchell, *The Living Dead* (Durham, N.C.: Duke Press, 1981). Twitchell provides a good summary of vampire folklore and the history of the literary vampire before the nineteenth century.

7. Frye, *Secular Scripture,* pp. 111–13.

8. On the development of modern science, see Herbert Butterfield, *The Origins of Modern Science,* rev. ed. (New York: Free Press, 1965); Richard S. Westfall, *The Construction of Modern Science: Mechanism and Mechanics* (Cambridge: Cambridge Press, 1971); and Alfred North Whitehead, *Science and the Modern World* (New York: Free Press, 1957). For a provocative discussion of the literary response to modern science, see Donald Ault, *Visionary Physics: Blake's Response to Newton* (Chicago: of Chicago Press, 1971). My discussion here reduces a very complex topic to a few sentences.

9. On the importance of "truth" as an essential factor in determining the worth of a piece of fiction, see Richard Stang, *The Theory of the Novel in England, 1850–1870* (New York: Columbia Press, 1959), pp. 9–11. Stang deals with the relationship between writers of fiction and the romantic conception of the artist as prophet or seer. Winifred Hughes, *The Maniac in the Cellar* (Princeton: Princeton Press, 1981), pp. 47–56, discusses the connection between realism and truth, and the equation of realism with good art in the nineteenth century.

Chapter One

1. Leslie Fiedler is the most important critic to have applied Freudian insights and categories to the Gothic, but the idea that the genre is a reflection of the unconscious mind is pervasive in its criticism, even if the term "unconscious" is not used in a strictly Freudian sense or very clearly defined. The relationship between the Gothic and romanticism is explored in Hume, "Gothic versus Romantic," and in Robert Hume and Robert Platzner, "Gothic versus Romantic: A Rejoinder," *PMLA* 86 (1971): 266–74. Hume argues that the genre is not romantic because it offers no transcendent vision. G. Richard Thompson discusses the tradition's relation to the cultural forces that formed romanticism in his introductory essays in *The Gothic Imagination: Essays in Dark Romanticism* (Pullman: Washington State Press, 1974), and *Romantic Gothic Tales* (New York: Harper and Row, 1979). In both essays, he emphasizes, not only the intellectual roots of the Gothic, but its classification as historical, supernatural, and ambiguous. For a further development of Hume's ideas, see "Exuberant Gloom, Existential Agony, and Heroic Despair," in *The Gothic Imagination*. On the conception of the Protestant Gothic, see Joel Porte, "In the Hands of an Angry God: Religious Terror in Gothic Fiction," in *The Gothic Imagination*, and Wilt, *Ghosts of the Gothic*, pp. 13–20. David Punter, *The Literature of Terror* (London: Longman, 1980), is an excellent general discussion of the Gothic, though the book includes a number of writers and works I have excluded from the Gothic canon by definition. Punter's argument runs parallel to mine at a number of points and shares with mine an interest in understanding the Gothic as a social and historical phenomenon. George Levine, *The Realistic Imagination* (Chicago: University of Chicago Press, 1981), makes a number of interesting comments on the relationship of the Gothic to realism, from the perspective of an argument about the nature of nineteenth-century realism (see particularly pp. 3–60). I read both the last two books late in my work on the Gothic, when my own argument were essentially complete; I have taken the instances of parallels in our views as confirmation of the soundness of my views.

2. For a discussion of Victorian fantasy other than Gothic, including Kingsley and MacDonald, see Stephan Prickert, *Victorian Fantasy* (Bloomington: University of Indiana Press, 1976). Prickert argues that for many Victorian writers, fantasy served as a way of expressing and resolving personal anxiety and escaping conventional society.

3. For a semiotic approach to the genre see Eve Kosofsky Sedgwick, "Character in the Veil: Imagery of the Surface in the Gothic Novel," *PMLA* 96 (1981): 255–71.

4. The conventions of the Gothic novel have been addressed by every writer who has dealt with the topic. The Faustian hero, the sentimental heroine, the use of the double, of incest, the supernatural, transformation and metamorphosis, the use of remote and exotic locales, the concept of Gothic atmosphere have all been well established as the central bundle of Gothic formulas. Its earliest critics focused very heavily on the establishment of the genre. See Edith Birkhead, *The Tale of Terror* (London: Constable, 1921); Eino Railo, *The Haunted Castle* (1927; reprint ed., New York: Gordon Press 1974); and Montague Summers, *The Gothic Quest* (1938; reprint ed., New York: Russell and Russell, 1964). I make no claim to having discovered any new conventions but, I hope, simply a new way of looking at their interrelationship.

5. Fiedler has developed the Faustian reading of the Gothic novel in great detail, *Love and Death,* p. 133 and passim.

6. MacAndrews, *The Gothic Traditions,* is particularly good on the relationship between the Gothic and the sentimental tradition, though I see the effect of the sentimental on the genre as less pervasive than she does. She also sees the Gothic as an expression of the unconscious and an exploration of the nature of evil.

7. See Frye, *Secular Scripture* pp. 65–93, for the sources of these styles of identity in the romance tradition.

8. My discussion of doubles and doubleness is informed by the examination of doubles in Daniel Hoffman's *Poe, Poe, Poe, Poe, Poe* (Garden City, N.J.: Doubleday, 1972), pp. 207–13. Both Wilt, *Ghosts of the Gothic,* pp. 62–95 and MacAndrews, *The Gothic Tradition,* offer discussions of the double. On the double in nineteenth-century literature, particularly in works outside the Gothic tradition, see Masao Miyoshi, *The Divided Self* (Berkeley: of California Press, 1969).

9. Oscar Wilde, *The Picture of Dorian Grey,* in *Minor Classics of Nineteenth-Century Fiction,* ed. William E. Buckler II (Boston: Houghton Mifflin, 1967), p. 274. All further citations are from this text.

10. William Godwin, *Caleb Williams* (New York: W. W. Norton, 1977), pp. 129–30. All further citations are from this text.

11. Sheridan LeFanu, "Carmilla," in *Best Ghost Stories of Sheridan LeFanu,* ed. F. E. Bleiler (New York: Dover, 1964), p. 339. All further citations are from this text.

12. Charles Brockden Brown, *Wieland; or, the Transformation* (New York: Hafner Publishing Co., 1960), pp. 95–96. All further citations are from this text.

13. Charles Robert Maturin, *Melmoth the Wanderer* (Lincoln: of Nebraska Press, 1961), p. 165. All further citations are from this text.

14. The dream origins of *The Castle of Otranto* are recounted in a letter from Walpole to Rev. William Cole, dated 9 March 1765, quoted in *Three Gothic Novels,* ed. E. F. Bleiler (New York: Dover, 1966), p. xi. Mary Shelley's account of her dream source for *Frankenstein* appears in the author's introduction to the 1831 edition of the novel and is reprinted in Mary Shelley, *Frankenstein* (New York: New American Library, 1965), pp. x–xi. Stevenson's account of the dream origin of *Jekyll and Hyde* is quoted in the introduction to Robert Louis Stevenson, *Dr. Jekyll and Mr. Hyde* (New York: New American Library, 1967), p. viii.

15. Brown's clearest statement of his desire to write American books appears in his prefatory remarks to *Edgar Huntley,* ed. David Stineback (New Haven: College and University Press, 1973), p. 29. All further citations are from this text.

16. Fiedler, *Love and Death,* p. 137.

17. For arguments in favor of the view that the Gothic offers a vision of the numinous, see Devendra P. Varma, *The Gothic Flame* (New York: Russell and Russell, 1965), pp. 206–33; Wilt, *Ghosts of the Gothic,* pp. 12–24; and S. L. Varnado, "The Idea of the Numinous in Gothic Literature," in *The Gothic Imagination,* pp. 11–22. Somewhat similar is the connection of the genre to the concept of the sublime, discussed in Keily, *The Romantic Novel,* pp. 12–17.

18. Horace Walpole, *The Castle of Otranto,* ed. W. S. Lewis (London: Oxford Press, 1964), p. 17. All further citations are from this text.

19. Mathew G. Lewis, *The Monk* (New York: Grove Press, 1959), p. 420. All further citations are taken from this edition.

20. Bram Stoker, *Dracula* (New York: New American Library, 1965), p. 40. All further citations are taken from this text.

21. My understanding of the detective story and the figure of the detective has been most heavily influenced by Cawelti and by Richard Wilbur, "The House of Poe," in *Poe,* ed, Robert Regan (Englewood Cliffs, N.J.: Prentice-Hall, 1967). Albert D. Hunter, "Dreams, Transformations, and Literature: The Implications of Detective Fiction," *Victorian Studies* 19 (1975), p. 181–210, points out that the rise of the detective story coincides with the appearance of real detectives and police forces; thus, the fictional detective does not have a purely literary geneology. This point is important, because it reenforces the interactive nature of literature, culture, and society. I would argue, though, that the creation of detective stories is possible, not because of the existence of real detectives, but because of the existence of a literary form that has a place for, and can make use of, a fictional version of the detective. Detectives, like scientists and psychologists, fit naturally into the "literary space" in the Gothic fantasy that is left by the disintegration of the romance quest hero. I think the literary transformation of the quest hero into the detective is, finally, the significant phenomenon here. Fictional detectives bear only a little more resemblance to real ones than real cowboys do to Gary Cooper and Randolph Scott.

22. Sir Arthur Conan Doyle, *The Hound of the Baskervilles* (Baltimore: Penguin Books, 1981), p. 38–151. All further citations are taken from this text.

23. Ibid., pp. 103–4.

24. For a discussion of the Gothic and comic effects, see Paul Lewis, "Mysterious Laughter: Humor and Fear in Gothic Fiction," *Genre* 14 (1981), 309–27. An interesting discussion of parody in *Northanger Abbey,* which parallels a number of elements in my discussion, can be found in Levine, *The Realistic Imagination,* pp. 61–80.

25. Daniel Hoffman, *Poe,* p. 228–40.

26. *Selected Writings of Edgar Allan Poe,* ed. Edward H. Davidson (Boston: Houghton Mifflin Company, 1956), p. 499. All further citations taken from this text.

✓ 27. Ellen Moers, *Literary Women* (Garden City, N.J.: Doubleday, 1976), pp. 137–40. In her discussion, Moers emphasizes the centrality of fear as effect and subject in the Gothic and the peculiar co existence of fear and pleasure in the genre.

28. Maturin, *Melmoth,* p. 165.

29. William Beckford, *Vathek* (London: Oxford University Press, 1970), pp. 119–120. All further citations are taken from this text.

30. Fiedler argues that "one of [the Gothic's] functions was to shock the bourgeoisie into an awareness of what a chamber of horrors its own smugly regarded world really was." He also calls the Gothic avant-garde and anti-bourgeois, as well as revolutionary and Faustian (*Love and Death,* pp. 134–45). He defines a plausible way of looking at the genre, and I would agree with him to the extent that I see it reflecting the contradictions, tensions, and problems of middle-class life. I would, though, insist that it is an essentailly bourgeois genre, and not avant-garde or revolutionary in any of the conventional senses of these terms. Fiedler describes one of the ways in which readers might use the Gothic fantasy, but we must always remember that its radical criticism of middle-class life and values is expressed indirectly as parody. The Gothic critique of bourgeois society came from within that culture, not from without, from a revolutionary avant-garde, and thus its function as a form of entertainment and as a psychic safety valve is every bit as important as its revolutionary function.

31. Prickert, *Victorian Fantasy,* pp. 1–34, provides a very complete discussion of the distinction between the concept of imagination and the concept of fantasy in the nineteenth century. Hume, in "Gothic versus Romantic," argues a distinction between the two traditions on the grounds that the Gothic is not the expression of a transcendent vision. My argument is indebted to both of these views.

32. Samuel Taylor Coleridge, *Biographia Literaria* (London: J. M. Dent and Co., 1906), pp. 159–60.

Chapter Two

1. On the family in the nineteenth century, see Lawrence Stone, *The Family, Sex, and Marriage in England, 1500–1800* (New York: Harper and Row, 1977), pp. 660–80. Though Stone's study formally encompasses only the first decade of the Gothic fantasy's popularity—the 1790s—he makes a number of comments on the family and sex in the nineteenth-century as well. Most significant for the purposes of my argument is his claim that what we think of as the classic Victorian family really began to take shape in the late eighteenth century. Literary history, with its sharp demarcation between the romantic, or Regency, era on the one hand, and the Victorian era on the other, tends to obscure the fundamental cultural continuity between the two. Also useful on the subject of the Victorian family is Anthony Wohl, ed., *The Victorian Family: Structure and Stress* (New York: St. Martin's Press, 1778), Particularly good on the figure of the patriarch is the essay by David Roberts, "The Paterfamilias of the Victorian Governing

Classes." General discussions of the Victorian family, sexuality, and masculine and feminine ideals appear in Walter Houghton, *The Victorian Frame of Mind* (New Haven: Yale University Press, 1957), pp. 341–94.; Richard Altick, *Victorian People and Ideas* (New York: W. W. Norton; 1973), pp. 50–59.; The BBC Third Programme, *Ideas and Beliefs of the Victorians* (1949; reprint ed., New York: Dutton, 1966), pp. 343–58; G. M. Young, ed., *Early Victorian England,* (London: Oxford University Press, 1934), 1: 1–245, contains a mass of information on Victorian home life. Also interesting is the short section on the family in Raymond Williams, *Keywords: A Vocabulary of Culture and Society* (London: Oxford University Press, 1976), pp. 108–11. On masculine and feminine styles of identity in the Gothic, MacAndrews, *The Gothic Tradition,* is particularly useful, focusing as she does on the sentimental ideal of feminine identity and on the masculine villain. In George Levine and U. C. Knoepflmacher, ed., *The Endurance of Frankenstein* (Berkeley: University of California Press, 1979), Kate Ellis's "Monsters in the Garden: Mary Shelley and the Bourgeois Family" is particularly good and has influenced my thinking, not only about *Frankenstein,* but about the family in all Gothic novels. Also interesting in this vein are two pieces of biographical criticism, U. C. Knoepflmacher, "Thoughts on the Aggression of Daughters," in Levine and Knoepflmacher, and Moers, *Literary Women,* pp. 140–57. Both deal with how Mary Shelley's own family experiences shaped her vision of the Gothic fantasy.

2. Twitchel, pp. 129–30, sees *Carmilla* as an antilesbian story. My own reading parallels the interpretation of William Veeder, "'Carmilla': The Arts of Represseion," *Texas Studies in Language and Literature,* 22 (1980), 197–224.

3. LeFanu, *Carmilla,* pp. 291–92.

4. Stevenson, *Jekyll and Hyde,* p. 54.

5. Walpole, *Otranto,* p. 35.

6. Ibid., p. 110.

7. Sheridan LeFanu, *Uncle Silas* (New York: Dover, 1966), p. 10. All further citations are from this text.

8. Ibid., p. 436.

9. The amount of critical work on *The Turn of the Screw* is immense. Particularly useful to me were the discussion in Dorothea Krock, *The Ordeal of Consciousness in Henry James* (Cambridge: Cambridge University Press, 1962), pp. 106–43, and Joseph Firbaugh, "Inadequacy in Eden: Knowledge and 'The Turn of the Screw,'" *Modern Fiction Studies* 3(Spring 1957): 57–64. Also important is Edmund Wilson's "The Ambiguity of Henry James," reprinted in *The Triple Thinkers,* rev. ed. (New York: Oxford University Press, 1948). Wilson argues the "repressed-to-the-point-of-psychosis" line; Krock and Firbaugh emphasize the problem of knowledge in the story, particularly the problem of children encountering adult knowledge. Firbaugh also emphasizes that Miles is a boy, caught in a feminine, family situation.

10. Henry James, *The Turn of the Screw* (New York: New American Library, 1962), p. 309.

11. Tompkins, *The Popular Novel,* pp. 62–66.

12. Brown, *Wieland,* p. 113.

13. Poe, "House of Usher," p. 111.

14. For a discussion of the androgyne in literature other than the Gothic, see Carolyn Heilbrun, *Toward a Recognition of Androgyny* (New York: Harper and Row, 1974).

15. Godwin, *Caleb Williams,* p. 323.

16. Ibid., p. 324.

17. My reading of *Dracula* as a story about families corresponds in its essentials to Judith Wilt's discussion of the novel. I also found Nina Auerbach's "Magi and Maidens: The Romance of Victorian Freud," *Critical Inquiry* Winter 1981, pp. 281–300. very stimulating. Professor Auerbach was kind enough to let me read her essay before it was published.

Chapter Three

1. My discussions of these films, particularly *King Kong* and *Halloween,* has been stimulated by the articles on them in Danny Peary, *Cult Movies* (New York: Delacorte Press, 1982), though ultimately my readings differ significantly from his.

2. The general decription of modernism I have used here is derived in part from Malcolm Bradbury and James MacFarland, *Modernism* (New York: Penguin, 1976), pp. 19–30. On a related topic, the Gothic and surrealism, see Varma, *The Gothic Flame,* pp. 66–73, and Summers, *The Gothic Quest,* pp. 383–89, 397–98, 411.

3. My thinking about Freud has been influenced by Auerbach, and by Stanley Edgar Hyman, *The Tangled Bank: Darwin, Marx, Frazer, and Freud as Imaginative Writers* (1959; reprint ed., New York: Grossett & Dunlop, 1966). Particularly important is Hyman's conception of Freud's intellectual life as a type of quest and that this was, in fact, the way Freud conceived of his work himself. Hyman also emphasizes that the development of psychoanalysis was also Freud's pursuit of his own identity. Most of the quotations from Freud used in this section I originally found in Hyman, though I have cited their sources in the standard edition of Freud's works.

4. Quoted in ibid., p. 310.

5. Thomas Kuhn, *The Structure of Scientific Revolutions,* 2d ed., enl. (Chicago: University of Chicago Press, 1970).

6. Sigmund Freud, "Civilized Sexual Morality and Modern Nervousness," in *The Standard Edition of the Complete Psychological Works of Sigmund Freud,* trans. James Strachey (London: Hogarth Press and the Institute of Psychoanalysis, 1959) 9:204.

7. Sigmund Freud, "On the Universal Tendency to Debasement in the Sphere of Love," *Complete Pyschological Works 11:* 186, 189.

8. Sigmund Freud, *Introductory Lectures on Psychoanalysis,* trans. Joan Riviere (New York; 1917), p. 354.

9. Sigmund Freud, "Future Prospects of Psychoanalytic Theory," *Complete Psychological Works 11:* 148; and *Ego and Id,* trans. Joan Riviere, rev. and ed. by James Strachey (New York: W. W. Norton, 1962).

10. Sigmund Freud, "Thoughts for the Times on War and Death," *Complete Psychological Works* 14: 300.

11. Philip Reiff, *Freud: The Mind of the Moralist* (New York: Viking, 1967), pp. 138, 181.

12. Philip Reiff, Introduction to *Dora: An Analysis of a Case of Hysteria,* by Sigmund Freud (New York: Collier Books, 1963), p. 10.

13. Sigmund Freud, "Psychological Consequences of the Anatomical Distinction between the Sexes," *Complete Psychological Works* 19: 257–58.

14. Sigmund Freud, "Recommendations for Physicians on the Psychoanalytic Method of Treatment," ibid., 12:118.

15. Ibid., p. 115.

16. Sigmund Freud, "The Uncanny," in *Studies in Parapsychology,* ed. Philip Reiff (New York: Collier, 1963), p 49.

Index